Thomas Baines

The Gold Regions of South Eastern Africa

Thomas Baines

The Gold Regions of South Eastern Africa

ISBN/EAN: 9783743417519

Manufactured in Europe, USA, Canada, Australia, Japa

Cover: Foto ©Andreas Hilbeck / pixelio.de

Manufactured and distributed by brebook publishing software (www.brebook.com)

Thomas Baines

The Gold Regions of South Eastern Africa

THE GOLD REGIONS

OF

SOUTH EASTERN AFRICA,

BY THE LATE

THOMAS BAINES, ESQ., F.R.G.S.

ACCOMPANIED BY BIOGRAPHICAL SKETCH OF THE AUTHOR.

With Portrait, Map, and numerous Illustrations and Photographs.

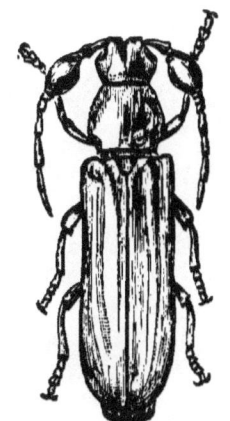

BOLBOTRITUS BAINESI.—NATURAL SIZE.

LONDON:
EDWARD STANFORD, CHARING CROSS.

CAPE COLONY:
J. W. C. MACKAY, PORT ELIZABETH.

1877.

THIS BOOK,

WHICH COMPRISES THE LAST AND GREATEST WORK OF THE INDEFATIGABLE TRAVELLER,

THOMAS BAINES,

IS DEDICATED,

WITH SPECIAL PERMISSION,

TO

His Royal Highness Prince Alfred,

DUKE OF EDINBURGH,

AS

THE FIRST OF ENGLAND'S ROYAL RACE

WHO HAS LANDED UPON THE

SHORES OF SOUTH AFRICA.

PREFACE.

The region described in the following pages was, until the last few years, when the explorations of Herr Mauch, Erskine, Elton, Chapman, and others somewhat dispersed the cloud of mystery in which it was enveloped, essentially a mythical one. Its geographical features were generally depicted in the manner described by Swift—

> "So Geographers in Afric Maps
> With savage pictures fill their gaps,
> And o'er unhabitable downs
> Place elephants instead of towns."

The name of Monomotapa (which means a place from which something valuable is derived), is seldom used except as a mediæval geographical term, found in old school geographies and obsolete atlases. It was supposed by its Arab and Portuguese discoverers and conquerors to include all the regions* south of the Zambesi, extending to the country of the Kafirs (Pays de Caffres) or even to the banks of the Orange River, the Vigita Magna of the old geographers, and the large towns supposed to exist in this region (shaken over the old Maps as if from a pepper castor) are frequently alluded to in the early records of the Cape Colony. We learn from these records, however, that several exploring parties were sent in search of rich countries during the latter half of the seventeenth century, but none of them succeeded in penetrating so far into the interior. The Seaboard or Coast Region was known under the name it still bears, that of "Sofala," which signifies in Arabic a plain or low country.

Sabia lies more inland behind Sofala, and is supposed by some authorities, including Josephus, and no less a personage than the

---

* The country north of the Zambesi is Lower Ethiopia. The land of the lakes was known as the Empire of Monoamugi.

author of the Koran, to be the ancient kingdom of the love-sick Queen, who visited Solomon when in all his glory, and of whom Mahommedan, Abyssinian, and Jewish writers relate such innumerable traditions. Several ruins of ancient buildings are found still in this region, which is drained by a river disemboguing on the east coast, still called "Sabia." These ruins will be adverted to in this work, and we furnish an excellent illustration of them. The memory of the Queen of Sheba is still preserved amongst the Arabs of Sofala, as well as among the Habesh of Gondar in their scandalous chronicles (vide genealogical tables of the late King Theodore.*) The site of the region of Ophir has from time immemorial been a bone of contention amongst Archæologists, and vast learning has been uselessly expended to prove its locality, whether in Arabia Felix, or Arabia Petrea, Socotra, the Persian Gulf, India, the Punjaub, Malacca, or the Moluccas of Spain. Even Peru, far away to the west, had its advocates, as we read in Ben Jonson—

> "Here's the rich Peru,
> And there within, Sir, are the golden mines,
> Great Solomon's Ophir."

Such a weighty authority as Milton, who surely ought to know something on the subject, is in favor of Africa. In "Paradise Lost," xi. 399 to 401, he says—

> "Mombaza, Quiloa and Melind,
> And Sofala (thought Ophir) to the realm
> Of Congo and Angola farthest south."

Our own opinion of the situation of Ophir is undoubtedly in favour of South Eastern Africa.

> "We have a vision of our own,
> And why should we undo it?"

---

* The Transvaal Boers, although not a very literary people, yet like their Colonial brethren, great readers of the Bible, especially the Old Testament, are firm believers in the realm of Sheba and Ophir, as bordering on their Republic; in fact, as they advance northward their belief is getting more confirmed, that they will eventually reach Palestine or the Land of Promise, via Egypt. Already one of the tributaries of the Limpopo running north has been called by them the Nylstrom. It is a very curious thing what a Judaical or Old Testament tint all the ideas of these people have taken since their migration from the Colony, or, as they prefer to call it, their "sojourn in the wilderness."

DESCRIPTION OF PICTURE OF TOWER.

REMAINS OF ANCENT TOWER IN "THE LAND OF OPHIR."—PORTION OF "THE HOUSE OF THE GREAT PRINCESS, OR PALACE OF THE QUEEN," 30 feet high, 15 feet diameter at its base, cylindrical to 10 feet from the ground, and then tapering upwards. No entrance observed by Herr Mauch. Formerly, at intervals of three or four years, the people assembled here for solemn feast and sacrifice. After the sacrifice the High Priest entered the Tower, sprinkled the place, and prayed that "Mali," or, the Father, would remove all disease. The Portuguese are of opinion that these Ruins are portions of the remains of the City and Palace of the Queen of Sheba.

Old Ogilby, in his ponderous folio on African Geography, principally however translated from Dapper, says "yet divers make Ophir the " same with Sofala because it has much gold and ivory, and if all " the main land included between the river Magnice and Quama and " submitting unto Monomotapa, be all as Barros calls it, Sofala, as " well as the rest on the sea coast, it can with great reason be judged " that this country be none but the Golden Ophir of Solomon, partly " because of the houses there to be found near the gold mines, not " built after the manner of the country, but seem the work of " foreigners, and partly because of the inscriptions being strange and " unknown. Moreover, T. Lopez, in his voyage to the Indies, affirms " that among the inhabitants of this country, there remain books which " shew that Solomon every three years had his gold thence. Besides, " the Septuagint Interpreters have translated the word Ophir into the " Greek word Sophira, which agrees very well with Sofala, and Josephus " the Jewish historian, calleth it Indian Ophir, adding, moreover, it " was called the Gold Country. Besides gold and ivory this region " produced apes (dog-faced baboons) in myriads, and if for peacocks, " we read ostrich feathers, and for almug trees we substitute ebony " or stink-wood, it leaves nothing to be denied." For a learned and exhaustive article on this subject we refer our reader to Notes and Queries III. Series, vols. 7, 8 and 9, and also to article "Ophir" in Smith's Bible Dictionary.

In our friend Baines' simple recital of his adventures in these regions there is no attempt at sensational writing, or any endeavour to arrest attention by exciting hunting adventures. As an artist, a geographer and an explorer, poor Baines distinguished himself, not as the useless and wholesale destroyer of hosts of the larger game. The country is, however, most truthfully described, and the thorough accuracy of the information renders it exceedingly valuable. Thomas Baines has been the pioneer of civilization in a great continent, and in that capacity has performed a work which can only be measured in aftertimes by results. Without fee or patronage he pressed forward through the wilds of Southern Africa, and it is principally by the exertions of his pencil and pen that we are made aware of the vast riches which await development in the fertile regions which intervene between the Limpopo and Zambesi rivers. The country described stretches upward to the most southerly portion of that delineated in the map of Captain

Cameron's travels; and this work, therefore, forms an essential volume in the series whose object is to describe the vast countries in the interior of the African continent.

The unhappy difference of Mr. Baines with Dr. Livingstone is specially referred to in Mr. Hall's biographical sketch, and forms an illustration of the old saying "Ne sutor ultra crepidam." Baines as an artist and an astronomer, or as an explorer to any expedition, would have been invaluable; in the capacity of commissariat officer or store keeper he was out of place.

We trust that the large and expensive Map published in this book will be fully appreciated by the scientific public. The data upon which it is founded are perfectly reliable, and the whole of it was originally laid down by BAINES himself on a very large scale. It is now presented to the world under the very able supervision of Mr. E. Stanford, of Charing Cross, and it will be found to occupy a very large void in the Map of Africa, and to fill up blanks in regions hitherto very imperfectly known.

The illustrations in this volume are principally copied from paintings by Mr. Baines, now in the possession of his old friend, Mr. Robert White, of London, which were objects of attention both in the Picture Gallery at the Crystal Palace and subsequently at the Dublin Exhibition, and are now on view at the Alexandra Palace. With regard to their merit, it is sufficient to quote Sir Roderick Murchison, who in an address delivered before the Royal Geographical Society declared that, "with an artist like "Mr. Baines, who has sent home such admirable coloured drawings "of South African scenes, particularly of the Falls of the Zambesi, "those of us, who are destined never to penetrate into the southern "part of Africa, may quite realise to our minds' eye the true "characters of that grand continent." * * * *
Dr. Kirk also says, "it gives me pleasure to record the high "opinion I entertain of the artistic merit and truthfulness of the "series of paintings by Mr. T. Baines, of the Victoria Falls of "the Zambesi." In a letter from the mother of Mr. Thomas Baines, addressed to Mr. White, of London, she says, "a number "of his paintings were sent to Windsor for the inspection of "Her Majesty and the Prince Consort." The note by Sir George Grey stated, "that Her Majesty expressed much pleasure in "inspecting them, and allowed the work to be dedicated to the

"Prince Consort." Mr. Glover, the Librarian, stated "that he never "saw the Prince more interested in anything of the kind than these "paintings. They kept them at Windsor a week, and Her Majesty "took her family into the room in which they were laid out, and "explained each to her children."

In concluding these prefatory remarks, we think it just to say that the Map and Itinerary have been carefully revised by Mr. Hall, F.R.G.S., and that the biographical sketch of Mr. Baines is from his pen.

MEMOIR

OF THE LATE

THOMAS BAINES, ESQ., F.R.G.S.

"HE was a man to whom the wilderness brought gladness, and the mountains peace." As a writer in the "Cape Monthly Magazine" well observes, "the death of this brave and distinguished man, whose name must for ever be associated with the explorers of the country north of the Cape Colony in the same rank as Livingstone, Chapman, Andersson, and Green, has been a greater loss to South Africa than is generally supposed. Toiling for years in the cause of civilisation and human progress, as well as in that of the honour and prestige of Englishmen in a barbarous country, enduring hardships and difficulties such as explorers only know, toiling honestly and diligently in the careful elaboration of plans and the acquisition of the scientific knowledge of this splendid wilderness, this fearless and accomplished man has, like Andersson and Livingstone, impressed the native mind with a conviction of English courage and superiority, and has now gone to his rest unrecognised and unrewarded, but not unlamented. If his value was unappreciated by the many, his friendship was prized by a few, and had not his death deprived Africa of a fund of information with regard to these regions, it would be needless for us to write these lines. As it is we shall say but little of the Matabili Proper, where the Gold Fields lie, but refer the reader to the following pages, the last work of Mr. Baines on this subject, wherein will be found full descriptions of the old mines and the native races who now occupy the land."

So far the writer in the "Cape Magazine," and as an old and faithful friend of poor Baines of more than 30 years' duration, we can only say, "And such an honest chronicler is Griffith," for we can fully endorse every word he says in praise of that truly honesthearted, unselfish, generous and simple-minded specimen of humanity, Thomas Baines, who was always in the front performing acts of kindness to his fellow-labourers, whether in sickness, semi-starvation, or any other difficulty they might be in, and died with the happy recollection that he was to his or their end the participator in the love and friendship of such men as Charles J. Andersson, James Chapman, Herr Mauch, Fred. Green, and dozens of other explorers early cut off, all like himself nature's gentlemen, and victims of the hardships and fatigues they had to undergo in their African explorations. We here, availing ourselves of the notes of his old friend Mr. Wilmot, of Port Elizabeth, and other early friends of Baines, together with our own personal knowledge, proceed to give a few sketches of his career in the Cape Colony. He was a native of that nursery of the Anglo-Saxon race, whose energy he so truly inherited, Norfolk. He was born at King's Lynn in 1822. His father, also a man of considerable energy, was the master of a small vessel belonging to that port, and no doubt his marine life as well as the striking scenery of the Norfolk coast, gave a tinge to the early artistic tendencies of his second son THOMAS, who received the rudiments of at least an excellent English education, although the art school he had to study in was of an humble nature, the heraldic department of a coach builder; but we must not forget Hogarth's early experience as a plate engraver of crests, or Stanfield and Roberts in the painter's loft in Drury Lane or Covent Garden theatres as scene painters. His first sketches that we can recollect were all on marine subjects, which he afterwards abandoned when his mind got thoroughly saturated with the love of travel, and the magical romance of African landscape and animal life. He arrived in the Cape Colony in 1842, and he soon made valued and attached friends, both in Cape Town and the Eastern province, whose friendship, to the end of his life, he always spoke warmly of. We need hardly say that for any man to earn a competent living by art in the Cape Colony is always an uphill task, and we fear poor Baines for a long time felt it so; but he was gradually enabled to abandon his heraldic work. By painting for a few patrons African landscapes, and groups of game and native figures, and by teaching drawing, he was enabled, by degrees, to earn a comfortable living. By cultivating the acquaintance of explorers, and reading works of travel in the South African Library, he began to feel that it was his vocation to explore the then nearly unknown region to the north of the Colony, and proceeding to the frontier during the Kafir wars of 1846-7, he had ample opportunities of employing his pencil, and, as it were, showing the Cape community what was in him. About this period we first formed his acquaintance in Graham's Town. Hearing that we were employed constructing a map of the Colony, he immediately called on us, and placed at our disposal the multifarious information and sketches he had accumulated in a previous trip to the country north of the Orange River, and we are happy to say we enjoyed his confidential intimacy and friendship from that time down to the period of his death, both in England, Cape Town, and the Frontier.

During the progress of the Kafir wars of 1848 and 1851, Baines was always in the front. He was in the field with the brave Col. Tylden during his brilliant campaign in the country now the division of Queen's Town, but then Tambookieland, where he got materials for some of his best pictures; and on the 6th Nov. 1851, he was present at the action with the rebel Hottentots in Water Kloof, when the lamented Col. Fordyce, 74th Regiment, was killed, and on every occasion, in front of the enemy, he was busy with his sketch-book, exposing himself, under heavy fire, with the coolest courage, to very great personal risk. In fact, wherever there was action or danger, Baines was always in the front, and being an unerring shot, no doubt his presence on these occasions cost the enemy dear; he was almost positive that he shot the Hottentot who killed Col. Fordyce, to whom he was close when he received his fatal wound.

At the conclusion of the war of 1854, Baines, who was always a welcome guest at the headquarters of the General and his staff, returned to England, and got attached to the exploring expedition to Northern Australia under Gregory as artist, and as usual took his full share of the dangers and fatigues. An unknown coast, an unknown ocean, and hostile natives, formed almost insuperable obstacles to the progress of the expedition, which were only overcome by the courage and energies of the parties forming it; and Baines particularly distinguished himself by navigating a ship's boat round the north-west shores of the Gulf of Carpentaria, showing himself a thorough seaman and marine surveyor; and his exertions were so much appreciated that he received the special thanks of the Colonial Government.

On his return to his native town, King's Lynn, in 1856-7, Baines was presented with the freedom of the borough, with an address under the corporate seal, testifying at least that in his case a prophet was somewhat honoured in his native country. In the meantime Baines' name was becoming well known to the scientific societies both of England and of Europe—not only as an artist, but as an accurate and scientific geographer, and this led to his appointment, at the recommendation of the Royal Geographical Society, as artist to the Livingstone Zambesi Expedition in 1858. He, however, unfortunately for himself, also accepted the somewhat inferior office of storekeeper, which led to some very unpleasant differences with Mr. Charles Livingstone, the Doctor's brother, and eventually with the Doctor himself. Without entering very deeply into the details of the case, we think it better, as it is little known, to place a few facts before the public, who will be enabled to judge how very harshly poor Baines was used in the matter. Prostrated by fever at Tete, after almost superhuman exertions to bring the little steamer through the fever-stricken marshes of the Zambesi Delta, he was there received into the Commandant's house, and treated by the Portuguese authorities with the greatest kindness, until he recovered. Grateful for this treatment, he conceived, as an artist, the best way of expressing his thanks was to offer to paint the portrait of his kind host and nurse. This offer was gladly accepted and executed. Conceive, however, his horror when he found this graceful recognition of his obligation converted by Mr. Charles Livingstone into a charge against him, made to the Doctor, as leader of the expedition, of embezzling, in the shape of the colours and canvas of the portrait, the stores entrusted to his charge; and, we regret to say, the Doctor never hesitated for a moment in accepting this accusation, and refusing to hear any explanation on Baines' part. It led to the secession, and eventually to the dismissal of the latter, as he could not remain, branded, as he was, with the name of a common thief, and it certainly does not redound to the credit of Dr. Livingstone, that to the last he did not honestly acknowledge his error, and absolve Baines from an accusation engendered only by envy and malevolence, and which no honest man could silently allow to rest on him. Into his conduct on this occasion he always challenged the strictest inquiry from his accusers, and was refused it. He appealed to the Secretary of State and to the Council of the Royal Geographical Society, but without effect. What could the friendless unknown artist do with the influence of a man like Livingstone dead against him? He could only await patiently, and leave his redress to the great avenger, Time. He did so, and never was man so completely acquitted. We know, in fact, that the great motive which actuated him in joining Chapman's Expedition to the Zambesi in 1861 was the hope of meeting Livingstone, and personally confronting him on the Zambesi, or at Tete; but the meeting never occurred. This expedition went from the West Coast overland to Victoria Falls, meeting Chapman on the way. Baines painted, shot and preserved the skins of animals, besides superintending the construction of boats, &c., they had brought with them. His series of pictures of the Victoria Falls, and other scenes on the Zambesi, are well known, and, as the property of Mr. Robert White, have been exhibited to the public at the Crystal Palace and Dublin Exhibition for several years, and are now on view at the Alexandra Palace.

On his return from this expedition, Baines again revisited England, and for some time had his studio in a spare room at the Royal Geographical Society's Rooms, in Whitehall Place, and in 1865 he published his drawings of African Scenery, and his Explorations in South-Eastern Africa, which acquired quite a European celebrity; and attention having been called to the existence of gold fields in the Tati and the ruined cities in the region North-East of the Trans-Vaal Republic, he entered into arrangements with a company formed for the purpose in London for exploring them, and obtained the friendship of the paramount chief, Lo Bengulo, the successor of the once dreaded Um Zelikatze,* who granted him, on account of the company he represented, many valuable concessions north of the Tati, which, unfortunately, were not always properly utilized through the mismanagement of the directors at home failing to provide the proper capital and machinery, &c. His last and greatest work, to which these few biographical notes are prefixed, fully describes this country, as well as the adjoining regions, all of which, collectively, imperfectly as they have been explored, may be said to comprise as rich an auriferous region as any in the world; differing, however, from those in California and Australia in their distance from a port, and difficulty in reaching them. Like too many other pioneers, poor Baines never reaped the harvest he had sown. A day will, and must come, when great and powerful communities will exist in these wealthy and fertile coun-

---

* The Moselikatse of Harris and Moffat.

tries, whose nature and capabilities are described in the present volume; but Baines' reward was only the fame of being the pioneer to point the way to them, and for him that was reward sufficient.

Mr. Baines encountered many serious difficulties from defective co-operation and want of support. Debts had to be satisfied, and his own subsistence even provided for, from the slender resources of the labours of his pencil; but throughout all his difficulties he never shrunk from a fixed determination to do the work which he considered had been allotted to him, and help to open up to civilization the great country of the Northern Gold Fields of Southern Africa. He knew that locked-up treasures existed there; he knew also that they required a golden key to open them, and want of funds crippled his energies, and weakened all his efforts, causing delays and disappointments that eventually affected his health, already seriously impaired, and tended to shorten his life; but at last it seemed as if his hopes were about to be realized by the establishment of a company at Port Elizabeth, who knew their man better than the London company did. In consequence, however, of the mining concessions from the chief, Lo Bengulo, having been made in favour of the London company, it was found impracticable to commence operations. Still undaunted, Baines made arrangements to proceed to the Fields almost alone, and to take with him a small quartz-crushing machine, which he had already purchased. The Rev. Mr. Greenstock, of Port Elizabeth, joined him. After having proceeded to D'Urban, Port Natal, a wagon was purchased, and every preparation made for the long journey, but God ordained it otherwise. The anxieties of mind he had lately gone through, as well as the injury sustained by the many years of hardship experienced in his travels, had fatally affected his digestive organs, and he at last, after a short illness, succumbed to a long and eventually fatal attack of dysentery, on the 8th of April, 1875, at the comparatively early age of 53 years. The same disease which killed Andersson, Chapman, and Livingstone, caused, doubtless, from the necessity for so many years of feeding on the tough and indigestible flesh of the elephant, rhinoceros, lion, and other larger game. He passed away quietly: " After life's fitful fever he sleeps well." To the end, perhaps, he would have preferred discovering the supposed remains of the Queen of Sheba's Palace to that of the richest gold mines in Ophir. As he, by all Englishmen who knew him, Baines was equally loved and revered by the natives of the country he explored, who would have followed him anywhere, or lost their lives in his defence.

We have in the above brief Memoir expressed not only our own, but the general opinion of all who knew him—of the many excellencies in the private character of poor Baines—and we consider it necessary now to review him as a public and well recognized contributor to science. Although never enjoying the benefit of what is generally known as a classical education, Baines was a sound English scholar. The diction of the volume he published, " Explorations in S.W. Africa in 1865," is singularly pure, and he published it without the usual polish and extraneous aid that the rough notes of travellers generally receive from their London editors and publishers. We all know what he was as an artist and field-sketcher. In that line no modern travellers could compete with him. As an astronomer, whose observations could be depended upon, the estimable Sir Thomas Maclear, of the Cape Observatory, considered him as second only to Livingstone—and indeed it was in that strict school of observation that Baines learned the use of his instruments, under Sir Thomas's own supervision. His sketch-maps of his travels in the interior of Africa are laid down and founded on facts, not imagination, and constructed on a scale so large that when reduced to that of maps in general use, all small errors would merely be eliminated, and this fact the great German geographers knew, and were not slow to recognize. As a geologist he made the best use of his powers of observation, and preferred facts to theories. As a botanist, ethnologist, and natural historian, he was equal, if not superior to many of his contemporaries. Of his particular excellence as an explorer, he was gifted with good temper, good health, and perseverance. Sufficiently educated to be able to make the most of letting the world know all he had seen and suffered, he possessed wonderful powers of observation. Not as good a linguist as Livingstone, he had, notwithstanding, such a colloquial capacity as permitted him to pass through hundreds of separate and distinct tribes, and allow himself to be understood; and, let it be remarked, not misunderstood, which is a very important point. He was well acquainted with all the native names of the botanical and natural history kingdoms. His English, written and spoken, was remarkably pure—wonderfully so in contrast with many magnates of the land, who looked down with contempt on the little East Anglian half-sailor, half-artist, from their elevated social condition. Poor Baines could take an accurate observation from lunars or occultation. He had a wonderful amount of reading in him, and there was hardly a subject in modern society to be discussed that he could not take a very prominent part in, as long as you did not allude to the Zambesi, for then he went off like a sky-rocket. In a ball-room, however, he might have been a failure.

As an artist, Baines' works are very numerous, executed, as too many of them were, very hastily, and almost to supply his daily and pressing wants. Objections have been made to his want of finish, and too great glare in their colouring; but it must be remembered that he was entirely a self-taught artist, and never had the advantage of any academical or gallery education. He also painted in a most brilliant climate, where all the varying tints of nature shine out in indeed very strong lights, and very often he was compelled to use colours of a very perishable and inferior nature. He was most successful in giving expression to the forms and attitudes not only of the wild tribes, but also of the wild animals of South Africa. His sketches of the immense troops of wilde-beests on the plains of the Free State are both in landscape and figure natural in the extreme, and the striking scenery of the Victoria Falls from several points of view, all visitors to the Crystal Palace must have seen and admired. As a portrait painter, his friends have several very excellent specimens of his art. He was particularly diligent as a naturalist in observing in the wilderness any hitherto unknown or undescribed species of plant, bird, insect, or animal. In this manner he observed and described the very curious genera of the "Welvistchia," nearly simultaneously with the first discoverer, Dr. Welvistch, after whom it has been called, and the beetle which graces our title-page. "Bolbotritus Bainesi," a new genus, described by Mr. H. W. Bates in the "Transactions of the Entomological Society, 1871," p. 175, was first discovered by Baines on the banks of the Mungone river, Lat. S. 20·45. Baines has also contributed a great deal to our knowledge of that plague of South Africa, the "Tsetse Fly," and in this work has given a most interesting account of his journey through a district infested with it, guided by an experienced hunter, with very little loss. Unfortunately Baines' discoveries in the botanical and natural history world are scattered through Cape newspapers and other periodicals, so that it would be rather a difficult task to collect them all. As a geologist, he generally takes a very clear and sensible view of the country he goes through, although not a professed mineralogist. His mechanical acquirements were just those an explorer ought to possess, and in common with Livingstone and Moffat, he could shoe a horse or refix a loose wagon tire, construct an improvised pontoon or repair a damaged gun-lock or stock broken to pieces by an enraged elephant or rhinoceros. In his nocturnal outspans his great pleasure was to amuse his followers by tricks, sleight-of-hand, and conjuring. The magic lantern and microscope were not forgotten —and also he composed for them comic songs of the Christy Minstrel school they all could join in; so that in connection with the cures he often effected of sometimes imaginary complaints, his followers seemed often to look on him as a being more than human, especially as they knew no matter how critical a situation he was in he never seemed to know fear— the great secret of respect amongst African savages.

Baines died unmarried, although eminently formed by nature for a domestic life. He always hesitated to ask any woman to share with him the discomforts of his wandering career. He left nothing behind save the regrets of a numerous and attached body of friends, his pictures, and the works which will always place him in the foremost rank of Explorers in South Africa.

H. H.

After the above notice of Baines' life was written, Sir Henry Rawlinson, President of the Royal Geographical Society, delivered his Annual Address on the 22nd May, 1876, and referred to Mr. Baines' career and death in the following manner:—

"THOMAS BAINES, the well-known African traveller and painter of African scenery, died at Durban, Natal, on the 8th May, 1875, whilst preparing for another of his numerous expeditions into the unexplored interior of the Continent. He was a man of marked individuality of character, a born artist and explorer, a lover of wild life, and skilled in all the shifts and resources of an explorer's career. Few men were so well endowed with these and other qualifications for successful African travel, and perhaps none possessed greater courage and perseverance, or more untiring industry than Baines. He was born at King's Lynn, in Norfolk, in 1822, the second son of a master mariner of that place. After receiving such an education as the views and circumstances of his parents admitted, he was placed with a coach-builder to learn the art of heraldic painting on carriage-panels; but a strong innate love of art soon led him to more elevated subjects, and he devoted much of the leisure time of his youth to sketching marine subjects from nature along the coasts of his native county. His ardent imagination fired him with a desire to see foreign countries, and in 1842 he left England for the Cape of Good Hope. It was in Cape Colony and in the neighbouring countries of South Africa that he was destined to pass the greater portion of his subsequent life; and it was here that he became better known even than in his native country. In fact, few men were thought so much of, or talked so much of, for many years in our South African Colonies as the Artist-traveller, Thomas Baines. His extreme unselfishness and willingness to oblige, his prolific pencil, ready for anything—African landscape, scenes of native war, animal and Caffre life, or portraits of his friends—and his fluent pen, kept him continually before the Colonial public and made him popular. It is to be remarked also that many friendships which he formed in the Colonies were kept with constancy to the end of his life. In 1846-7 he left Cape Town and proceeded to the then nearly unknown regions to the north of the colony for the purpose of sketching the scenes and incidents of the Caffre war then waging. Again, in the subsequent wars of 1851-3, he was busily engaged on the frontier in similar work, he having been attached to General Somerset's staff during the campaigns, through the intervention of his faithful friend, Mr. R. White. Several hundred sketches, displaying great vigour and vivid local character, were the results of his labours; many of which have since been on exhibition, with his other works, in London and Dublin. On the 6th November, 1851, he was present at the action with the rebel Hottentots at Water Kloof, when Colonel Fordyce, of the 74th Regiment, was killed; and in fact, Baines, in his desire to sketch faithfully scenes of actual battle, generally strove to be in the front, and he was rich in anecdotes of adventure and narrow escape in presence of the savage enemy.

"At the conclusion of the war in 1854 Baines returned to England, and was soon after his arrival, at the recommendation of our Council, appointed artist to the North-West Australian Expedition, under Mr. Augustus Gregory. During this arduous undertaking he distinguished himself and earned the approval of his leader and the Colonial Office by the zeal and ability with which he carried out a special mission with which he was entrusted, namely, a voyage in a schooner from the Victoria River to Java to procure fresh provisions for the Expedition, after their traverse by land from the Victoria to the Albert Rivers. The large series of sketches in oil made by Baines during this, as well as the subsequent Zambesi Expedition, were afterwards divided between the Kew Museum and our Society. On the termination of the Expedition in 1856, Baines returned to England, and in revisiting his native town was presented with the freedom of the borough by the Corporation.

"When the Zambesi Expedition, under Dr. Livingstone, was organised, early in 1858, Baines was selected to accompany it as artist and store keeper. An unhappy disagreement with Mr. Charles Livingstone, the brother to the great traveller, led to Baines' retirement, much against his own will; and he proceeded to the Cape. His love of exploration was at this time as keen as ever, and having become well versed in the use of astronomical and surveying instruments, under the supervision of Sir Thomas Maclear, Astronomer Royal at the Cape, he accepted the invitation of his friend, Mr. Thomas Chapman, an ivory-trader, to accompany him in a journey from the south-west coast to the Victoria Falls of the Zambesi. An account of this journey was published by him in 1864 on his return to England, under the title of 'Explorations in South-West Africa; being an Account of a Journey in 1861-2 from Walvisch Bay to Lake Ngami and the Victoria Falls.' Besides a complete route-survey, and very numerous sketches, Baines made on this journey a collection of objects of natural history. He spent several weeks at the Victoria Falls, making drawings and measurements; and published, besides the narrative just mentioned, a folio volume of coloured lithographs of this remarkable cataract.

"The years 1864-8 Baines spent in England, employing himself in bringing out the works above mentioned, lecturing, writing, and drawing illustrations for various periodicals. His industry was without limit. Early and late he was to be found in his painting-room, or at the desk, and his time and abilities were at the service of any one who needed them, with or without payment; for amongst his most striking characteristics was an utter indifference to worldly considerations. At the end of the year 1868 he again went out to Africa, under engagement with a Company to explore the Goldfields of the Tati, recently discovered, or re-discovered, by Carl Mauch and Mr. Hartley. He succeeded in obtaining the friendship of Lo Bengulo, the successor of the celebrated Moselikatze, the paramount chief of the region in which lay the Goldfields. From him he obtained valuable concessions for the Company he represented ; but nothing came of all his toilsome journeys and successful diplomacy ; the distances were too great, and the Company had no capital. Baines was never reimbursed his expenses, and had, on his return to Natal, to toil again as an artist to obtain a livelihood. The results of his explorations in the Gold region were, however, of considerable importance to Geography. He mapped very carefully the country, and the route thither from the capital of the Trans-Vaal Republic, and wrote a description of the region, which is now about to be published under the editorship of his old and tried friend, Mr. H. Hall, of Cape Town. A reduction of his map was published in our ' Journal,' vol. xli., in illustration of an abridgment of his Journals by Dr. R. J. Mann. In 1873 our Council recognised the value of Baines' geographical services by presenting him with a testimonial gold watch. He undertook, subsequently, other journeys into the adjoining Caffre countries, always mapping most carefully his routes, and sketching scenery and people. After a visit to Port Elizabeth he planned a new journey, almost alone, to the Gold district north of Tati, taking with him a small quartz-crushing machine ; and had prepared all his outfit and wagons for the journey when he was struck down by the old enemy of so many African travellers — dysentery — at Durban, and died, as before stated, on the 8th of May, 1875."

CONTENTS.

CHAPTER I.

THE TATI, OR VICTORIA GOLD FIELDS.

                                                                                    PAGE

The Zambesi, or Monomatapa Gold Fields—The Tati, or Victoria Gold Fields, Matabililand—Position and Extent of the Tati Gold Fields—Distances and Routes—Height above the Sea—Vegetation—Sanitary Conditions—Cost of Living—Medicines . 1

CHAPTER II.

THE NORTHERN GOLD FIELDS.

Departure from Natal—Journey up Country—Arrival in Matabililand—Reception by the Great Chief—Description of Scenery—The Mashona People—Old Diggings—The Hartley Hill Quartz Reefs—Ordered to leave the Country 12

CHAPTER III.

ELECTION OF THE MATABILI KING.

Lo Bengula proclaimed King—Coronation Ceremonies—Exploring for Gold—Elephant Hunting—" Willie's Grave"—Ancient Gold Fields—Visit to the King—Return to Matabililand—Lo Bengula signs the Grant 32

CHAPTER IV.

THE NORTHERN GOLD FIELDS, MATABILILAND.

Journey through the Fly Country—Opening the New Road—Adventure with Lions—Difficulties of Travel—Hunting Adventures—The Limpopo River—The Nylstroom—Bricks from an Ancient City—Return to Pretoria 53

CHAPTER V.

THE GOLD FIELDS OF THE TRANS-VAAL REPUBLIC—MARABASTADT, EERSTELING, LYDENBURG, MACMAC, AND PILGRIM'S REST.

PAGE

Mr. E. Button's Journeys—Ruins of an Old Town—Migrations of the Dutch Boers towards Canaan—Climate of the Gold Fields—Alluvial Gold Fields—Various Quartz Reefs—Information for intending Diggers 71

CHAPTER VI.

PROGRESS OF DISCOVERY.

Residence in the Trans-vaal—Anecdotes . . . 101

CHAPTER VII.

PROGRESS OF DISCOVERY.

Mr. George Pigott Moodie's journey to Delagoa Bay—Country between the Gold Fields and the sea—Boundary between the Trans-vaal and the Portuguese 105

CHAPTER VIII.

PROGRESS OF DISCOVERY—JOURNEY FROM PRETORIA TO NATAL via MARTHINUS WESSEL STROOM AND UTRECHT

Coal in South Eastern Africa—Crossing the Drakensberg—Quartz Reefs—Arrival in Natal—Summary of Distances . . . 111

CHAPTER IX.

PROGRESS OF DISCOVERY—THE LYDENBERG GOLD FIELDS—MACMAC OR MACAMAC AND PILGRIM'S REST QUARTZ REEFS AND ALLUVIAL DIGGINGS.

Discoveries of Herr Mauch—Ancient Ophir—Extensive ruins at Zambaoe—Adventure with Lions—First Discoveries of Gold—Position of the Gold Fields 120

CHAPTER X.

THE PRODUCE OF THE LYDENBERG GOLD FIELDS.

New Alluvial Gold Fields and the Finds 128

CHAPTER XI.

THE WORKING OF THE GOLD FIELDS.

PAGE

Dawn of Prosperity—Produce of the Fields—Big Nuggets—Finds at "Macmac"—Large Finds—Prospecting—Waterfall Creek Rush 131

CHAPTER XII.

THE GATHERING OF MINING COMMUNITIES.

General and Provisional Government—Mode of working—Establishment of Townships—Formation of Roads—Locality and season as affecting health—The Tsetse Fly—Routes and Distances—Mining Laws—Hints for Gold Diggers—Tests for Gold—Letters from Diggers—Conclusion 143

Itinerary 164

THE GOLD REGIONS

OF

SOUTH-EASTERN AFRICA.

THE VICTORIA FALLS OF THE ZAMBESI RIVER.—FROM AN OIL PAINTING BY MR. BAINES.

CHAPTER I.

THE TATI OR VICTORIA GOLD FIELDS.

THE following brief sketch of these regions is not intended as a narrative of their re-discovery, and the recent attempts to work them, but rather as a reliable compendium of information respecting their position, probable richness, sanitary condition, facility of reaching them, and cost of living there. It will, perhaps, be best to take them as nearly as possible in chronological order, and commence with the earliest known, which appear to be

Section I.—The Zambesi, or Monomotapa Gold Fields.

The country of Monomotapa, a name which in itself signifies a place whence something valuable is derived, lies to the southward of the Zambesi, or, as Vasco de Gama called it, when he discovered it in 1498, the " river of good signs." It may be roughly stated as lying between the parallels of 16° to 19° south latitude, and the meridian of 30° to 35° east longitude. The country, according to the early historian, abounded in gold, which in great quantities was extracted from veins in many of the provinces, especially in the kingdom of Torva, where also remained the ruins of ancient stone buildings, which for splendour and magnificence were reported to bear comparison with those of ancient Rome. The largest of these was traditionally supposed to have been the Queen of Sheba's palace, and the Moors of Sofala were said to have written testimony that Solomon derived his gold from the Torvan mines. A large and well equipped expedition was sent from Lisbon in 1650 under Francesco Barreto to explore these gold fields, but from sickness, opposition of the natives, and hardships and perils of the way, never reached them. The Portuguese subsequently settled on the Zambesi, and in an ancient work (accessible in Natal), it is stated that the quantity of gold sent from their possessions amounted to 2,000,000 metigals, estimated at £1,001,854 sterling. In later times we know that 130lbs. per annum have been sent home, but in the palmy days of the slave trade the annual expeditions to the Luenya and other rivers in quest of alluvial gold were discontinued. Nevertheless, the Mashona and other tribes south of the Zambesi continued to bring in small quantities of gold in vulture quills, which they sold at 3 dollars, or 13s. 6d. per onza, which is somewhat less than our ounce. In 1868-9, I had gold offered to me in exchange for calico, and saw the native goldsmiths belonging to Senhor Tito de Secard, casting it into ingots and making very neat rings, chains, and other ornaments. Gold is still brought down in small quantities to the Portuguese settlements along the coast.

Section II.—The Tati, or Victoria Gold Fields, Matabili Land.*

The discovery of these and of the northern gold fields was so nearly simultaneous that it is hardly possible to separate them, yet as the Tati claims precedence by a month or two, it will be well for the sake of clearness to consider it first.

We had heard for many years amongst the Dutch emigrants rumours of gold found beyond the Zoutpansberg, and about 1865, Mr. H. Hartley, while hunting in Matabili land, observed groups of ancient diggings, and connecting these with the current stories,

---

* The Zambesi Gold Fields are situated north of the watershed line, between the Zambesi and Limpopo rivers; the Tati Gold Fields South of same (*vide* map).

he invited Herr Carl Manch to accompany him on his next trip; and in 1866, the then young and almost unknown traveller, announced the discovery of a gold field eighty miles in length by two or three miles in breadth. Various companies, or rather exploring parties, were formed in South Africa, one of the first being headed by Captain Black, and another of ten men under Mr. MacNiel, of Durban, Natal, besides many smaller ones. A party of 34 Australians was equipped in Natal in 1869, and sent up to test the richness of the reputed gold field. A party was also sent up from Port Elizabeth, but I am not aware that it discovered much at Tati.

In 1868, the London and Limpopo Mining Company, headed by Sir John Swinburne, Bart., and Captain Arthur Lionel Levert, left England, taking with them an expensive equipment, including a traction engine, which, however, was left, and subsequently sold in Natal. They reached the Tati on the 27th April, 1869; set up their steam engine and opened a store. Sir John and Mr. Le Vert proceeded to Myati. The former obtained leave to proceed to the northern gold fields—the latter returned to Natal, and had a stamping machine constructed there by Mr. Gavin, of Durban.

About this time quite a little village had arisen on the north bank of the Tati river. As nearly as I can ascertain, the following were the companies at work :—No. 1, Dr. Coverly's party; No. 2, Rocky, Dalton, and James, with three small stampers worked by the Limpopo Co.'s steam engine; 3, Burril's party; 4, King Williamstown party; 5, a section of do.; 6, Old Charley's party; 7, The Pretoria party, Brown and others; 8, Two carpenters; 9, London and Limpopo Mining and Trading Co. The company of 35 Australians, sent up from Durban, went about 32 miles up the river and located themselves on "Todd's Creek." Several of the shafts were 50 feet deep; but, though 150 tons of quartz, some of it apparently rich had been got out, the crushing machines that had been extemporised did not succeed. Nevertheless, specimens had been sent home, and Messrs. Johnson and Matthey's, assayers to the Bank of England, certified as under :—

"Assay Offices and Ore Floors, May 7th, 1870.

"Certificate of Assay. For London and South African Bank we have examined the samples of mineral, marked as under, and find the following to be the result :— Sent by J. J. Dickenson D'Urban.

"No. 1.—Specimen of rock cut through to meet the quartz; no gold.

"No. 2.—New Zealand reef, average stone, produce of gold 4·900 oz. per ton of 20 cwt. of ore, silver traces.

"No. 3. X.—New Zealand reef, produce of gold, 10 oz., produce of silver, 0·900 oz. per ton.

"No. 4, X.—Alliance reef, produce of gold, 65·250 oz.; produce of silver, 5 oz. per ton.

"No. 5, X.—Burrell's reef, average stone; produce of gold, 0·500 oz. per ton; silver traces.

"No. 6, X.—Pioneer reef, produce of gold, 39·725 oz.; produce of silver, 3·250 oz. per ton.

"No. 7, X.—Reef produce of gold, 3·250 oz. per ton; silver traces.

"No. 8, X.—Blue Jacket Reef, produce of gold, 4·700 oz. per ton; silver traces.

"From Mr. Bayne.

"No. 9.—Five pieces of quartz, produce of gold 20·250 oz.; produce of silver, 1·250 oz. per ton.

"No. 10.—One piece of quartz marked satisfactory, gold evenly dispersed; produce of gold 52·250 oz. ; produce of silver, 3 oz. per ton. "Signed

"JOHNSON, MATTHEY & Co."

Beside these, another specimen was received by a mercantile house in London, and when tested by Mr. Claudel proved to contain 26·8 oz. gold, and 31½ oz. silver to the ton.

Early in 1876, Captain Levert returned to Tati, and had the crushing machinery erected; and the following is the certified result by Mr. B. N. Acutt, of the first quartz subjected to anything like a fair test upon the spot :—

Name of Reef.	Quartz crushed.	Yield of Gold.	Yield per ton.
Blue Jacket	19 tons 10 cwt.	42 oz.	2 oz. 3 dwts. 1 gr.
Australian Reef A	2 tons 10 cwt.	16 oz. 10 dwts.	7 oz. 12 dwts.

Captain Levert also certified during the same year that 125 oz. had, to his knowledge, been produced from the reefs at or near the Tati.

Mr. Bromwich, of Durban, reported that the Australians had gone down 80 feet, but the vein did not widen out as they hoped. Nevertheless, out of 2 tons, 10 cwt. 2 qrs. 24 lbs. of quartz they had obtained 25 oz. 3 dwts. 12 grs. of gold. Besides this, they were about £70 indebted to the Limpopo Company, and sent down, as they reckoned, quartz enough to pay it, and to their gratification they found it not only quite sufficient, but their messenger brought them back a surplus of 22 oz., valued on the Tati at £77 more.

One of the party wrote to Mr. J. D. Wotherspoon in 1871, " We crushed five tons of quartz here at the end of last year, and received as the proceeds forty-three ounces of retorted gold, or over 8 oz of gold per ton of stone, and we expect the forty or fifty tons of stone raised since then will yield the same average."

Several of the smaller properties had been bought up by Sir John Swinburne, who left Mr. August Greite to work the Blue Jacket reef, and during his visit to London in 1870-71, had engaged Mr. C. J. Nelson (originally the Mineralogist of the South African Gold Field Exploration Company), to come out and take charge of mining operations for him.

Most of the working parties, being unprovided with funds sufficient for the long and laborious processes of mining till they reached the gold, and then requiring to provide machinery to crush it, had sold out or abandoned their claims, and yielded to the more brilliant attractions of the diamond fields; and in the beginning of August, 1871, only Messrs. Nelson, Acutt, Franklin, and Brown remained at Tati; Mr. Greite and assistant at Blue Jacket; and three of the Australians at Todd's Creek. The arrival of Mr. Hart with his engine and stamping machine, made also by Mr. Gavin, of Durban, with Mr. North as engineer, Mr. Arkle, engineer of the Limpopo Company, and others, re-enlivened the place a little.

Mr. Greite had gone about 70 feet deep, and had reached water, which, however, did not much inconvenience him. He had raised about £300 worth of gold, and had 150 tons of quartz lying on the surface in assorted heaps, of which the most promising he thought would yield 10 oz. of gold to the ton. He showed me several specimens of quartz of almost fabulous richness ; one piece he estimated at about 1,500 oz. to the ton. Of course these were picked specimens, but the mass must be rich from which such could be selected.

I was told on good authority that out of 74 tons of quartz raised by the Australians at Todd's Creek, 226 oz. were obtained ; 170 of which were from the first 40 tons. More than 400 oz. had at that time, been sent from Tati. Since then Mr. Hart has left the Tati, as there were not miners in the fields to supply quartz to keep his machine at work. The machine itself was bought by Mr. Cruikshank, and I believe now lies at Ba Mangwato. Mr. Nelson has been working steadily on, despite the difficulty of procuring labour and the imperfectness of his machinery ; and towards the close of 1872 I was informed by Mr. Acutt that between 1,500 and 2,000 oz. of gold had been sent home from Tati. In November of that year, Mr. Nelson brought down 250 oz., and is, I believe, now working on in expectation of the arrival of more complete machinery from England.

I am not aware that alluvial gold in any appreciable quantity has been discovered near the Tati. Deeds of grant and agreement were made to the Limpopo Gold Mining Company.

On May the 14th, 1870, Captain Levert called the residents at Tati together, and read to them the grants and agreement, and then informed them, that in virtue of these deeds, the Tati district was virtually his property, and that of the company he represented; but that he intended throwing it open to all who would subscribe to the laws made by the community, that all their hitherto acquired rights would be respected, and that the only difference would be that instead of dealing with the Matabili they would have to deal with him.

He claimed, however, 1st, to be perpetual chairman of their assembly. 2nd. That the company should have the power of leasing auriferous or other land, water rights, and licensing machinery. 3. That on every newly-discovered reef the company should claim one-fourth, allowing only three ordinary claims to the discoverers. 4. None of the company's claims should be liable to be "jumped" for any reason whatever.

Section III.—*Position and Extent of the Tati Gold Fields.*

The Tati district, as described in the grant made to Captain Levert, is a triangle, of which the southern side, formed by the Shashi river from its source to the junction of the Ramoqueban, is about 85 miles in length; its north-western, formed by the mountains in which those rivers rise, about 60, and its north-eastern, defined by the Ramoqueban river, about 85 miles.

The Tati river flows between the two previously named, and enters the Shashi on its northern side, four miles above the junction of the Ramoqueban. The settlement is about 20 miles up the Tati river. On the north bank its latitude, by my own observation, is 21° 27′ S., and by that of Edwin Mohr, the German explorer, 21° 28′. Its longitude, very carefully taken by Mr. Mohr, with more time at his command than I had, and with superior instruments, 27° 51′ E. The London and Limpopo Company's store is conspicuous on the west or left hand side of the road on the north of the river. To the north of this, on a rounded hill, is the house of Mr. Nelson, and a little to the east, that of Mr. Brown, of the Glasgow and Limpopo Company. Near these once stood Flagstaff Lodge, the trading store of Messrs. Coward, that of Mr. and Mrs. Hart, and several others; while to the east of the road, in a valley separated from the river by a small hill, stood "The Ranche," once tenanted by Dr. Coverley and his party and three or four others; while a mile below them stood that of Mr. Arkle, engineer to the London and Limpopo Company, and the crushing machine under his charge. Near this also was Mr. Hart's engine during the short time it remained there. I suppose few of these houses now remain, and I cannot tell how far they have been replaced by others. On a small range of hills north of the settlement remain the mines of the various parties, all of them containing quartz more or less auriferous, but now deserted because the owners had exhausted their means in sinking down to the reefs, and had not capital either to go on working their mines, or to provide machinery for crushing the quartz. About three miles north-west is Blue Jacket mine, formerly worked by Mr. Greite. Eight or nine miles north is Halfway Reef, and about 35 miles up the Tati from the settlement is Todd's Creek, formerly worked with very good results by the Australians, equipped from Natal, but in 1871 deserted by all except one or two of the party.

Section IV.—Distances and Routes.

The distance of Tati Settlement from Plough Hotel, Market Square, Pietermaritzburg, as measured by myself with tracheometer is, *via* Potchefstroom, 829 miles, 5 furlongs, 191 yards, and from Durban 883 miles, 5 furlongs, 191 yards. From Port Elizabeth it is estimated, I believe, by Mr. John Bell at 1,086 miles, *via* Hope Town, Kuruman, and Ba Mangwato.

Of the Port Elizabeth route I can only partially speak from experience, but I believe there are extensive tracts north of Hope Town, in which grass and water are excessively scarce in the dry season. The Natal road is better supplied, but in the month of July, when snow lies on the Drakensberg, the cold is so intense that the cattle and native servants suffer greatly. This may, however, be avoided by starting in the end of February or beginning of March.

We left Pietermaritzburg on 13th March, 1869, reached Potchefstroom on 27th April, left it on 12th May, passed Ba Mangwato May 29, and reached Tati on the 9th June, travelling easily, and with one span of oxen to each wagon.

At Ba Mangwato the two roads from Port Elizabeth and Natal

meet in what is called the Doorst, or Thirst-land, extending about 100 miles from the Limpopo in the direction of the Tati.

The rivers affluent of the Limpopo flow through a granite district, and are generally crossed where they are to appearance deep worn channels, filled for many miles in length by broad flat beds of sand. During the rainy season heavy floods rush down, and when they pass away leave the sand saturated with moisture, so that water may be obtained cool, clear, and pure by merely scraping with the hand ; but as the dry season advances this drains off, and unless a supply be retained by some inequality of the underlying rock forming a reservoir, the sand, by the end of June, is completely dried, and the traveller must enquire carefully of natives, or others, where small supplies of water are still likely to remain.

Section V.—Height above the Sea,—Vegetation,—Sanitary Conditions,—Cost of Living, &c.

The boiling point of water at Tati settlement, below the houses, was on the 9th June, 1869, 207°.0, barometer 26·22 ; and height above the sea level, 2623 feet ; the thermometer averaged 45 to 62. The maximum was 90 and the minimum 43. The houses standing in the valley were rendered hot by reflection of the sun's rays from the hill sides. The dense fringe of mimosas and acacias along the river banks also screened them from the breeze ; those houses built on the heights of course were cooler. The necessity of kraaling the cattle at night within the village, gives birth to immense swarms of flies, which, settling on the eyes of native children afflicted with opthalmic disease, are very apt to convey infection to others. In 1870, I think, three or four persons died of fever, but I feel tolerably sure that dwellers in houses, built on heights, exposed to the free breeze, at a distance from any accumulation of filth, would be in very little danger.

The hills and valleys supply all sorts of wood for building purposes. The Moparri or banhinca, a resinous wood, which white ants will not attack, is most useful as supplying poles for wattle and daub or palisade houses. The Umgarno, of which the Kafirs make their bowls and dishes, serves for many purposes in place of softer wood. The Mimosa gives firewood or thorny branches for kraal fencing, while the kameel-doorn, knopjies doorn, wagt-een-beetje, and other acacias, afford timber for wagon work or for machinery. I have seen a log 8 or 10 feet long and 30 inches thick cut for the basement of Mr. Hart's stamping machine.

Among the wild fruits the Marula, as large as a peach and with a kernel almost like one, has a pleasant flavour, and may be eaten from the tree or cooked for pastry, or preserved ; and a kind of strychnia, called the Kafir orange, has a moderately hard shell, a pleasant pulp, and seeds that had better be rejected. It makes when steeped in a little water and fermented, a pleasant wine, which the addition of a very little spirit and some sugar makes extremely palatable. A kind of wild spinach affords an excellent table vegetable. A garden was started by the London and Limpopo Mining Company, and everything that did not require a cold climate succeeded there.

Boer's meal (wheaten) which makes excellent bread, is taken up by traders from the Transvaal and sold at about £4 per muid, Natal sugar about 1/2 per lb., coffee, raw, 1/6 per lb. and other groceries in proportion. Transport from Natal was in 1870 about £2 10s. to £2 15s. per cwt., and the increase of cost in other articles may be estimated by this. We reckoned that it would cost £6 per month to provision a man according to the navy scale, and miners were at that time asking £2 10s. per week and rations, or £3 10s. without. Kafir corn, or millet, mealies, pumpkins, tobacco, a round nut giving excellent oil, &c., may be bought from the Makalakas ; also goats and slaughter cattle. It is usual to equip a wagon and make a trip of from 40 to 90 miles among the villages, taking beads, brass wire, brass rods, knives, snuff boxes, stout unbleached calico, voerchitz, blankets and clothing. It is contrary to Matabili law to sell guns to Mashonas or Makalakas. Game of all kinds, including the various antelopes, buffalo, eland, giraffe, lion, rhinoceros, and elephant are to be found in the Tati district, but the professional hunters make them, especially the elephant, scarce and shy, and though good sport may be had by a well mounted man or good pedestrian, no one could trust to living on the produce of his rifle.

Section VI.—*Medicines, &c.*

We had no serious illness during the whole of our expedition, during which 6,000 or 7,000 miles of all descriptions of country were traversed, and therefore most of our medicine was given to others less fortunate, but I have found the following most useful :—First, quinine dissolved in good spirit of any kind, a dram to be taken before breakfast, in any climate where fever is likely to be prevalent. N.B.—When you open a case of brandy do not trust to mixing your quinine as you want it, but at once set apart as many bottles as you think you will require, and put in quinine enough to make the spirit unpleasant to drink, except in small quantities, as a tonic.

I once relieved a poor woman from intense agony with a bit of chalk out of the tool box, a few drops of opium, and a spoonful of sugar. At another time a man was brought me bitten on the ankle by a serpent described as deadly ; indeed, he seemed to be already benumbed and falling into a state of torpor. I told his comrades to scarify the wound freely, but the blood would not flow. I gave them ammonia to wash it with, and then mixed a strong dose, but knowing that the natives think if a patient die it is the medicine that has killed him, I called the rest of the men, and said, "Now you have brought this man to me bitten by a deadly snake, so that he must die if I cannot help him. I will do my best, and you see me drink some of this medicine to show you there is no harm in it. Now let him drink the rest of it, and I have done my part ; after that he is in God's hands to live or die." They answered, " Yes, we see, and no blame can come to you if he die." He remained torpid all night, but was well next morning.

In cases of incipient fever among native servants, I never waited till the disease took a decided form, but as soon as a man complained of headache, disordered bowels, furred tongue, &c., I gave him five or six grains of tartar emetic, put him off duty for the day, and generally found him all right in the morning. Epsom salts, or other aperient medicine, should be provided rather plentifully, chalk and opium in case of dysentery, and powdered ginger, nutmeg or cinnamon for milder forms. Emetic powders are useful occasionally, and sulphate of zinc to mix with water tempered with a little opium for an eye wash. Eau de luce, or strong ammonia, in case of snake bites : scarify the wound to let the poisoned blood flow out, wash with ammonia, and take 10 or 15 drops diluted with water as a draught.

I once used one pound of carbonate of ammonia, dissolved in a bucket of warm water, to wash four horses during our passage through the Tsetse fly. I cannot assert that this saved them, but I have every reason to believe so. Nine or more of our oxen died, but not a single horse.

The natives will constantly apply for medicines, generally a dose of salts. A good strong emetic or an application of eye water, serves the purpose, but many come with imaginary diseases, and would be offended if medicine were refused ; to such I have often given cayenne pepper. The strength of my medicine became renowned, and patients flocked from all quarters to test its efficacy. To some of my own men who came with slight ailments when I really had but six small doses of fever medicine in case of real sickness, I have given curry powder, telling them to make a fire, boil some water, drink the mixture I gave them, and wrap themselves up warm for the night. In the morning they have been quite well. When, had I told them I had no medicine and sent them away, I really believe their imagination would have created an illness for them before morning.

MATABILI WARRIORS.—NORTHERN GOLD FIELDS.—COPIED FROM A PAINTING BY THOMAS BAINES

CHAPTER II.
THE NORTHERN GOLD FIELDS.
MATABILI LAND.

The discovery of these fields in 1866 and 1867 followed that of the Tati only by the interval of the few weeks necessarily occupied in travelling 350 miles more to the north-east, but the difficulty of exploring and ascertaining their reality increased at every step. Even during the first-named year the suspicions of the Matabili were aroused, and Mr. Hartley* dared not openly assist Herr Mauch in searching for reefs, because, whenever he attempted to do so his native servants would ask, "What have you to do with seeking stones? The king gave you leave to shoot elephants! Why do you not attend to your own business, and not meddle with things for which you have no liberty?"

Nevertheless, by his own scientific skill and perseverance, by the guidance of a Mashona, a retainer of Mr. Hartley's head man Inyoka, by such assistance as the hunters dare give, and chief of all by the immunity which almost all savages concede to men whom they believe "demented," Mauch was able to visit and make a hasty examination of several reefs in the vicinity of the Umvute and Sarua rivers, as well as between the Quæ-quæ and Bembesi.

* Mr. Hartley, formerly of Bathurst, Lower Albany—a well known elephant hunter.

"There," to use his own words, "the extent and beauty of the gold fields are such that I stood as it were transfixed, and for a few minutes was unable to use the hammer. . . . Thousands of persons might work on this extensive gold field without interfering with one another."

A second visit in 1867 confirmed the impressions of the former year, but the fears of the Matabili had been excited to the highest pitch. They were aware that the knowledge of the richness of their country had already spread among the white men, and they expected that a rush of fierce and lawless desperadoes from all parts of a world more extensive than they had ever before dreamed of, would set in at once and drive them from their land. Their anger was kindled against all who had helped to spread the gold news. Mr. Hartley himself, notwithstanding the personal friendship and favour of the great chief Umselekatse, was at one time in danger of falling a sacrifice to the popular fury, but owed his life partly to the respect his honest manliness had earned among the people, and partly to the tact and knowledge of native character shown by Rev. Mr. Lee, missionary to the Matabili, in pleading for him.

The news of these discoveries, backed by the exhibition of specimens of quartz more or less studded with gold, roused the public of Natal into action. The Durban Gold Mining Company, composed chiefly of members of the Durban Volunteer Artillery, and commanded by Lieut. McNeil of that corps, left town on the 14th October, 1868, and proceeded first to Tati, and next to Manyami's outpost, whence they sent in to ask permission to enter that part of Matabili land inhabited by the tribe, and in due time received permission. Accompanied by a letter from the Rev. T. M. Thomas, the missionary at Inyati, who rather unfortunately advised them, "Be careful not to say much about your gold search. Ask for permission to hunt and see the King's country."*

At the military kraal of the Twong Endaba they were visited by Umbeko, the Induna or commander of that regiment, who, after conversing some time, became satisfied of their peaceful intentions, and remarked that the alarming reports (for which Mr. Lee was blamed) could not be true. On the 6th of March, 1869 they reached Inyati, latitude 19°40'48", longitude 29°13'30"; height above the sea 4,115 feet, and 1,041½ miles from Durban, the station of the London Missionary Society, where they were gladly welcomed by a number of hunters and traders, among whom was

---

* The Matabili warriors are divided into regiments generally distinguished by the colour of their shields.

Herr Mauch himself. The Rev. Mr. Thomas was ill with fever, and his family were also more or less affected. A party of Griqua hunters had lost one of their number, and as the healthy season would not open for at least a month or two, it became necessary to decide how to shelter themselves till then. Some proposed building a large hut, but eventually they took possession of a delapidated house vacated by the Rev. John Moffat about four years previously. It was then damp, leaky, and surrounded by swampy ground, and signs of fever soon began to appear among the unfortunate party. Mr. Baker, who had dug a well with the double purpose of supplying the mission with water and of ascertaining whether gold bearing strata existed below the surface, was first taken ill, and shortly afterwards Messrs. McNeil, Guthrie, Will, Davis, and Hobson. On the night of the 3rd of April Baker passed away quietly, and McNeil, who lay insensible in the same room, knew not till morning that the spirit of his fellow-sufferer had fled. On the 4th the survivors made a coffin, and "as the sun was sinking to the horizon lowered the body of their friend to its resting-place, standing with uncovered heads around while the solemn service for the burial of the dead was read by one of them." On the 7th they removed to a small hill about a mile away, and the sick appeared to benefit by the change, but Mr. Guthrie died on the 14th, Mr. Hobson next day, and Mr. Davis on the 17th, and were buried by their sorrowing comrades beside poor Baker.*

When the unhealthy season had passed the propriety of going on to the north-east was debated, but though McNeil himself still weak, and two others voted for doing so, four took the less heroic but certainly more sensible view, that in their enfeebled state it would be more prudent to return; and I can only say that from the weak condition in which I saw the convalescents I think they adopted the proper course. Their expedition, however, was not without effect. By upright and straightforward dealings they had removed the strong prejudice that existed against gold seekers, and showed the natives that the much-dreaded diggers were men as honest and as peaceful as the hunters or other Englishmen they were accustomed to.

Meanwhile the letters of Herr Mauch announcing the discovery of the gold fields arrived in Europe, and were given to the public under the sanction of scientific societies in Germany and in

---

* In 1871 I took up from Natal a stone suitably inscribed, and delivered it to the Rev. J. B. Thompson, who, I have no doubt, has long since placed it on their tomb.

England. The glowing language he employed was considered open to discussion, but it proved fortunate, for it roused the public to action when a more sober relation of facts might have fallen flat on inattentive ears.

Small specimens of quartz and gold dust were exhibited at the Royal Geographical Society and elsewhere. One piece assayed by Johnson and Mattheys gave a proportion of 1·185 oz. gold and 60 oz. silver to the ton ; and a specimen possessed by the Chamber of Commerce in Port Elizabeth was stated by my friend, Dr. Atherstone, to be worth at the rate of £12,000 per ton.

During the year 1868, Sir John Swinburne, Bart., in conjunction with Captain Arthur Lionel Levert, and some other gentlemen, associated themselves under the title of the London and Limpopo Mining Company, and with a steam traction engine, a quantity of other appliances and stores for personal use or for training, left England for Natal. Almost simultaneously a number of gentlemen interested in that colony enrolled themselves as " The South African Gold Fields' Exploration Company," and offered the command of their expedition to me. Mr. C. J. Nelson, a Swedish mineralogist who had travelled and worked for 16 years in California, was placed in his proper capacity on our staff, and Mr. R. J. Jewell was appointed secretary. I left London in the steamship Asia on the 2nd of December, but after buffeting head winds and seas with an overloaded vessel till the 6th, we bore up and narrowly escaped shipwreck on the Isle of Wight, returned to Gravesend for repairs, where the passengers unanimously voted to Mrs. Blaxell, the captain's wife, a piece of plate in testimony of their admiration of the womanly devotion, fidelity, and courage with which she had assisted her husband during that trying time.

On the 19th December we finally left Falmouth ; anchored off Natal on the 14th Feb., 1869, and landed on the 16th at the Point. We proceeded by rail to Durban, a couple of miles north-west upon the shore of the inner bay, in latitude 29°52', longtitude about 31°1·30, and only 22 feet above the sea. The town is encircled by a range of wood-clad hills, dotted with suburban villas, sweeping round from the Berea, near the sea coast on the north, to the bluff which guards the entrance on the south, and displays its revolving light to guide the approaching mariner. We received a hearty welcome from the colonists, and every possible assistance from Mr. C. Behrens and the inhabitants generally ; the more especially as at this time a rush of Australian diggers had come over, and were now expressing in strong terms their disappointment at finding that the reported gold fields were perhaps a thousand miles away, and "not one ounce of gold had yet been brought in from them." They and the leading colonists were urging on the Government to take some steps to ascertain the actual value of the discovery, and now all parties looked with confidence to the well-known scientific and practical skill of Mr. Nelson to settle this important point. But the efforts of the colonists were not confined to helping us, and wishing us God speed upon our journey. Meetings were called, and money (about £3,000) subscribed, and a party of thirty-four miners* equipped, to follow on our track and explore the reputed auriferous country. At the same time, Messrs. Burke and Babe had arrived from America (*viâ* England, I believe), bringing with them a London waggonette, the newest repeating rifles, and the ideas generally current at home

ENTRANCE TO THE HARBOUR OF NATAL, WHENCE MR. BAINES PROCEEDED ON HIS OVERLAND JOURNEY.

of the savage wilderness they were going into. They were rather surprised to learn that most of their equipment might far more suitably have been provided here; that they might travel hundreds of miles without occasion for weapons of defence, and that even when a rifle is taken the colonial traveller lets his native attendant carry it, instead of keeping it slung on his own shoulder for fear of treachery. Another idea gleaned from experience in California (and confirmed since by our recent finds in the Lydenburg district) was that their best chance of finding alluvial gold was to skirt the " Foothills," on the sea-face of the Drakensberg. Fortune at the diamond fields, however, compensated their want of success, but I

---

* This is the party alluded to in page 3.

cannot close this brief notice of their expedition without paying a tribute to the memory of my friend, Mr. William Martin—a true colonist, a sincere Christian, and a warm-hearted philanthropist— who had travelled extensively already, and who, after the close of their journey, undertook another overland journey to Delagoa Bay. On the 12th Sept., 1869, he was found by some Portuguese gentlemen on the Manice, or King George's River, about 30 miles from Lorenzo Marques—his "placid features" still unchanged— some fragments of manive and a few beans only in his pocket. In the diary, traced by his enfeebled hand, the words, "Sunday 5th .... Patience must have her perfect work ..... I commend myself to the watchful care of Him who reigns on high." The Portuguese buried him with all possible respect and reverence, preserving the diary and articles necessary for the identification of the unfortunate traveller.

Here, also, we had the pleasure of rejoining and frequently meeting our German friends, Edwin Mohr and Adolph Hubner, bound also to the gold fields. Our four wagons standing side by side, flying the British and North German flags, like a little squadron busily fitting for a long voyage, were for many days a centre of interest upon the market square of Pietermaritzburg.

On the 13th March our expedition left Maritzburg,* and wended its way north-west, through the colony of Natal, passing Howick and the Umgeni waterfall, Mooi River, and Bushman's River at Estcourt, by substantial iron bridges; the Tugela River at Estcourt by the Pont, and the remaining streams by drifts or fords, till we climbed the Drakensberg at Van Reenen's Pass, and on its ridge, about 5,400 feet in height, passed from Natal into the Republic of the "Orange Free State," where we rested for a few days at the town of Harrismith,† with the giant Platberg rearing its castellated cliffs about 2,000 feet higher to the eastward.

Here we bought a willow log for fuel, ere we commenced our journey over the bleak, undulating, grassy, treeless highlands of the Free State. Replenishing our larder, by shooting a few of the numerous wilde-beest that still maintain a desperate struggle for existence with the unsparing skin-hunters, we crossed the Vaal River at Lause's Drift, and reached Potchefstroom, the capital of the Trans-Vaal Republic, where our wagons again stood side by

---

* Lat., 29·35·; long., 30 23·; and 2,080 feet above the sea.

† Harrismith, lat., 28·16·28; long., 29·5·; altitude 4,950 feet; **distance from Pietermaritzburg, 148 miles.**

side with Mr. Mohr's, by the circus in the grounds of the Royal Hotel, which Mr. Mohr's observations, taken with superior instruments and ample leisure, placed in latitude 26°43′, longitude 27°33′40″, altitude, 3,900 feet ; distance from Pietermaritzburg, 365 miles 2 furlongs. Its streets, like those of most South African towns, cross each other at right angles, with channels of fresh clear water running on either side, and its dwelling-houses, its stores, and public buildings, peep forth from among rich orchards or groves of tall willows, with their branches drooping in long and graceful curves, till their tips nearly sweep the passing vehicles.

Crossing the Mooi River, meandering through the wide alluvial valley, we proceeded north, visiting the famous limestone caverns and subterranean river at Wonder Fontein; and, at Thorndale, south of the bold ranges of the Magaliesberg, we visited Mr. Henry Hartley. He and I had long known each other by repute; but he had heard, some years before, of my death, and now would hardly be persuaded that I was not a ghost, until the justice I did to the good fare he set before us convinced him of his error. He was himself preparing for his journey, and volunteered to be our pilot along the road; an offer which I gladly accepted. And here, I may say, in brief, commenced one of the most gratifying friendships I have been privileged to form, which has endured through many a changing scene of life in trouble and in joy.

I must pass rapidly over the incidents of our journey. We visited Rustenburg* with its coffee farms, its fruitful orchards, and its experimental plots of sugar cane, crossed the Marico River, travelled along the forest clad banks of the Limpopo, crossed the Nomani river, and then, striking across a broad dry flat, reached the cross roads under the hills of Ba Mangwato,† the native town of Shoshong,‡ being about 10 miles west north-west. The chief Matchen, impressed with the general idea that all gold seekers were on the sure and speedy road to fortune, was already levying a tax of one sovereign upon prospectors, but this I declined to pay because I did not intend to work at the Tati, over which he claimed jurisdiction, and also because he was only a tributary chief to the Matabili affecting temporary importance since the

---

* Lat., 24·41·: long., 27·30·: height, 3,367 feet; 454 miles 6 furlongs 188 yards from Pietermaritzburg.

† Lat. 23·6·54; long., 26·58·; height, 2,800 feet; 628 miles 2 furlongs 79 yards from Pietermaritzburg.

‡ The Moselikatzi of Harris and Moffat.

death of their great chieftain Umselekatze.* An arduous *trek* across the "Doorst land" crossing several rivers either quite dry or scantily supplied with water, kept cool and clear in reservoirs of rock beneath the broad, dry sandy beds, brought us to the Great Shasha and then to the Tati river, where we out-spanned near the store of the † London and Limpopo Mining Company, where we were warmly welcomed by my friend, D. M. Kisch, and by the other miners, whose names will be found in the section already devoted to the Tati. We crossed the Ramoqueban, the Impaque, the Umkwesi, and a small branch (afterwards called ‡Sawpit Spruit) of the Mangwe river. Here Mr. Hartley introduced us to Mr. Lee, who not only perfectly understood the language and customs of the Matabili, but was privileged to hunt and reside in the South Western district, had long enjoyed the confidence of the late chieftain Umselekatze, and was generally regarded as his agent in all business affairs with white men. I told my errand, and showed the letter of introduction given me by the Governor of Natal, and Mr. Lee said he had often told the old king that the English Government would do nothing underhand, but that any of its messages would be sent openly and above board, and now he regretted the king was not alive to see the truth of his words.

We now left the quartzose country, and passed through ranges of picturesque granite hills with forests at their base, and huge rocks, bearing often a grotesque resemblance to animals or other familiar objects. Crossing their summits we reached Manyama's Kraal¶ on a spruit of the Shashani, when Mr. Lee explained to him the general purpose of my visit, and desired him at once to send forward special messengers to announce my arrival, and to call together the council of the nation to hear the contents of His Excellency's letter. We remained here from the 16th June till the beginning of July, when two petty chiefs were sent by order of Um Nombata from Umbeko's Kraal. They showed much curiosity respecting my business, and the contents of the letter.

---

* These native towns are constructed of the most perishable and fragile materials, and in case of their destruction by invasion, or fire, future travellers may, in vain, look for their remains.

† Lat., 21·28·; long., 27·51·; height, 2,623 feet; 829 miles 5 furlongs 191 yards from Pietermaritzburg.

‡ Sawpit-Lees farm, lat., 20·44·40; long., 28·13·48; height, 3,470 feet, 888 miles 2 furlongs 36 yards distance from Pietermaritzburg.

¶ Manyamas outpost, lat., 20·37·10; long, 28·19· ; height, 3470 feet; distance from Pietermaritzburg, 887 miles 2 furlongs 134 yards.

I desired Mr. Watson, my interpreter, to tell them that the letter could be read to no one but the chief or chiefs in council of their nation, but that I recognised the name of Um Nombata as the great and venerable councillor of their late king, and had read of him in the works of Englishmen (the Rev. R. Moffat and Captain Cornwallis Harris) who had written in terms of respect and friendship of him ; also that in general terms I had no objection to tell them that my business was friendly, and that it had relation to the metal, gold, of which they had recently heard as having been found in their country. When Mr. Lee arrived he reproved them for exceeding their duty as messengers by endeavouring to learn from me that message which should only be communicated to the chiefs, and they acknowledged he was right, but said they thought it no harm to test me by trying whether I would reserve my words or scatter them abroad upon the hills. Manyama was then called, and Mr. Lee showed the outside of the letter, with the title of our great Queen and royal seal upon the envelope, and pointing to the royal arms upon the waggons, told them it was sufficient they should see these tokens and know that my business was friendly. He then explained as much as he thought needful of my plans, and arranged that on the 6th July they should be in readiness to escort us.

We crossed the Shashani and climbed to the "top of the hill" or watershed between the Limpopo and Zambesi systems. Brooklets trickling to the former on our right and to the latter on our left, while proteas of considerable dimensions bordered our path. We crossed the Kumalo or Royal River (a principal source of the Gwali which I had visited near its junction with the Zambesi in 1862), and after we had outspanned were met by Captain Levert's wagon coming from Sir John Swinburne at Inyati, and bound to Natal for machinery. Here, on account of the exhausted condition of the oxen, I found it necessary to leave Jewell and Watson with one wagon "en cache" under the protection of the young Prince Lo Bengula, while I with Mr. Nelson and Mr. Lee proceeded with the other. We crossed the Umthlambo Boloi (the Bath of Majesty) on the Um Kosi or King River, and spanning out at night on a waterless flat were aroused by the attack of a lion on our cattle. Of course every one sleeps outside to spring up fully armed at the first alarm. The cattle in terror were already breaking out of the kraal when I heard them, and drove them back. My companions stood to their posts to guard the horses or other points of attack. Little Jack barked as lustily as if his small voice were backed by the power of a wolf hound. The lion circled round to the bivouac of our guides, and they, igniting the grass they had used for their bedding, tossed it up high overhead, filling the air with scattered sparks and flame, and firing on the lion when the light revealed him. One only of the Ba Mangwato boys sought inglorious safety by diving under the wagon, and he was chaffed unmercifully by the heroes of the night, and told that in future the post of honour where the lion must kill his man before getting at the cattle would be assigned to him. The horses strayed in the morning, but were brought back by the people of the next village. Mr. Nelson while out looking for them saw the lion, but being armed only with a revolver did not fire on him.

At the military kraal of the Twong Endaba Regiment, numbering, perhaps, 800 men, and entrusted with the care of some thousands of the national cattle, we saw Umbeko, and as Mr. Lee insisted on reading the letter to none but the great chief of the land, or to all the chiefs in council, it was at length decided that the Regent Um Nombata was, in his own person, sufficiently empowered to hear it, and consider my application. We, therefore, took the straight way through the country, and leaving Inyati on our left, reached Emampanjene* or Umbanjin on the 19th. Our guides went forward to report us, and in less than an hour, word was sent that the chief was ready to receive us.

We attended at once and found the old chief sitting perfectly naked (a royal privilege) before the door of his hut. He received us in a friendly unaffected manner, and after a little pleasant conversation, proposed to adjourn to the kotla, or place of council, to grant the formal audience ; his bodily strength had completely failed, and he had to be supported even while he walked so short a distance, but his mental powers appeared as vigorous as ever. When he announced his readiness to hear us, I requested Mr. Lee to say that I had been sent by a company from London, the city of our great Queen, many thousand miles across the great water, to pay him a friendly visit, and to ascertain whether the report, that his country contained gold, was true. Also that I was the bearer of a letter from the governor of the English in Natal, asking him to give me leave to travel and explore, and to protect me in doing so, in order that I might ascertain and report the truth, so that if the gold really existed, his excellency might make laws to regulate the conduct of

---

* Emampanjene, lat., 14·42·30; long., 29·44·30; height, 3,900 feet; distance from Inyati, 35 miles 102 yards.

those who would come to seek it, or if I found none he might make the fact known, and advise them not to undertake the journey.

The chief thanked me for coming so far to bring the message and the letter, and expressed his gratification at finding the English the same people he had always known them; he had twice been sent by his great chief Umselekatze to our country people. First to the residence of the Reverend Robert Moffat, and, secondly to Cape Town, where our governor lived on the shores of the great ocean.* He gave me liberty to travel and explore freely, and promised me a man to go with me to act as guide, and to be a visible proof to all that I went by his permission and authority. He exacted but one condition in return, and this was, "You must also make me *one* promise, you must not go out of my country by another way, but must come back to me, and tell me truly whether you have found gold, so that I also may know what to say to your governor, when we make laws upon the subject." I then offered the usual tribute on entering the country, a musket with a supply of ammunition, and presented a handsome railway rug, as a personal gift. Next day he sent me word that I might retain the gold that I found.

When Mr. Lee returned to his farm, I sent down for a fresh span of oxen, as it was impossible for ours to proceed further, and while waiting for them, I received a letter, written by order of some of the other chiefs, to inform me that Um Nombata was considered imbecile, that his permission was of no avail, and that I could not be allowed to travel because they had bound themselves not to let any but Sir John Swinburne and his party do so. I rode over to the mission station at Inyati, where I was kindly received by the Reverends T. M. Thomas and W. Sykes. I found six men who had been sent to fetch me back, but I told them that having received permission from their great chief, Um Nombata, I should not pay him so poor a compliment as to ask any one else, but should hold his promise valid till he recalled it with his own lips. Jewell brought me the new cattle and took back some that were wearied out. I received a guide named Inyassa, after the old Regent, to whom I made a present of a good warm coat, when I went to pay my parting visit.

It is not my purpose to lengthen out this narrative by anecdotes of hunting adventures, but to give as accurate and concise an idea

---

* His memory of the visit was exceedingly minute and clear. Among other things he witnessed a marriage in St. George's Church, and remembered distinctly which finger the bride wore the ring upon.

as possible of the known capabilities of the gold fields, and the manner in which permission to explore, and privileges to work them, were obtained ; therefore, I shall confine myself chiefly to details bearing on that subject. In the vicinity of Um Nombata's kraal, Mr. Nelson, our indefatigable and skilful mineralogist, found several large quartz reefs, one, five miles north north-east, a hundred feet wide, striking north 35°, west, with a south-west dip of 70° or 80° ; and about four miles south-west, two large, and several small reefs. The first did not look very favourable, but the others appeared better and contained much oxide and sulphuret of iron, as well as brown hematite or peroxide of iron. Want of time and means prevented Mr. Nelson breaking up much of this quartz to examine it for gold. An explorer on foot, with two or three natives to carry his and their own bedding, provisions, and tools, cannot do much, besides which the Matabilis had not quite got over their alarm, and we did not like to irritate them by searching in the immediate vicinity of their villages. Mr. Nelson's opinion, however, was that some of these reefs were gold bearing. He washed gravel and sand in the Changani and M'Nyami rivers, and readily found several specks of gold in every part, proving that considerable quantities of fine gold had been washed down from the upper parts of the rivers. He tried the river thirty-five miles down with the same result, and found gold also in red ferruginous gravel, about five hundred feet from the river. From these indications, Mr. Nelson thought that payable alluvial gold might be found in the Lhangani or its various feeders, and was inclined to regard this district as one of the most favourable for mines he had met with in South Africa. A band of talcose chloritic, and hornblende schist, with numerous quartz ledges. in which Mr. Nelson obtained a fair prospect of gold, lies eight or ten miles south-west of the village ; and this he also includes in his favourable opinion. On the 6th August, 1869, Mr. Nelson and I, with one wagon, trekked northward across country, with wild hills composed of immense blocks of granite, on either side. We struck the hunters road west of the Umbanga river and hills, and met Mr. Samuel Edwards coming out to fetch supplies for Sir John Swinburne, who was in advance of us. We held on to the eastward, turning gradually more north, and crossed the Um Vung, the U'Gwelo River, the Gwailo,* and the Ingwainya or Crocodile River, and taking a road which carried us too far north, had to turn south-east again, and join the main one at the Quacquae River, near which we found

---

* Gwailo River, lat., 19·11·15 ; long., 29·50·10 ; height, 3,792 ; distance from Pietermaritzburg, 1,042 miles, 3 furlongs, 198 yards.

extensive slate and schistous rocks, striking north by west and south by east, with numerous quartz-reefs, some of which Mr. Nelson found to be gold bearing. The country was park-like and beautiful; the graceful matchabela, which in its young leaf presents a rich yet delicate crimson tint, changing by various gradations into green, as its foliage is matured ; the leghondi, which buds forth in golden yellow, and the mimosas, acacias, aloes, and occasional euphorbias added an ever-varying charm to the scene ; while the higher lands were adorned with large white flowering proteas, and other plants suited to their altitude. We crossed the Bembesi River and the Sebaque* near the junction of which eight or ten miles north, many apparently rich quartz reefs exist, which were subsequently visited separately by Mr. Nelson and myself. Mr. Nelson tried the river and found a trace of gold, and I remarked galena in several specimens of the quartz.

Hitherto the chief features of the country had been granite ; but to the north-west of our course greenstone schist was found, and beyond that a dark slate formation, striking north and south, and upright enough to enclose the stream between high bluffs. Mr. Nelson found alluvial gold in two places in the river ; but it was very fine, and not enough to warrant him in calling it payable. We observed the first palm-tree at Sebaque. Here the country is chiefly fine-grained granite, intersected by green stone. On our right, or south-east, appear the ridges of the Thaba Euzimba, and the other highlands, forming the watershed between the Zambesian tributaries we were daily crossing, and those of the Limpopo and Sabea, flowing from their south and eastern slopes.

The drift of the Umnyati, or Buffalo, was guarded, as it were, by castellated granite hills, among which a small baobab or two, and the beautiful coral-blossomed *erithrina kaffra*, mingled with the acacias and mimosa, while cranes and waterfowl waded on the sandy beaches, or sported in the pools, and the hippopotamus and crocodile occupied the deeper reaches below. The Umgesi, a few miles onward, was a bleak unsheltered mountain river, rushing and babbling over accumulated rocks and stones, clear and cold as we experienced when we waded knee-deep across it. At Umgesana we found the brothers Jennings with Mr. Saunders and Mr. Gilliewie, outspanned by a clump of trees and dwarf palms, and received valuable information from them. And at the drift of the Umz-

---

* Sebaque, lat., 18·55·7; long., 30·24·; height, 3,420.

wezwie (beautifully overshadowed by bold groups of forest trees) Mr. Nelson found gold among the stones, and sand in the broad bed which only the flooded river could fill.

The hills of the watershed upon our right sweeping round like a vast amphitheatre from east to north, forced us still more in that direction; and camping in a soft wood grove near Zizina, or Mud Spruit, we lost an ox from weakness and exhaustion; and here, saddling up my horse—kept only for great emergencies—I rode on to overtake Mr. Hartley. Crossing the Zinbindasi rivulet, and the broad and sandy Um Vuli river, I reached the Sarua and halted for the night. I observed the glare upon the clouds from fires in the direction of Sir John Swinburne's camp, three or four miles south-west of me. Next day I crossed much quartz ore and well wooded country, intersected by several rivulets; and during the forenoon reached the wagons of Mr. Hartley, the brothers Wood, and Mr. McMaster. The hunters were absent, but Mrs. McMaster and the other ladies welcomed me, and spread upon the skin that did duty for a breakfast table, so many little delicacies, created from the rough materials at their command, that I seemed to have fallen into the very lap of luxury. A train of Matabili and Mashonas arrived, loaded with ivory and elephants' flesh, and as the camp was shortly to be moved I rode back early next morning to hasten on the wagon. I met it at the Sarua river, in which Nelson found a little gold.

When we returned to the hunter's camp at the Imbecta River, Mr. Hartley gladly received us, but dared not promise me any help in gold seeking until his head man, Inyoka (or the Serpent), had ascertained from mine that I had received full permission to explore from Um Nombati himself. So soon as this information was given he at once invited me to ride with him on his hunting expeditions, and also promised to show me such quartz-reefs as he knew of. Beyond this river no wagon road existed; but the hunters had already marked the direction. We proceeded north-north-west, crossing the Inzinghazi River, and halting to form camp upon a large river called the Ganyana,* where a huge block of granite, big enough for a comfortable cottage, is supported on three or four smaller ones, so as to form a massive canopy over a space in which a goodly company might sit or lounge at pleasure. Mr. Nelson found several quartz-reefs to the westward of the road; one strik-

---

* Ganyana River, lat., 17·44·56; long., 30·41·20; height, 3953 feet; from Pietermaritzburg, 1,195 miles.

ing north to west was 150 feet wide, forming several hills in line, which were visible from afar. He did not think this was gold-bearing, but considers it, nevertheless, well worthy of examination.

From Um Nombatis' village we had been travelling through a wilderness desolated by the marauding expeditions of the Matabili against the former inhabitants—the Mashonas—a people rich in cattle and of peaceful and industrious habits—of whose villages and cattle-folds the ruined walls, built of dry stone, still remain among the granite kopjies. Their formerly extensive rice and corn fields present long reaches of ridge and furrow, causing the ox-wagon to pitch like a boat in a short sea, and so trying to the horse that an elephant in these old gardens very often baffles the hunter.

Here we were visited by a number of Mashonas, from the village, about thirty-five miles to the north-west, and as they informed us that there were pits in the vicinity, from which their forefathers used to dig a kind of metal, of which they professed ignorance, I accompanied them on their return, and it may interest our countrymen at home to know that we do not, on such occasions, go armed to the teeth, and in constant fear of treachery. I rode at a walking pace, about the centre of the long procession, my head man, Inyassa, carried my rifle, and two or three other men my blankets and other necessaries, we crossed large tracts of well wooded granitic country, alternated with belts, in which quartz reefs of considerable extent prevailed. When we reached Maghoondas Village,* it seemed to me that I had reached the borders of the Zambesi population with whom I had been familiar in 1859. The chief sent me a dish of meal paste, and a little pot of meat, rather high in flavour. I slept in a little arbour below the village and the next day a guide went with me to shew me the pits from which the precious metal used, in old times, to be extracted. The reef bordered by clay slate, and other rocks, traversed a valley shut in by rounded hills, and the pits were in groups of six or eight together, three or four feet wide, and some of them ten feet deep. My guide jumped into one to fetch 'me up a specimen, and as his gaunt weird figure disappeared, I wondered whether his forefathers had ever done the same, at the bidding of Solomon's merchants, and thus afforded material for the legends of Djinns, Afreets, and Demons, who were said to be subject to that powerful monarch.

---

* Maghoondas Village, lat., 17·33·30; long., 30·17·40; Miles from Maritzburg, 1,230

The customs of the Mashonas, as I have said, seemed all familiar to me, they are more negro like than the Kafirs, the Zulus, or the Matabili, their hair is naturally crisp and short, but they cultivate and increase its length by tying it up in small tufts with red mimosa bark, plentifully anointed with fat, or with vegetable oil, mostly from the ground nut (*arachis*) ; these tufts are arranged in ridges, from back to front, giving a dandy, with his hair in curl, a ludicrous resemblance to our clowns; but when the locks are nearly a foot long, they are taken " out of paper," dressed with charcoal, and nut-oil, parted in the centre, and allowed to hang down on either side the face, confined only by a bandeau, reminding one of the drawings on Egyptian monuments. Of course the head cannot be allowed to touch the ground, and to keep the well oiled locks from being soiled by dust, every man carries with him a neck pillow, like a little stool, which suffers not the head to come within eight or ten inches of the ground. Their arms are the bow and arrow, and the assegai or short spear in many forms, from the blade, meant to inflict a wound two inches wide and two feet deep, upon an elephant, to curious little instruments of torture, intended to penetrate the human form, and by means of thirty or forty ingenious reverted barbs to remain fixed and rankling in the wound.

The law observed by Portuguese hunters, was in force among them, *i.e.* :—That the half of any slain animal that touched the ground belonged to the chief, and till he had taken his, the hunter must not touch his own share. I had expressed my opinion, ten years before, that English hunters would not submit to this, and now the question was settled, without even being proposed to the white men. The Matabili camp followers, indignantly repudiated the bare idea. " Our own master, the great chief, " our late king Umselegazi, never took a tusk from an English- " man, and shall you Mashonas, who are only our dogs, dare to " claim that which he refrained from ?" At one time I found that they had debated on the propriety of terminating my earthly career, while they had me in their power, to give the white men an idea of their prowess. I had observed Inyassa gathering his weapons, and my own closer to me, but went on eating my mess of pap till I should learn more, and I believe gained more credit for coolness than I might, had I known the object of their discussion. As I returned I saw several other quartz-reefs, and groups of diggings, in all of which gold bearing stone had evidently been found. I was requested to put my horse to speed, that the villagers, who had never seen such an animal, might have some idea of his power.

Spending a night at another stockaded village, perched on the top of a rugged clay slate hill, with quartz reefs at its base, I reached our camp, supplying my followers with flesh, by shooting a rhinoceros and two antelopes, on the way.

On our return journey, Mr. Hartley brought us by a more direct road, crossing the Simbo rivulet, just above its junction with the Umvuli. Some of our wagons were damaged in the drift, and we halted for repairs, under a group of granite hills, with quartz-reefs at their base. Here Mr. Hartley picked up several specimens, in which we afterwards found gold. He informed me that extensive diggings were near us, but as he wished his head man, Inyoka, to

SLAYING A RHINOCEROS. FROM A PAINTING BY THOMAS BAINES.

show them to me, I refrained from visiting them until we had persuaded him to go with me next morning.

The reefs seemed to be the greater part of a mile in length, but were so covered with refuse, thrown from the old surface workings, that their exact limit could not be easily determined, the holes were three or four feet wide, and sometimes ten or twelve feet deep. Here and there a group of holes had been worked into one, forming a large pit, and in many of these mimosa and other trees, from three to ten inches thick, were growing, proving that many years must have elapsed since they were worked, but not establishing for them a high antiquity. One of Inyoka's followers remembers that a house stood some distance north, and in his father's time, it was inhabited, and gold dust was sold there. Perhaps, it might have been the residence of some one combining the occupation of trading with the office of Catechist, or teacher from the now deserted Jesuit mission, at Zumbo on the Zambesi. Mr. Nelson, who had been out in another direction, inspected these reefs, and was so pleased with them, that I delayed the wagon as long as I could for repairs, to give him opportunity for examination.

Nearly a mile to the south Sir John Swinburne had encamped, and with the help of his head miner, Mr. August Griete, had sunk two shafts about twenty-five feet deep, from which he had obtained some very rich, and visibly auriferous quartz, some white and crystalline, some coloured red or yellow with oxide of iron. Mr. Nelson and I returned on subsequent days to examine the Simbo reefs, and at length determined to mark them off in the presence of our head man, as the first claim for which we would ask the new King when he should come into power, and as an acknowledgement to our friend, who had first shewn me the locality, I named the station "Hartley Hill,"* the north side is bounded by the Simbo rivulet, the north-east by the "Hartley Hill," and the south by large ant heaps with marked trees growing from them.

Mr. Nelson, in his official report, thus describes the place we had selected :— .

"Profitable quartz mining depends largely on the facilities for working and crushing quartz; here these are very good, an unlimited supply on the ground, and a fine stream, the Simbo, within a few hundred yards, with constant water, which can probably be used as a motive power.

"The rock strata enclosing these veins are gneiss and a mixture of talcose and chloritic schists striking north-east and south-west or thereabouts, and these dip westward at an angle of 70° or 80° judging by the dip and strike of the rocks lying close on both sides of the hill.

"Just where the reefs are the underlying formation is so covered with soil that it cannot be seen.

"Everywhere in the northern mining district the stratified rocks are so hardened and metamorphosed, that their geological age cannot be ascertained. I believe they belong to the lower palæozoic epoch.

"On the north-eastern boundary of the chain are several kopjies, or small hills of igneous rocks (Hartley hills), which have burst

---

* Hartley Hill, lat., 18·31·39; long., 30·49·20; height in feet, 3,079; 1,157 miles from Pietermaritzburg.

through the rocks containing the quartz veins, and pressed them aside; hence, though by the line of old workings, the reef No. 1, appears to have a north and south strike, its real course is north-east and south-west. Prospectors in South Africa will find it to their interest to explore places where the stratified rocks have been invaded by the igneous rocks, as precious metals are most likely to be found there.

"I cannot tell the breadth of these veins, as they are hidden by refuse quartz from the old workings; but I believe it to be considerable. They are larger and more extensive than any others I have seen in Africa; and nowhere else did I find silver-bearing galena disseminated through gold quartz.

"I brought samples of quartz from these mines, and have assayed them; some gave low results, some high.

"From one piece of quartz taken from vein No. 1, the result was at the rate of sixty and three-quarters ounces of gold, and seventeen one-hundreth (17·100) ounces of silver, to the ton; but this was taken from a very choice piece.

"Since my arrival in London, Messrs. Johnson, Matthey and Co. have made six different assays of quartz, taken at various places from the old workings, with the following results:—

Sample (a) - 0·225 ounces of gold to the ton.
,, (b) - 1·450 ,, ,, ,,
,, (c) - 3·125 ,, ,, ,,
,, (d) - 3·150 ,, ,, ,,
,, (e) - 3·500 ,, ,, ,,
,, (f) - 0·975 ,, ,, ,,

The samples a and b were taken from vein No. 2, c d e f were from vein No. 1. These assays do not afford sufficient ground for estimating the value of the mine; but they prove, beyond a doubt, there is rich quartz in them.

(Signed) "C. J. NELSON.
Mineralogist, assayer, and practical miner to the S. A. G. F. E. Co."

We were now able to delay no longer, for orders had been sent that all white men were to quit the country for a season, and leave the natives uninterrupted to deliberate upon the choice and mode of installation of their future king. Mr. Nelson prospected, and found abundant proof of auriferous country as we came away; and reaching the village of Inyati, we found Jewell and Watson waiting for us with the other wagon. After a day or two I rode with Mr. Watson as interpreter, and my head man, Inyassa, to

Inthlathlangela,* to make my report to the venerable chief, Um Nombata.—

Inyassa was rigidly examined by the assembled Indunas as to whether I had not asked leave to go in as an elephant hunter, and then sought for gold ; and, also, whether I had not dug holes in the country without permission ; but his testimony completely cleared me, and old Um Nombati himself, turning round upon the council, exclaimed : " Why have you tormented me so long with your accusations ? It is not my man that has done wrong, but yours!" He then asked me whether I had found gold, and I told him " Yes;" but showing him a specimen, I pointed out how small was the proportion contained in a quantity of stone, and how great would be the labour of extracting it. He set apart a hut for me, not far from his own, and his son, Umthlabba, and his principal attendant, came and assured me that, though I must make a show of going out of the country, in obedience to orders, their hearts were too friendly to me to drive me further than just a little past their village ; in fact, they said they were my advocates in the council, and I ought to give them a blanket each for their good offices. I asked whether this would not amount to bribery and corruption ; but as they seemed not to understand my line of argument, I postponed the discussion, and gave them the blankets.

From Tati I sent Mr. Nelson, with one wagon and the specimens, to report to the Company's agent in Natal, and obtain the means of continuing our work. And thence he proceeded to London, to confer with the directors in person ; while I returned to Lee's farm, Mangwe river, to spend the summer. By the exercise of my pencil, I earned enough to supply the party with food for a considerable part of the next season.

Meanwhile, the deliberations respecting the succession of Umselegazi had been going on. It was believed that Kuruman, the real heir, had been sent out of the country in his youth, according to ancient custom, to prevent his forming attachments among the people he was to govern. Efforts had been made in every direction to find him ; and, at length, he was supposed to have been discovered in Natal ; but when Mr. Shepstone asked the individual in question, "Are you Kuruman ?" he replied, "No ; I am not!" The Rev. W. Sykes, of Inyati, on receiving this information, communicated it to the chiefs, and the old men who had affirmed that Kuruman was dead said, " Now is the time to bring forward our proof."

*Inthlathlangela, lat., 20·19·30 ; long., 28·47·30 ; height, 4,421 feet.

THE RAPIDS—VICTORIA FALLS, ZAMBESI RIVER.—FROM A PAINTING BY MR. BAINES.

CHAPTER III.

ELECTION OF THE MATABILI KING.

A council was called; and it was stated that while Umselegazi was pushing his conquests as far as the Zambesi, he was informed of a conspiracy to dethrone him, and appoint Kuruman, his heir by the royal wife, chief in his stead. He at once returned, and by night invested the Kraal of Intbaba Inisduna (the hill of the chiefs), attacked it, and slaughtered all the inhabitants, except Lo Bengula, one of his children by another wife, but created a royal child by adoption. One Induna had been specially charged with this duty, and he saved the child by lifting him into the shield house. In the morning it was found that Kuruman was not among the slain, and his father sent for him to Zwong Endaba, where he was staying with his regiment; he came attended by his servant, Gwalema, and the King ordered a Basuto, named Gwabaiiyo, to take him out and kill him. "Not to stab him with a spear, nor bruise him with a kerrie, nor to strangle him with a reim, but to take his head between the hands, and kill him by twisting his neck;" so that the body of a royal child might not be disfigured. The two men were produced, and Gwabaiiyo said he killed him according to order; but Gwalema said:—"You did, indeed, kill him, but not according to order; for when you failed to twist his neck, you broke your kerrie in striking him, and then took bark off a tree, and made a rope of it, to strangle him with." Both, however, agreed that he was dead; and other witnesses testified that, as boys, they had been put through the ceremonies of mourning for the death of their young companion. Lo Bengula then said: "If you are satisfied my brother is dead, I can no longer resist your entreaties. The chieftainship is mine by descent, as well as by your choice, and you must do as you desire with me."

A NATIVE WOMAN.— FROM A PAINTING BY MR. BAINES.

On the 25th of Jan., 1870, Mr. Lee received a message requiring his presence at Inthlathlangela, and I should have been glad to accompany him, had it been thought prudent to do so. On Wednesday, 26th, he returned; and next morning informed me that the destiny of Matibililand had been satisfactorily settled: Lo Bengula having been proclaimed king, and successor to his father, Umsalegazi.

On Monday, the 24th, the warriors (to the number of 9,000 or 10,000) assembled, wearing towering head-dresses of the black body-plumes of the ostrich (so arranged as not to hide the issigook, or head ring, which is the mark of a tried soldier), and large capes of the same, giving to their shoulders a great apparent increase of breadth, but dwarfing their lower limbs. They bore bandeaux of otter skin upon their foreheads; tails of white cattle upon their arms and legs, and strips of black and white catskin for their kilts; being armed with their short stabbing assegais, and covered by their large war-shields of ox hide, black, white, red or speckled, with all those colours according to their regiments. They were marshalled in the circular space, probably 800 yards in diameter, surrounded by the town of Inthlathlangela. The warriors formed a dense circle fifteen or twenty deep; but all the available force was not present; for numbers had paid their homage and departed. The Zwong Endaba, and other disaffected persons, numbering perhaps 1,500, were absent. The ceremonies commenced with a song in praise of the king, the full deep chorus swelling as grandly as one of our cathedral chants. This was accompanied by the striking of spear shafts upon shields, and the stamping of feet in unison, like soldiers marking time. Occasionally single warriors of known bravery were permitted to dash forward and to go through a pantomime of their own exploits, giving one stab in the air for every man, woman, or child they had killed; and going through the whole action of a battle; the stealthy approach; the wild charge; the hand to hand fight; the retreat; the rally; and the final overthrow of the victim. A great feat is to spring forward off the ground, and, while still in the air, strike the shield successively with the point and butt of the spear, and with both knees and feet. Proud is the man who can keep this up the longest. Each of these aspirants sung the praises of Lo Bengula, declared his readiness to die for him, defied all pretenders, especially "The man in the Sea" (at Natal), as well as all the writers, bringers, and even readers of letters concerning him. Lo Bengula, attended by forty majokkas, or young soldiers, crowding as a body guard round his horse, and followed by eight or ten mounted white men, arrived by the north-east river, and entered the town, the white men taking their stand on a little eminence outside; the Rev. W. Sykes, Mr. Lee, and Willie Hartley standing inside, under a tree near the kotla. The king elect, dressed in drab or brown moleskin and cord, and wearing a high crowned felt hat, with a single tall feather of the kapi crane, and a gaudy handkerchief tied round his head, rode into the kotla, or court of assembly, and there performed his first act of sovereignity, by superintending the slaughter of cattle brought as offerings to him. Each tribe contributed a small troop, and from each lot six, ten, or a dozen were selected. The black were killed first; then the black and white speckled; and, lastly, the coloured ones. The first were offered to the *manes* of his father; the second to the Molimo, or Great Spirit; and the rest for other purposes. The King made a short speech as he pointed out each victim; and then the sacrificer, holding his assegai just as one would hold a pin, placed its point low down behind the shoulder blade, where it does not spoil the skin for a shield, and assuring himself by a gentle titillating motion that it was rightly directed

Of course, the slaughter of so many oxen, in so confined a space, was a work of difficulty, especially when some had fallen, and the rest maddened by the sight, and smell of blood, made frantic efforts to escape, but there was no confusion. The place where the king had dismounted was kept clear by a circle of Majokkas, bound in honour to die upon the spot rather than let him be incommoded; others formed rings around each lot of cattle, and when two heaps had fallen, and there was no room for more in the kotla, the rest were killed outside, as the king successively devoted them. In the evening the carcasses were skinned and cut up, and next day the king distributed the meat to his newly-acquired subjects.

The king sent me a message of remembrance. He confirmed to Mr. Lee the rights granted him by Umselegasi, and at another visit he told Mr. Lee he was satisfied with all that I had done, and added, "Mr. Baines can have the northern gold fields."

In April, 1870, Jewell, Watson, and I, accompanied by Mr. Lee, went in and encamped near the king's new town of Gibbe Klaik,* where we found Lo Bengula in his wagon, dressing to visit us. Other wagons stood near laden with presents that had been made to his father, Umseligasi. Beads, guns, pistols, Colt's and other revolvers, corroded into masses of rust, and every conceivable article of use or luxury that a traveller could offer to a barbarian monarch, among which I will only mention a splendidly mounted Scottish garter dirk, and a pair of magnificent ram's horn mulls, mounted in massive silver. A couple of earthen cauldrons were simmering on the fire, and a stalwart warrior approaching these, took off the lids, drove a sharp stick into a filthy looking mass, and finding it sufficiently cooked, harpooned and hauled out the contents,

* Gibbe Klaik, lat., 20·18·11; long., 28·52·00; height in feet, about 4 000.

and heaped them on two great wooden dishes, laying on each some twigs that had been boiled as charms against evil influence, with the meat. The cook now intoned the praises of the king, the hungry warriors joining in the chorus. One of these vessels shaped its course towards us, steered by the kneeling functionary, and he, drawing his knife, cut off large slices, from which we pared the filthy outside, and found the remainder excellent.

On Saturday, April 9th, the king paid us another visit, when Mr. Lee repeated to him in proper form the whole history of the expedition from its commencement. He examined my compass, and asked me to make a sketch of Kapaes, the court jester. We next had visits from the princesses royal, who graciously accepted presents all round, until the king sent to call me and Mr. Lee. He asked to see my sketch of Kapaes, and, recognising it at once, turned it to his admiring subjects, who, of course, re-echoed the praise his majesty had bestowed on it. Beer was offered to us, and the great dishes of meat again went their usual round. Kapaes, the jester, came in blowing his horn, when Lee suddenly confronted him with his portrait. Nowise abashed, he pointed out his hat, feathers, and big horn, saying, "Now, I too shall go, like other great men, to be seen by Kuruman and the white people!"—an allusion that would probably have cost another man his life. The meal, at length, was finished, and the guests having sung the praises of the king left us alone. Mr. Lee then approached, and intimated to the king that I was present, on which he invited me to make my request. I then said that I had entered the country by permission of Um Nombata; had explored it; according to my promise, had reported what I found to him; and had also sent Mr. Nelson to report to our governor. Now, if he were disposed to grant me a portion of the country on any terms, I was prepared to treat with him. He asked me to state my boundaries, and Mr. Lee added a hint not to make them too small. I therefore requested him to grant me from the Gwailo to the Ganyona rivers. He answered, that being but newly seated in his father's throne he could not at once sell land, or define boundaries; but that he would give me leave to go in and seek for gold anywhere within those limits, with permission to dig or to introduce tools or machinery for crushing rocks, and free passage for all wagons in the service of the Company. Mr. Lee told him that I should require a house to live in, and storehouses, as it would not be possible for the company to carry backward and forward every season the heavy machinery required for gold quartz crushing.

He answered that all these things were included in his permission to dig for the gold; that it was my business to know what was needful, and that all details were covered by his general grant. But he also expected I would not exceed his permission, or do anything which would cause him to regret having made such a concession in my favour. I requested Mr. Lee to say that when Um Nombata had given me permission to explore, I had pledged my word to comply with the terms on which it was granted, and had duly returned to report to him; and now I would also give my word to him not to exceed his permission; but if I required other privileges I would come and ask them, and await his answer. He said the feelings of his heart were most friendly towards me, and would remain so, unless I should do anything to forfeit his friendship. He was well disposed to grant me all the favour in his power; but most likely other white men would come and make other requests. Mr. Lee explained that I had now made my request for my company, and he was doing his duty as agent for it, but neither of us were seeking to prejudice any other person.

If others came, the king would, at his own pleasure, grant or refuse their requests, but he (Mr. Lee) had introduced me because I was the first person who had come to him, duly accredited from an English company, and was also the trusted bearer of a message of friendship and good will from the governor of the colony of Natal.

The king's supper was now ready, his "plate" was laid on the wagon chest, his knife and fork, supplied only for himself. He invited us to draw out our own, and use them freely. A small basket of beer was brought and often replenished, the king requiring us to drink fairly with him, forgetting that our capacity was not equal to that of a native. When we returned to camp we discussed the subject of a present, and the only thing I had was my salted riding horse, for which I had just given £75, and I determined to present this, sending at the same time for a saddle, bridle, and rifle to make the value of the present £100.

On Sunday, Mr. Lee told me that the rain makers objected to the flags, which we generally shewed on holidays, over our wagons, as they were likely to drive away the rain, and as no point of honour was involved I thought it best to humour him. We had a little conversation with the king, who was free from prejudice on the subject, but who very reasonably urged the impropriety of offending his people, while he was yet not formerly settled in his power. Subsequently, I found that only the white bordered union jack was objectionable; there was no harm in the red ensign so long as it hung quietly, and did not flutter in the wind. White shirts and trowsers also could not be spread out to dry, without frightening away the rain clouds, but dark clothing might be hung out *ad libitum*. We also discussed the supposed power of these rain-makers, and the king said he knew that neither the man nor the crocodile's scales, and other ingredients which he burned, could make rain; "But," said he, "this is our way of asking for it; just as you ask for it with a book." I imagine, however, that his majesty's views on these points are far more enlightened than those of his subjects. He was very fond, also, of looking over my sketches. He distinguished very readily, not only the different forms of men and animals, but slight details which would escape the eye of many white men. The amount of finish bestowed upon the oil paintings especially attracted his notice, and he would remark, "Ah, these animals seem almost alive;" while I have known some of his subjects, in criticising a picture of myself, seated on the carcass of a hippopotamus, and paddling it across a river, after referring to the more obvious details, point to the indications of muscular action, and say, "Look how the arm is working."

We went down from the cold bleak heights, where the south-east fog-laden wind came keen and chilly from the Indian ocean (three hundred miles away), down to the valley of the Inzingwaine river, where the king was building a new village, in a milder climate. Here we were joined by the Rev. J. B. Thompson, the newly arrived missionary of the London Society. On Sunday we were considering the best manner of proposing some observance of the day, when the king himself asked "Whether we were not going to make Sunday?" My tent was cleared out, its front spread open, and several of the Indunas and people having collected, Mr. Thompson, aided by Watson as interpreter and Scripture reader, held his first service in Matabililand. We remained about a week on the most friendly terms; Mrs. Thompson and her white cat being objects of almost equal admiration. The king supplied us freely with beef. The royal ladies called freely to our cook for coffee with sugar in it—signifying their readiness at any time to accept gifts. At parting, it was ludicrous enough to see all the high-born beauty of the land bedecked in such garments as we had to spare;—white jackets, vests, blue striped shirts, and other habiliments being distributed among them; while the king, with real kind feeling, walked a mile out of the village, and told us his heart would be lonely now his white friends had left him.

ARRIVAL AT HARTLEY HILL REEFS.

We left on the 25th April, pulled up the long hill, passing several reefs and quartz ore indications, halted for breakfast next morning at Gibbe Klaik, and proceeded by a more easterly road to Inyati, whence we again left the main road, and turned east to Emampangena to buy corn; sticking fast in swamps, sinking not only to the axles, but to the bed planks of the wagons, making good sometimes three-quarters of a mile a day, and once having to off load the wagons, and lift them by the aid of screw-jacks on a foundation of stones and timber laid beneath them—breaking our gear time after time, even then, in the attempts to haul them out.

I must pass over our journey and hunting adventures, until we reached our location at Hartley Hill; where I first verified, and again marked, the boundaries formed by Mr. Nelson; and then commenced building a house, with two rooms of fourteen feet square and a six foot passage between them, the wall-plate being ten feet in height, and the roof twenty. My object being to give plenty of air in case any of the party should be attacked by fever and unable to quit his bed. Watson, with a gang of Kafirs, undertook the task of felling mopani poles—a hard wooded banhinea, with a resinous gum which the white ants will not touch—and he soon thinned the forest in the immediate vicinity.

I made a trip of about five and twenty miles down the Umvuli river; finding several quartz reefs, and returned to work at the house, hoping to have it ready to receive Nelson and the working party; when two horsemen, who proved to be Maloney and Leask, arrived. All our hopes of a cheerful re-union were dashed, as with a thunderstroke, by the sad intelligence that of the little party of hunters who had come in about a month before us, no fewer than seven had died of fever, while all the rest were more or less affected. Mr. George Wood had lost his wife, his infant, and his mother-in-law; Mr. Jebe, a very intelligent German explorer, had died next, having first, in the delirium of fever, destroyed his journals. Then followed Mr. McDonald, and Toris, a half-caste wagon driver; and lastly, Willie Hartley, a fine young hunter, who bade fair to rival the fame of his well-known father. His grave was about 13 miles E. S. E., and the camp about nine miles S. E., of my house. Next morning I set out to visit our friends, Mr. Wood kindly sending a horse to meet me on the way, and it was sad indeed to see so many men, whom I had known so recently rejoicing in their strength, now so enfeebled in body and in mind, that they dared hardly ride a mile, even in fine weather, for the benefit of their health, and could not remember with distinctness the details of the terrible ordeal through which they had just passed. Mr. McGilliwie, with Jennings's party, died subsequently. Many remained for a long time too weak for much exertion; and even this loss, fearful as it seemed in our little community, was a trifle to what we afterwards heard had taken place in other districts.

On the 8th of June, Jewel and I took two wagons and proceeded south-east, crossing the watershed 4,703 feet high, and reached the village of Umtigesa,* a Mashona chief, situated among granite hills, on the Kitoro and Sepowie rivulets, which flow eastward to join the Sabia

NATIVE HUTS.—FROM A PAINTING BY MR. BAINES.

river. The Mashona villages are usually perched on the most inaccessible peaks and rugged hills, as a refuge from the Matabili. Many of their huts are built on isolated boulders, that can be approached only by a rough pole, serving for a ladder; the foundation being secured by plastering a ring of stiff clay upon the bare stone, into which to stick the poles which form the walls. The rocks too small to build huts on serve to support granaries and store-houses. The Mashonas are clever blacksmiths; but I saw no trace of gold, not being yet below the granite on the Sabian side; but the name, Umtigesa, I believe, means tin. We bought corn, goats, and pack oxen here, and returned to Hartley Hill, followed for about 50 miles by lions, which one night caught and fatally injured an ox, but were driven off before they could take it from us. Near

* Umtigesa, lat., 18·47·16; long., 31·40·60; height 4,060 feet; distance from Hartley Hill, 92 miles.

Hartley Hill Watson had shot a crocodile—a rather hazardous act, as the Matabili think the liver can be used for witchcraft, and are at liberty to kill any person who may be suspected of having it in his possession. I cut off the head and preserved it, but left the carcase.

Jewell and I made another trip down Um Vuli river about 25 miles, finding several reefs, which had been formerly worked by the Mashonas. Mr. Hartley arrived about the 20th of August, naturally overwhelmed with grief for the loss of his favourite son, and I was also much disappointed at learning that Mr. Nelson and the working party I expected had not returned with him. I bought horses from him, and shortly after we went out, under the guidance of Mr. Leask, to visit poor Willie's lonely grave; but on our way we found elephants spoor, and Mr. Hartley, at once sacrificing his own feelings, to the general interest, gave the word to follow. The spoor, singularly enough, led us within half-a-mile of the grave, and yet the father might not turn aside to visit the spot where his much-loved son was lying. Late that afternoon we came up with the elephants. Mr. Hartley shot two, and the other three hunters one each. And on another expedition we reached the spot without hindrance, left our friend in solitude for a few minutes to indulge in feelings too sacred to be shared by others; and afterwards I made a sketch, and Jewell a photograph, of the little heap of bushes which under a tree marked, W. J. H., 29/5/70 * were all that marked the early grave of the gallant boy.

Again I rode with Mr. Hartley about 21 miles N. W. by N., and saw several groups of very extensive abandoned gold workings.† There were the ruins of a house that had been occupied by white men 45 or 50 years ago; but we did not at that time find them, because elephant's spoor again led us away, and we followed it till the herd escaped into the Tsetse Fly. Sweeping round to the east of our station, we found an elevation admirably adapted for a sanatarium, which I propose to establish when we commence working; and, on our return, I mustered the wagon drivers and Kafirs, and commenced breaking out quartz, and searching for gold-bearing specimens. I must say, however, that my unskilled attempts very inadequately represented the practised operations of Mr. Nelson, who would have found more gold in an hour than I did in a couple

---

* W. J. Hartley, 29th May, 1870. Lat., 18·16·40; long., 30·59·10; distance from Hartley Hill, 13 miles.

† Abandoned workings, lat., 13·0·0; long., 30·36·0; from Hartley Hill, 21 miles.

of weeks. Still, I saw quite enough to convince me that Mr. Nelson's report was justified by the richness of the reef. Mr. Hartley helped me now and then, and so did Inyassa; but the chief value of his services rested in the fact that they afforded proof that I was acting by the orders and permission of the king.

On the 9th September, I rode with Mr. George Wood, who had come to invite me to his camp, about 60 miles N. N. W.,* where he had bought from the Mashonas a few grains of gold in a quill, and now very kindly presented it to me. At night we halted by a large quartz hill, and next day reached his wagons in a country extensively quartzose, with old workings all round, and a renewed working in sight of the camp. We were about six miles east of Maghoonda, whom I visited last year, and the enquiries I then made had, it appears, stimulated them to seek out their old workmen and renew their ancient industry. G. Wood took me to a place in which he had seen a heap of quartz burned, and another heap, piled with wood among it, ready for burning. The crushing stones, like a printer's slab and muller had also been lying in a hut near, but at the time of my visit these were removed, and the calcined quartz also, but the other heap had been fired and now lay mingled with the charcoal ready for crushing. The country around bore such evident marks of inundation by the summer torrents that it seemed absolutely certain that a rich alluvial field must exist at the first plain where the speed of the rivers could abate. I considered Wood's gift invaluable, not that it shewed me more than I knew in 1859, but as the means of proving the existence of a gold field, worked by the natives, to our company at home. We made enquiries for more, but the poor wretches seemed to be in as much dread as if they had committed a mortal crime, and dared not confess that they possessed riches of any kind lest the Matabili should plunder them. I trust when our works are in full operation, I shall be able to employ a number of these people, and of course, as far as possible, shall deem it my duty to protect them, and to ameliorate their condition.

During the homeward journey Mr. Hartley shewed me several reefs, and one day I had the pleasure of riding close up to a herd of about two hundred elephants, and being in at the death of seven out of eight that were shot. I did not carry my gun, not having a licence to shoot elephants. Near the junction of the Benbisi and

---

*Renewed workings, lat., 17·31·30; long., 30·32·6; from Hartley Hill, 60 miles.

Sebaque rivers, I saw several rich reefs, but I was so successful in shooting, that the men were too well fed to care about going on to the principal reef I wanted to see.

At Inyati we were warmly welcomed by the Rev. Mr. and Mrs. Sykes, as well as by Mr. and Mrs. Thompson. The latter had already grown and reaped a fine crop of wheat; and I found the fact of the King's having given me the northern gold fields so generally known and recognised among the Matabili, that once when I expressed some anxiety to see the King, his brother, M'Poetlo, answered "Why need you be troubled, do we not all know the king has given "you the country?" The chiefs Kokotoi and Umtigoran also, when conversing with Mr. Lee, had said "Yes, we are glad the king has given Mr. Baines the gold fields. One thing can only be given to one man, but they are given, not to him personally, but to the great white men who sent him."

During their absence the king had, after as much forbearance as possible, met and defeated the disaffected Zwong Endabas, and had destroyed their town; but he stopped the slaughter as soon as the battle was over, and drafted the survivors into different regiments that were faithful to him.

Mr. and Mrs. Thompson accompanied us to the king, and we visited on the way a spot selected on the highland range for a mission station, to be called Hope Fountain. Mr. Lee met us at the king's, and, I am happy to say, rendered very material assistance in explaining the principles and working of a missionary society, and in obtaining the grant of land selected for a station. Watson also assisting in interpreting and illustrating Mr. Thompson's arguments on the necessity and benefit of religious instruction. Mr. Thompson held services on two consecutive Sundays in Dutch and Kafir for the natives, and in English for the white men, all of whom attended gladly; and the grand Old Hundreth Psalm, sung by eighteen or twenty powerful manly voices, brought the Matibili running from all quarters to listen; not a few of them expecting that after the song we should perform a war dance.

I consulted seriously and frequently with Hartley and Lee as to the propriety of asking a written document or deed of gift from the king, and decided not to do so, but to trust his verbal promise. His word formally made known to the chiefs and natives, passes into law, and is held sacred and irrevocable. The grants of hunting privileges made by Umzelegasi are held in remembrance, and their words are discussed as closely as points of written law are among us. And I have good reason to believe that, had I then asked for a document, he would have regarded it as an attempt to overreach him, and deprive him of his land.

He examined the quartz I had brought down, and readily perceived how small the proportion of gold was to the mass of stone, and what labour would be required to extract it. He said he was perfectly satisfied with the manner in which I had acted, and would not withdraw his favour until I should do something to forfeit it. He wished to see the picture of Willie's grave (in the absence of Mr. Hartley), and asked, "Does that belong to Oude Baas?" "Yes," said I, "I have given it to him as a memento." "But," he added, "will that not keep his heart very sore?" I told him "Yes; but, nevertheless, we always prized such relics of those we loved and lost." He went carefully through all my sketches, and showed some little anxiety to know whether I had indeed left the liver of the crocodile untouched; but I knew I was not in much danger, because he shoots crocodiles himself on the quiet, and only respects the superstitions of his people in public.

On the 23rd November, 1870, the king visited me early, and in the presence of Mr. Lee, Mr. Thompson, and Mr. Hartley, asked me the details of my journey, and fully confirmed all the privileges he had already granted me. He was particular to guard against any infringement of his territorial rights; and I told him that I had given him my promise not to exceed his permission, and this promise I would keep. That our company would not ask me to break it, but even should they so far forget themselves, I would resign my appointment rather than do so. I asked what gift or tribute I should pay him, but he refused to name any sum lest it should seem like parting with his right to his country; and I therefore told him I would annually make him such a present as I thought he would be pleased with, adding that I felt sure the report of his liberal conduct would secure for him the friendship of the Colonial and British Governments. Mr. Kisch had given a dinner the night before, and some days after Mr. Hartley and I gave one in return; the King and his sister were present at the first, and Mr. and Mrs. Thompson at the second. Mr. Carter furnished wine enough to serve for loyal and general toasts; and songs and recitations enlivened the rest of the evening. The remembrance that a missionary and his lady had graced our table, exercising a marked and beneficial influence over the remainder of our festivities. We had an excellent opportunity of seeing the discipline and war dances, or rather parades, of the Matabili; two divisions of the army having just returned from a raid on the Mashonas, in which they had killed more than two hundred men, women, and children, and taken eight thousand head of cattle.

The limits of this little work forbid my giving any lengthened details of the rather imposing military displays, or the animated scenes during the distribution of the cattle which followed; but I may mention, that on the fifth or sixth day, the ceremonies were concluded by the presentation of a stout and fierce young bull from the king to his warriors, that they might show their own ferocity by eating it alive upon the spot. They had thrown their victim on the ground, and were making their first incision, when, maddened by the pain, he made one tremendous effort, shook off the savages that clustered round him, and broke away. I was not present at the moment, nor aware of what was going on, till I heard that the infuriated animal had fatally gored one of my horses, a "salted" or acclimatised animal, which had cost me £45, and which it was almost impossible to replace. The division of the spoil seemed to be arranged on well understood and tolerably equitable principles. A number of cattle were distributed as prizes to the captors, and a hundred and fifty were given to the "doctor," for having charmed the shield and persons of the warriors against hostile weapons. The greater number were reserved and given to the King as national property, to be herded by such regiments as he might trust, and to be used by him for public purposes. A smaller herd was apportioned to him for the support of his household and retainers, and for affording hospitality to guests; and I believe he was allowed several cattle as private and strictly personal property. The hardship to the poor Mashonas, of course, was never taken into consideration; but I hope, when our workings are established, and centres of industry are formed on various quartz reefs, we may be able to convince the King that it is more politic, as well as more humane, to protect these harassed tribes, and let their labours minister to the general good of the nation, rather than plunder and destroy them.

During my stay here I received a letter from His Excellency Senhor Carlos Pedro Barrahona E. Costa, governor of Quillimane, informing me that the land north of the Limpopo was a part of the district of Sofala, in the province of Mozambique, and that I could not be allowed to explore for gold, or to make treaties with the natives, except by permission, to be first obtained from his most faithful majesty the King of Portugal. To this I answered that, "while I honoured the memories of the early Portuguese voyagers for their achievements, I was not aware that they ever held territorial right in Matabili Land; and that if they had, the country was long ago abandoned, and had been conquered by Umzelegasi, whose son, Lo Bengula, had conferred on me the right of working in it."

On reaching Potchefstroom I had the honour of meeting His Excellency, who showed me a map, on which the different districts were defined, and I pointed out the position of Lo Bengula's grant to me, as being so far west and south-west of the boundaries of Sofala and Tette, that it not only did not approach the Portuguese territory, but was so far distant from it that a broad belt of independent native population actually existed between us. His Excellency, however, made a general claim to all South Africa, from the Indian ocean to the Atlantic, in virtue of a cession made by the conquered Emperor of Monomotapa three hundred years ago, and I answered, that if conquests were a valid right, Umzelegasi had conquered, forty years ago, the country now called the northern gold fields, and his son, Lo Bengula, had given it to me. His Excellency said he had done his duty by protesting, and should not take any active measures to hinder me. Mr. Forssman, the Portuguese Consul, advocated liberal measures, and proposed that Portugal should rather encourage us in developing the gold fields, by opening its ports to us—pointing out the fact that Captain Elton had already explored a road down the Limpopo from Tati to Inhambane, and that I should probably do the same from Hartley Hill to Sofala.

I find an old friend of mine, Mr. Richardson, is minister of the Church of England here. He is desirous that a bishop should be appointed for the Transvaal. I asked him to have the gold fields included in his diocese, and we will give him all the help that influence, interpretation, or hospitality can afford. I cannot stay to dwell on, as I could wish, the kindness we received from Mr. and Mrs. Hartley at their farmhouse at Thorndale; from Mr. Reid and Mr. Forssman, and many other friends at Potchefstroom; or tell how we took to pieces our wagons, and made rafts of the bed planks, to carry the cargoes over rivers too deep to ford; but must leave all the details of a journey during the wet and flooded season to the imagination of the reader, and state briefly that I reached Pietermaritzburg on the 30th of January, 1871. Here I found that our "exploration" company had not yet completed the negociations with the "working" company that was to succeed it; and that, however valid the privileges granted me verbally by the king might be in Matabililand, the company wanted a document, duly signed and sealed, in testimony of the reality. I pointed out the risk of offending the King and exciting his suspicions, by appearing to doubt the validity of the verbal promise; but as the company pressed this point, I applied to some of my colonial friends, and by their kind assistance I was able to refit the expedition so as to leave Pietermaritzburg again for the North on the 16th May, 1871.

I found that the person in Natal supposed to be heir to the Matabili kingdom, had retracted his former denial, and now asserted that he was really Kuruman, and intended to go up and claim his right.

The Hon. T. Shepstone, Secretary for Native Affairs, by desire of his Excellency the Governor, entrusted me with a letter to Lo Bengula, informing him that this person claiming to be Kuruman, and whose identity had been attested by several refugees from Matabili land, had decided to go up and claim his inheritance; that the Colonial Government did not send him, but had no right to prevent his doing so on his own responsibility. That it abstained from any participation in a matter which could only be properly discussed in a full council of the chiefs and people of Matabili Land, and that it warned all British subjects not to commit any breach of neutrality, or to interfere in a matter which concerned the Matabili nation only. The letter concluded with an expression of his Excellency's gratification at the friendship Lo Bengula had shown to me and other travellers, and a hope that the Matabili would calmly consider and peacefully determine a matter of so much importance to themselves.

As far as Vaal River I had the pleasure of travelling in company with his Excellency F. Van Leller, the plenipotentiary of the Crown of Portugal, who was on his way to Plerona to ratify the treaty of 1869, respecting the boundaries between the Portuguese possessions on the east coast, and those of the Trans Vaal Republic. I overtook our friend Hartley beyond Rustenburg, and was again indebted to him for many acts of kindness which were of the greatest possible service to me.

At the Limpopo river we came up with the wagons which were conveying a steam engine and quartz-crushing battery for Mr. Hart to Tati, where we found Mr. Nelson actively engaged in preparations for gold mining in the interests of Sir John Swinburne, who had purchased the right to the "blue jacket" and other mines from the earlier diggers, this right being confirmed in 1872 by special deed of grant from the King. At Tati I took leave of Mr. Hartley and my other friends. On Friday, August 11th, we reached Gibbeklaiko, and found that the King had gone down the valley, somewhat beyond the kraal he had built last year, on the Umzingwaine river.

We reached the kraal next day, and after a preliminary visit I was invited to an audience, at which the King received me with his usual friendship, and listened with marked attention while I read the Governor's letter and Mr Lee translated it. He remarked that it was serious news and could not be answered hastily, but he thanked the Governor for writing and me for bringing it, and before I left he would ask me to take down his answer in writing.

The King removed to his valley residence of last year and we stayed several days with him, Mr. Lee cautiously feeling his way towards asking for the written confirmation of the grant—a task of considerable delicacy, which I leave entirely to his tact and knowledge of Matabili etiquette. The tributory chief, Matcheu of Ba-Mangwato, who had assumed considerable independence since the death of Umselegasi, had recently sent a defiant letter to Lo Bengula, who, on that account, preferred not to risk the lives of the messengers he wished to send to Natal, by bidding them go down the usual road. I offered to take them with me and to guarantee their lives with my own, telling him that wherever the flag of our great Queen flew none dare molest those who were protected by it, and that if Matchen was ever to murder me or the ambassadors who were covered by our flag, our Government would certainly call him to account for it. Bengula admitted this, but said that he feared treachery rather than open violence, and it was impossible for me to guarantee the lives of his messengers against secret murder. He told me that a more direct road existed to the southward, through the Tsetse Fly, but that some of his father's people knew of passages by which the danger might be avoided, and to his great gratification I consented to open the road by going that way.

At length Mr. Lee had informed me that the king had intimated his willingness to let me have a written ratification of his grant, but that it would be advisable for me to ask it personally; and a few days afterwards, when we had been talking about medicine for a boy of the royal household, and the conversation began to flag, Lee told me that he thought it would be a good time to introduce the business, and I commenced by telling the king that I was quite satisfied with his word and had perfect confidence in it, and that my friends who knew me had also perfect confidence in mine; but that in carrying on the work I should have transactions with perhaps many hundred persons, whom I should never see and who would not even know me, and, therefore, could not hear from my lips the word the king had given me, and it was also possible that I might die, and then doubts might arise as to the exact words he had used. And, therefore, for the satisfaction of those to whom I could not personally speak, and for the avoidance of any possible uncertainty I begged that he would be good enough to let me have in writing the word he had already given me with his own lips. To this he replied : " Yes ; I know it is the custom of white men and you shall have a writing." I thanked him, and from that moment rested in perfect security and mentioned it no more ; but I consulted Mr. Lee, and we agreed that in drawing up the document I should avoid any attempt at legal phraseology, and write it as nearly as possible in the words the king had used. I must also do Mr. Lee the justice to say that he was anxious I should write it in a fair and equitable manner, and not introduce, for the sake of advantage on my side, any expressions that could afterwards be interpreted to mean more than the king might understand at the time of signing the document.

For some weeks I was occupied at intervals in writing for the king letters to the Governor of Natal, the President of the Trans Vaal Republic, and various native chiefs, and when all these were finished a day was appointed on which they were carefully read over and interpreted to him, after which he signed them with his —X—mark, and signed them with a signet of box wood, on which at his own request, I had engraved his name, "Lo Bengula." Finally, his own correspondence having been duly signed, enclosed, directed, and handed to me for delivery, he asked me, " Have you the writing ready that you wished me to sign for you ? " I brought it forward and read it by short sentences, Mr. Lee interpreting, and the King giving signs of assent or recognition occasionally. When the rivers constituting the boundaries of the grant were named he asked me to repeat them, and making another sign of assent he heard the document to its end. He then affixed his sign manual in the proper place ; Mr. Jewell spread the wax, and he impressed on it the royal signet. Some of our friends who were present then signed as witnesses, and the business of the day was considered as having been satisfactorily concluded. The king desiring Mr. Lee to tell me that " I had a very good memory " for " those were the exact words he said."

I append here a copy of the document :—

Ratification of Grant, made verbally by Lo Bengula, Supreme Chief of the Matabili nation, to Mr. Thomas Baines on behalf of the South African Gold Fields Exploration Company (Limited), on the Ninth Day of April, 1870.

I, Lo Bengula, King of the Matabili nation, do hereby certify that on the 9th day of April, 1870, in the presence of Mr. John Lee, acting as agent between myself and Mr. Thomas Baines, then and now commanding the expedition of the South African Gold Fields Exploration Company (Limited) I do freely grant Mr. Thomas Baines, on behalf of the above-named Company, full permission to explore, prospect, and dig, or mine for GOLD in all that country lying between the Gwailo river on the south-west, and the Ganyana on the north-east, and that this, my permission, includes liberty to build dwellings or storehouses, to erect machinery for crushing rocks or other purposes, to use the roads through my country freely for the purpose of introducing and conveying to the mines, such machinery, tools, provisions materials, and other necessaries, and for the removal of gold so obtained ; and it also includes all lesser details connected with Gold Mining.

In making this grant I do not alienate from my Kingdom this or any other portion of it; but reserve intact the sovereignty of my Dominion, and Mr. Baines engaged on behalf of said Company not to make any claim contrary or injurious to my right as sovereign of the country, but to recognise my authority as King and to apply to me for such protection as he might require, and I engaged to grant such protection to Mr. Baines as should enable him to enjoy all lawful and proper use of the privileges granted him by me; and I also certify that when in November of the same year, 1870, Mr. Baines asked me what tribute or payment he should make me in return for said privileges, I declined to name any sum, but left it to the judgment of Mr. Baines to make me annually, on behalf of the said Company, such present as might seem proper to him and acceptable to me.

Among the Matabili the verbal promise of the King has always been regarded as a sufficient guarantee, and many white men now enjoy privileges in virtue of grants made by my father, Umzelegazi, which I regard as binding on me.

I also regard my verbal permission given to Mr. Baines as valid and binding on me and my successors; but finding that the customs of white men require that such grants or promises should be made in writing, I now hereby solemnly and fully confirm the grant verbally made to Mr. Baines on behalf of his Company. In witness of which I hereto append my sign manual.

LO BENGULA.   X His mark

(Here his seal was affixed.)

Signed the 29th day of August, 1871.
Signed the same in witness hereof.

G. A. PHILLIPS.
F. BETTS.
ROBERT J. JEWELL.
JOHN LEE.

We now commenced preparations for our homeward journey. I selected a present for the King, with which he was well pleased, and all our friends came to bid us good-bye and receive a parting present. Next day the king was absent and the people as usual somewhat unruly and troublesome, and looking out sharply for a last chance of getting something. One man opened the tool chest and ran off with the jack plane, but was pursued and made to drop it. And I appealed to Umthlabba and Umtigoan to preserve order among the people, and the manner in which they assisted me will serve to show how well defined is the power of each Induna in his own jurisdiction, under the general authority of the King. They did not attempt to coerce those who belonged to other regiments or kraals, but each ordered his own retainers to stand back to a distance from the wagons, and that left us only a minority of others whom we could ourselves more easily deal with.

On the 31st the King visited me, and told me to send up to his place for meat. I sent the wagons away, and went to his hut to say farewell. He sent some men with a good supply of beef after the wagons, bought Mr. Jewell's gun, and Mr. Lee's horse for ivory; and desired Mr. Phillips to accompany us to Gibbeklaiko and make the payment there, and bade me "Go pleasantly and come back quickly," we shook hands, bade him "Rest pleasantly," and followed the wagons, and after a hard pull up the long hill reached Gibbeklaiko (or Bulo-waigo as it is also named), on Friday, September 1st, where we had the honour of an interview with the Royal widow of Umzeligasi the reputed, but not the actual, mother of Lo Bengula.* A fine wagon stood covered with a thatched roof to be preserved unused as long as it would hold together because Umseligasi himself had ridden in it, another is going to pieces in another part of the Royal precincts, one or two were destroyed at the burial of Umzeligasi, and the people felt sure their late Sovereign would rest in peace because at that time "*the lightning flashed out of a clear sky,*" and twelve people fell dead. Of course we understand perfectly that the blades of the assegais are meant by "the flashing lightning," just as they speak of "thunder without clouds," when the lion roars. In the King's wagon-house was a quantity of ivory which he had sent down as a present to Mr. Shepstone, but Matchen having turned back the wagon, it had never reached its destination.

* Bengula's mother was not the Royal wife, but when she presented the infant, Umzeligasi said to her although you have borne this child it is not yours. I take it and give it to the Queen as a Royal child, but you may nurse and rear it for me.

I gave the Queen mother a blue blanket, and went to pay my respects to Um Nombati who seemed very weak, but with his intellect as clear as ever. He told Gee, my wagon driver, who speaks Zulu very well, that I was the first man who had come to him duly accredited by a letter from the Governor to ask leave to explore for gold, and after recounting various incidents of the expedition, he desired Gee to say to me, "The country is yours."

In the afternoon we rode to Hope Fountain, three miles distant, where Mr. and Mrs. Thompson, living in a comfortable, though temporary, house of wattle and daub, built upon the spot selected last year, very gladly welcomed us; their little patch of green corn in the valley looked quite refreshing. On the 2nd September I delivered the grave stone, intended to be placed over the poor fellows of McNiel's party, who died at the Inyati Mission Station, and Mr. Thompson promised to see it taken there and placed in its intended position.

Hope Fountain is a real "Highland" home, the top of the ridges, which forms the continuation of the Drakensberg being only 200 feet higher, and it affords a splendid view over the low country to the south-east in which direction the trade wind comes up cold, cutting, and laden with the salt sea mists from the Indian ocean 300 miles away. My observations for height were :—

Sept. 2.—Boiling point 203·9 ; height 4274 feet
Sept. 3.—   „   203·9 ;   „   4274 „
And for latitude
Sept. 2.—Alpha Lyra, obs. alt. 62·13·50 ; lat. 20·15·30
Sept. 3.—   „   „   62·14·00 ; lat. 20·15·25

2] 40·30·55

Mean latitude south 20·15·27

I proceeded with the wagons to Mr. Lee's farm at Mangwe, we rode over to Tati with Jewell to post our letters, and found Mr. Hart busy in putting up his machinery, and Mr. Nelson and Arkle putting shoes, or blocks of iron, on the worn out stampers of the London and Limpopo Company's quartz crusher. We returned to Lee's to make preparation for our journey through the Fly Country.

A VIEW OF THE ZAMBESI FALLS. - FROM A PAINTING BY MR. BAINES.

CHAPTER IV.

THE NORTHERN GOLD FIELDS, MATABILILAND.

My journey through the Fly Country.—Opening the New Road.

As an indispensable preliminary I made observations at Mr. Lee's house, which fixed our starting point at lat., 20·44·20 ; long. 28·14·20 E. ; boiling point, 205·3; height in feet, 3,526, being about half-a-mile north-east from the saw-pit, which is in lat. 20°44·40, and long. 28·13·48 E.—the boiling point being 205·2, and height 3,580 feet. I engaged Carl Lee to drive Jewell's wagon, and on Sept. 26th Mr. Lee gave us an early breakfast, and we exchanged farewells and turned our faces to the south (a trifle easterly) following the course of the Mangwe river between granite hills of picturesque and fantastic form, sometimes they were bare hemispherical mounds of immense size, at others great piles of irregular blocks with which grass, trees, and bush were mingled, and not unfrequently they seemed like pyramidal bases for loggans or rocking stones ; immense pillars, obelisk or castellated piles looking in the dim morning or evening light like feudal strongholds, such as Ehrenbreitstein or others that overhang the Rhine. Some of Mr. Lee's relatives and our friend Mr. H. Biles had preceded us, and when we overtook them the next evening we found they had killed two giraffes, but the second not proving fat they had returned to the first when Christian Herbst noticed that the shot in the shoulder was rather too high up to be effective, and said we had better kill it or it will run away ; they off-saddled, and then Herbert took hold of the horns, and next moment was raised several feet into the air, and thrown with violence to a distance. As soon as he recovered he caught up his gun, but only inflicted a flank wound, and they had to catch their horses and give chase again before they killed the animal. I have heard of elephants supposed to be killed rising suddenly, and shaking off a whole party in the same way. Lions were occasionally seen, and we caught a little Lemur, called by the Dutch, Batapie, or Uil Apie (Bat or Owl Monkey) on account of its large ears. I put it into a side bag in the wagon, feeding it with gum, and at night led it out with a long tether, and gave it flies, locusts, moths, or any insects I could catch, or which were unwary enough to trust themselves within reach of its cord. It would come to me and lap drops of water off my finger, giving me a tolerably sharp nip as a hint to wet it again if it got too dry.

On Saturday, 30th, we reached the junction of Mangwe with Semokhie river, and in the afternoon met Mr. Jennings and other hunters at New-Year's Tree—lat., 21·11·24 ; long., 28·25·10 ; boiling point, 207 ; height 2,623 feet. Here the hunters informed me of a tree they called the South African mahogany, and promised to get mê its leaves and a piece of wood. It is red, with a short grain, and I think I must have seen it on the Zambesi. We travelled on, going in front with axes to cut a path when the bush was thick, and on the 7th October crossed the Shasha river, below the junction of the Semokhie—lat., 21·33·20 ; long., 23·39·40 E. ; height, 2,359 feet ; 85 miles, 4 furlongs 174 yards from Lee's house at Mangwe, and 54 miles, by hunters estimation, east-south-east of the Tati settlement.

I must not omit to acknowledge an act of kindness on the part of our friend Biles, who, seeing me trying to buy oxen from Mr. Jennings, and not quite able to make a settlement for them, came forward at once and said, "I will buy the oxen myself and lend them to you."

Here Herbst, Schmidt, and our Dutch friends left us, but Mr. Biles declared his intention to go through. At 5.30 A.M. on the 9th Gee and I, with four kafirs, started on foot to find a safe road before bringing the wagons on. We breakfasted under a leafless Baobab, about 40 feet in circumference, and passed others begining to show young foliage, some of them 50 feet in girth ; we saw a rhinoceros, two giraffes, and several antelopes, but men making a march and carrying blankets and provisions cannot turn aside and lose time in following game to any distance.

In the afternoon we fell in with some guinea fowl, and were trying to pick off one with a rifle bullet for dinner when we heard a low growling in the bush, and just in front of me half-a-dozen or more young lion cubs—of two sizes as if they belonged to two litters—came tumbling out into the open space, just beyond them a lioness uttering threatening growls against the invaders of her solitude, and a lion and lioness were disappearing behind a bush to our right. I raised my rifle and let mamma have the bullet which sent her off followed by her family in such haste that as we ran

PALM TREES IN THE INTERIOR OF SOUTH AFRICA.

after them her footsteps strewed fragments of earth, thrown back as if from the hoofs of a galloping horse.

By this time we were thirsty, and as the Kafirs expressed it, the water did not stop at this season in the rivers but it went and stayed by itself on the top of the great stones, we searched among the granite hills, and on the very summit of a great bare mound we found a hole four feet long, 3 wide, and about 3 deep, in the bottom of which there were 6 or 8 inches of water, shewing that rain must have fallen recently ; at night we crossed the broad sandy bed of the Macloutsie river but could find no water and made coffee of the little we had brought in our tin buckets.

Tuesday 10th passing several clumps of wild date and fan palms from 8 to about 25 feet high. We searched the river for water but could find none, till, probing the sand of a small tributary, our ramrods came up wet, we dug down with our hands and then left our little well to fill and clear itself; and while coffee was being made I cut down dwarf palms and scooped out the "cabbage" at the root of the young leaves.

We followed the river to the Eastward of South, narrowly watching every insect lest it should prove a Tsetse, when we saw two Buffaloes at a distance, we followed them until they dipped into a little gully, but when we reached the bank and looked down they were so close under us that we dared not move for fear of disturbing them, and so hidden by the foliage that we had to fire almost at random into the little patch of dark stem that was visible, they turned at once towards us and rushed past so close, that though the leading bull glared viciously from under his massive horns, his impetus carried him away before he could turn upon us, we reloaded and followed but could not get another shot. Somewhat farther South as we were searching a small patch of rock that contained a few pools of water, in the sand of the river, the boys started back with an expression of alarm, and looking in the direction they indicated I saw two noble yellow-maned lions within 15 yards. I caught my rifle from the bearer but the lions were already retreating, and I had to run round the clump of mimosas to get a shot at them as they bounded away through the long grass—it appears they were lying on the sand when first seen, and had the boys quietly given us our guns we might probably have killed one.

We wounded several pallahs at long ranges but were not able to run them down, and should have slept supperless had not I shot a monkey off the topmost branches of a tree, probably 100 feet high.

October 11th we returned by a pass through the hill about a mile west of our yesterday's track, and found no fly nor obstacle to a wagon. Gee noticed a dragon fly hovering; over a rock and springing up, found a cleft with water enough to serve us for breakfast; at night we slept on the Shasha river and reached the wagons in the morning.

Friday 13th we brought on the wagons, keeping, by Mr. Biles's advice, still further to the west, so as to keep clear of the hills as some of them were known to be infested by fly, and next day we drew up the wagons in a fine grove of Kameel doorns and palms upon the Macloutsie river, very picturesque but so suggestive of swamp and fever that had we arrived in the wet season instead of the dry, I would not have stayed a night in it.*

The next three days were devoted to endeavour to trace the spoor of a wagon which had apparently gone in on a hunting trip and had again passed out to the southward. Mr. Biles shot a pallah and the sight of the vultures hovering over our camp brought a few masaras, or poor natives, who in this district represent the bushmen of the deserts to the west. By cautious questioning we learned from them that the spoor was that of a Trans-Vaal hunter, named Du Venage (commonly called Devenaar) who was reported to know a safe track between the various patches of fly that overspread the country. We tried to hire some of them as guides, but they asked a musket each which we were not able to give even had we chosen to risk breaking the law of the Republic we were on our way to. We tried to tempt them with other articles, but they said Machin's people were hunting to the south and would kill them if they shewed us the road. On Tuesday we brought the wagons across the river and rode out to find the tracks of Du Venage's wagons, keeping a sharp look out upon our own and each others horses to see that no "fly" settled on them. The Tsetse is easily known by the manner in which he folds his wings one over the other like a pair of scissors, as we have before observed, giving him an appearance of narrowness and length, differing from other flies which settle with wings half expanded, there are some which close their wings at an angle of forty-five like the roof of a house, but none of these are the Tsetse. On Wednesday 18th, we moved to a little knoll overlooking the river, apparently safe from fly, and likely to be healthy even in the wet season, being thinly clad with bush, sufficiently elevated, and of gravelly soil, with pebbles or quartz agate of great beauty and coarse Malachite. In the afternoon Lee and I had a long walk in search of game and finally discovered a herd of buffaloes, chased them about three miles, firing whenever we could get within range, and wounding some, at length they turned to the river and crossed it in a cloud of dust. Lee threw himself down and thrust his arms in the sand up to the shoulder, but could feel no moisture, and we continued the practice till a wounded beast separated from the herd and charged viciously as we approached, but as he menaced one of us, he afforded a fair mark to the other, and two or three

---

* First outspan on Macloutsie river, acacia palm grove, lat., 21°57′45″; long., 28°35′ E.; B.P. 208; height, 2094 feet; distance from Shasha, 28 miles, 2 furlongs, 109 yards; distance from Lee's 116 miles, 3 furlongs, 64 yards.

shots terminated the contest as the sun sunk below the horizon. Taking the head and as much meat as we could carry, we turned homeward, so spent with fatigue and thirst that the water flowed over our parched tongues without refreshing them, and it was only by continued washing, rather than by drinking, that we could restore a grateful sense of moisture to them. I observed two stars at night:—

  A Andromedæ obs. alt 79·23·50 ; lat. 21·58·11
  A Eridani   ,, 108·11·50 ; ,, 21·57·55
              2] 116·6

     Mean latitude south 21·58·3

  Thursday, Oct. 19th, we moved the wagons nearly six miles east by south along the course of the Macloutsie, when the spoor suddenly turned and doubled back upon itself. This rendered us suspicious, and halting at once we sent the drivers with the cattle to the most open place in view, and instituting a search we found Tsetse in a little granite kopjie, thickly clad with bush about a mile from us. We also found castor-oil plants in the river bed, a sure sign that we were coming to as low a level as we dare risk; we were in hopes of finding the "commando path" of the Emigrant Boers, where in old times they cleared away the bush, 100 yards on each side of the road, but we found reason to believe that this was still east of us, and we knew no safe way of reaching it. I saw a suspicious looking insect on Jewell's white horse, I washed the place with ammonia, but as the horse did not flinch, I hoped that even if the insect had been a Tsetse it had made no puncture.

  Mr. Biles and I agreed to go ahead on foot to-morrow and explore the path, and Gee and Carl Lee were ordered to take all the oxen and horses, with four kafirs, and make a kraal a few miles back upon the road, near any water at which the oxen could drink clear of fly, in case they could find no pool we told him to bring the cattle to the water near the wagons after sunset, and get them away before daylight, but on no account to let them remain till after sunrise. Jewell remained with one boy in charge of the wagons.

  Tuesday, Oct. 20th, Mr. Biles and I, with four kafirs, went back and found spoor turning out to the west, and then trending southerly. In an hour and a half we reached a place where wagons had stood two days and where the hunters had shot buffaloes and had pegged the skins out to dry. This led us to hope that we might safely bring ours there, but we caught a tsetse and saw two or three more, and we subsequently learned that Du Venage having, during his last journey, gone too near the fly and got his oxen "stuck," had afterwards wandered wherever game led him, knowing that their death was certain, and further care useless, and thus his tracks were actually leading us into the danger which we hoped to escape by following them. An hour and a half more south we found water in the hollow of a rock, and from it saw hills on the south side of the Limpopo or L'Oorie, as it is here called. At 12·45 we crossed a river with sandy bed quite dry (the Little Tuli), and in a grove of fine acacias and mimosas found a deserted camp, where wagons had remained for several days, while large game had been shot and their skins pegged out to dry. We caught a glimpse of a Masara woman, and sent some of our boys to persuade her to come, but they feared her husband would bewitch them, and made no effort to induce her. A smaller rivulet named Pakwe joined the Tuli, and the path turned south-east up the bank of the former. We walked till after sunset, passing several fine baobabs, and halted under a granite hill, which we climbed to look for water but could find none, and therefore, contented ourselves with half a pannikin each, reserving a little for the morning.

Saturday, Oct. 21, we climbed a larger kopjie, where a gigantic baobab grew among granite blocks as grey, as huge, and as rugged as itself. I had frequently in Australia cut out junks of baobab wood and chewed them for the sap which they contained; but in those growing between Lake Ngami and the Zambesi I had failed to find sufficient moisture. We tried the experiment here, and were glad to find that the wood contained sap enough to allay our thirst while the act of chewing it cleansed our mouths from the dry hard incrustation that covered them. We had seen a huge bare granite mound about a mile to the west, and had sent a couple of kafirs to look for water in the fissures. We saw a kaross waved in token of success, and walking thither we found they had really discovered a treasure—a crescent shaped fissure in the rock, at which we might water all our cattle with a bucket, while the steepness of its sides would prevent wild animals exhausting it, unless Elephants, whose signs were visible around, should be able to suck it up with their long trunks; a "glorious godsend" in the wilderness Biles called it, and I laid it down upon our track chart under his name.

Here, to our great joy, we found the track turning South again, and as we proceeded we fell in with several baobabs, the largest of which measured 63 feet in girth, and here we again saw a small troop of the real short-horned gemsbok, (*oryx capensis*), which previous to this year we had thought was confined to the deserts West of Bamangwato. We found another "stand place," with huts, kraals, and other indications of lengthened occupation ; and in a branch of the Pakwe river to the south in a grove of mimosas and long weeds we found some pints of water in a hollow under a limestone bank ; at night a shower came on and we took refuge in one of the deserted huts.

WOUNDED RHINOCEROS.— FROM A PICTURE BY MR. BAINES.

Sunday, Oct. 22nd, as our provisions were exhausted and we had no certainty of reaching any village on the Limpopo, which was evidently much farther South than the best and latest maps placed it, we commenced our return and Mr. Biles shot a small steinbok and a quagga, which was received as a welcome supply ; the latter seemed intermediate between the bonte quagga (*equus Burchelli*) of Vaal river, and the full striped quagga (*equus Chapmanni*) of the Zambesi. Its legs, instead of being white like the first were very faintly striped, its ears slightly marked, and its tail tufted with black but covered with white hair, so as to make it look grey instead of being white like Burchell's or black like Chapman's. I believe there is a regular and almost imperceptible gradation between the two. We went on to Biles' pool and halted for the rest of the day, and while we were lying under the shadow of a rock, Mr. Biles whispered, " Here comes a camel," (*i.e.* camel-leopard or giraffe), we slipped out of sight at once and watched the stately animal emerge from the bush and approach one of the shallow rain pools on the bare granite flat, then halting and directly facing us, it prepared to drink ; now the male giraffe is six feet in the leg, 6 feet to the withers and 6 more to the top of the head, the head being about 3 feet long, he therefore lowered his body by gradually shuffling the fore feet apart till the hoofs were seven feet from each other and then the lofty head and neck came sweeping downward like a falling mast, until the lips reached the water.* Some times the giraffe kneels to drink by the river side, but is rarely seen in the act, and we have to-day witnessed what many hunters, ten years or more in the country, have never seen.

† On Monday 23rd, we reached the wagons at 5 p.m., and sent word to have the oxen kept away till after dark, we set fire to the grass and to heaps of rubbish to drive away the Tsetse, a few of which we saw. Gee had seen a fly upon one of the horses, he touched the place with ammonia and the animal started with pain, a sign that there was a puncture and that the ammonia had entered it. I had about a pound of carbonate of ammonia, and dissolving the greater part in warm water, I had all four of the horses washed. We observed some of them flinch as if the remedy had found its way into punctures, and it speaks well for our experiment, that up to the present time, so far as I am aware, not one of those horses have died. I had not enough to wash the oxen, but I sprinkled them with tar water in hope of keeping the fly off, but without effect.

Tuesday, 24th, we inspanned before the moon rose, and took a south-west course to clear the fly. We had passed the Tsetse Fountain and were crossing a little gully when the loose oxen pushed Gee's span out of their course, and the near wheels sinking into a hollow my wagon launched forward and capsized. I sent the horses and spare cattle on with Jewell, and unloading the vehicle unshipped the dissel boom, passed it as a lever between the axle and the feltoe of the after wheel, got a tackle on it, and made three yoke of oxen fast to the fore wheel, righted the wagon, reloaded, and at 11 a.m. overtook the others outspanned at the junction of the Tuli and Pakwe‡ rivers, where some of Matchen's people, who were out hunting, endeavoured to terrify our kafirs with threats and make them

---

* The largest giraffe I have measured was 19 feet 6 inches high including the horns which were about 9 inches.

† Last outspan on Macloutsie river, lat., 21·59·5; long., 28·44 E.

‡ Little Tuli and Pakwe, lat., 21·9·10 ; long., 23·43 E.

desert us. I gave the drivers charge to watch strictly lest any of the oxen should be driven away, and remained up myself nearly all night, observing stars, and keeping an eye on our visitors. We halted to drink next day at Biles'* pool and slept at the Great Baobab† after passing several others, in full foliage, adorned with beautiful white pendent flowers, peculiar to the African tree.

Oct. 26 we reached the limestone fountain on Pakwe‡ river, and were ten or fifteen miles south of the Limpopo, as placed on the latest maps, but in fact had not yet reached the river on the 27th, therefore I took Gee and two or three kafirs and again marched ahead, tracing the spoor south-east for thirteen and a half miles to an outspan, beside a dark dense line of thorn trees, and pushing our way through thick thorny underwood, mingled with date palms and tall reeds, at length looked down on the still deep waters of a narrow branch of the Limpopo, as it lay reflecting the tall green trees that over-arched it. The hunters had formed a bower by clearing a space under a small tree, whose branches, bearing bright green leaves and yellow fragile flowers, drooped nearly to the ground all round us. In this we ate a small meal cake each, rejoicing in being at last able to moisten it in real Limpopo water, and meanwhile letting every insect buzz round or sting us undisturbed, while we watched narrowly whether it were or not a tsetse. The wagons seemed to have turned up the river to seek a drift, and in following their spoor we exercised the same vigilance with regard to every winged insect that approached us, either at the drinking place, where the water flowed in streamlets over the rocks, or on the long red sand bank that we passed on our return to our camp. On again —saw some real gemsboks, but could not shoot them. We were somewhat tired for the day had been hot, and we had walked eleven hours, performing an actual distance of twenty-seven miles, besides the various casts we made to recover the spoor when it was so faint that we could not certainly keep it. Thus walking the whole distance three times over, besides hunting, sketching, writing my journal and letters for the directors at home. besides mapping and astronomical observations leaves me barely three hours for sleep out of the twenty-four when we are in the fly country.

Saturday, 28th. Inspanned at daybreak, and in five hours reached the Limpopo, and Carl caught a fine barbel for breakfast.

---

* Bile's pool, lat., 22°17′40; long., 28°35′30 E.
† Great Baobab lat., 22°19′41; long 28°39′10 E.
‡ Lime Fountain, Pakwe, lat., 22°27′1; long., 28°39′10 E.

Gee found a kraal of Masaras, who, on his assurance that we were English and not Boers, consented to come to the wagons, and Mr. Biles persuaded them for a reward in powder and lead, to show us the way through the fly. It is unlawful to sell ammunition to them, but when the choice lies between the probable loss of all our cattle, and a slight infraction of a powerless law, I fancy very few will blame us for thus securing their services. The reason we have to travel so far up the bank of the Limpopo to the south-west is that we may avoid a patch of fly that holds the bank opposite to our present outspan. Our elevation above the sea is now 1935 feet, and we expect to go no lower, but to ascend gradually as we travel southward. Our spirits is now expended, and I have to boil the thermometer with chips of wood or a candle end, a dirty and uncertain method of getting the boiling point. We caught several fine barbels, which in our scarcity of meat are very acceptable. I fed my little lemur, Jeannette, on young locusts. I have kept a bag full of them for several days, and instead of dying of suffocation they live on, generating so much heat that there is no wonder that the crowds of them that gather on the bush and tufts of grass survive the rigour of the coldest night.

Monday, Oct. 30th, under the guidance of our Masaras we travelled $4\frac{1}{2}$ miles South West, then breaking through the belt of tall trees we saw the noble river more than a hundred yards in breadth, flowing smoothly over its sandy bottom with a current of about two knots per hour, occasional shoals or reedy islets giving diversity to its surface ; to an English reader this may seem common place enough, but after such a country as we had recently passed, the sight of a broad flowing river was so pleasant and refreshing that we could hardly imagine a description of it would be tedious to others. We crossed and outspanned on a place *reported clear of fly, but after Mr. Biles had killed and brought home a pullah, we saw a "fly" on Jewell's hat but failed to catch it. We brought up all the cattle and horses immediately and rigidly examined them, tied up the horses, posted a kafir to watch every insect that approached them and fired several shots to recall Gee, in a short time he came followed by a kafir bringing another pullah and I went out to meet him at a distance and make sure that he brought no "fly" upon his game. We saw one on Plait's fore leg but could not kill it, we washed the place with ammonia, and saw probably the same "fly" on Mr. Biles's horse, we tried to

* Outspan on Limpopo, lat., 22·35·31 ; long., 28·41·10 E; height 1935 feet. Drift of Limpopo, South side, 22·37·40   long. 28·38·0.

catch him with the edge of a knife so held as to cast the narrowest possible shadow a little away from the insect, but the Tsetse was too quick even for this, at last Biles struck him to the ground, and I secured him in an envelope to be sent to London.

Here our guide asked payment as he wanted to go home, and we at first looked upon this as a breach of his engagement, but Gee, who spoke a little of the language, at length made out that he had brought us out of the limits of his own tribe and into the country of the next. Our first care was to ascertain that the head man on whose domain we had entered would take over the charge, and we then agreed for a bar of lead and a flask of powder and paid our first man off; a little hastiness here would have spoiled everything, and we should have looked upon our first guide as a breaker of the engagement he had made with us. In the afternoon we moved a little more than five miles up stream to Peerie's *village. Next morning, Tuesday, 31st Oct., I went to sketch the waterfall at Impopo Mini, the noise of which we had heard all night. A ledge of granite formed a rugged barrier 8 or 10 feet high across the river and down the various hollows of this the clear waters rushed or rippled in various rills, cascades or rapids, bubbling and eddying among the great masses of rock below, in many of which (like those of the Zambesi) great holes were worn by stones which during the floods had settled perhaps in small hollows, and by continual whirling round had increased them to circular cavities six or eight feet deep and perhaps half the width. Sometimes two or more of these form beside each other and increase till the partition walls become thin, and finally break away below leaving the upper parts like arches, spanning the vault beneath them.

Biles, Jewell, and Carl went to a pool to watch for tsetses but did not secure any. In the afternoon one of the herdsmen told me a crocodile had seized an ox by the Dewlap as he went to drink, but they had driven him off with sticks, stones, and hideous yells. I went with him and saw the crocodile again lying in wait, his head nearly submerged, but with a portion of his body and tail above water; the watchful creature detected our approach and was already moving off when I gave him a bullet in the flank, making him writhe and struggle as he launched into deep water, but he was not killed, for when the cattle went to drink he was again in position watching for them.

Wednesday, Nov. 1st, our first track of nearly 7 miles brought

---

* Peerie's village, lat., 22°40'55; long, 28°34'10 E.; Impopo Mini, or the Waterfall over granite ledge 8 or 10 feet high.

us to a place where hunters' wagons had stood for some days, and where they had evidently hunted giraffes with horses, and the second track of about $4\frac{1}{2}$ miles more brought us nearly abreast of the Tslagool hills (the Silika or Siloquam of the maps) on the opposite side of the forest fringed river. I feared we were pushing on too early, but was relieved by seeing the sun sink down below the hills. At 7 p.m. it was quite dark, and we thought it safe to span out till the moon rose and enabled us to see the nearly effaced tracks of the hunters' wagons. At 12.10 we moved on again, but it is difficult to see a track by moonlight, and more than once we lost it and had to scatter in all directions to recover it; at 1 a.m. we passed a granite hill covered with bush and infested by the dreaded "fly"; at 3.15 we outspanned and I obtained an altitude of "Canopus"—observed altitude, 120·29·40. Latitude, 22·50·4, approximate longitude, 28·22·40.

Thursday, Nov. 2nd. The morning revealed the dark dense line of trees that bordered the Limpopo still upon our right. We travelled eight miles and seven furlongs beside it during the day, caught a barbel three feet six inches in length, a welcome addition to our scanty larder. We had now paid off and parted with our guides, and in our evening track we found the spoor turn south, away from the Limpopo, and begin to scatter. We feared that this indicated the proximity of fly, through which every one had sought his road by night as best he could, and we halted and searched with lanterns till we found a definite track again.

I observed "a. Eridani," alt., 110·13·00; lat., 22·58·32; and as soon as the moon rose high enough we went on again. I walked in front with one of our kafirs as usual, till I became so oppressed by continued want of sleep, that I was obliged to mount Mr. Bile's wagon, and stretch myself upon his "kadel," or swinging bed frame; but the road was now more definite, and about midnight we came to a pan, whence we took a little water for our next meal, but there was none for the oxen, nor dare we halt till daylight as we were still within the limit of the patch of fly.

Friday, Nov. 3rd, we outspanned near a hollow, and Gee and I went forward, passing a grove of fine Baobabs in full leaf. We found an old woman and a girl gathering locusts (Voet-gangers), and four or five men and boys joined us, they told us the pan in front was called Madlala, and a day's journey beyond it was "Schimmel Paard Pan," there was fly between them, but no water, and there is fly also beyond Schimmel Paard Pan. But we must leave it before dark so as to be able to get into a definite track, and yet not so soon as to rush into the fly till it has retired for the night. It is a day's journey to Maghaliquain River, through which we must not cross as there is fly between it and Madzalana River, but after this we are past all danger, and reach Matlalas in two days, and Makapans in four. From Maghaliquain there is fly to the west, between us and the Limpopo.

We moved on to Madlala Pan, intending to rest all Saturday and Sunday, but found only a scanty drink for the oxen, so that this was impossible. Gee shot a Sassaybe, or bastard hartebeest, and one of the boys killed a quagga; we gave the Masaras a share of the flesh, and tried to tempt one of them with beads, powder or lead, to become our guide, but in vain.

The Matchopong mountains were visible to the north-west, and as they are also seen from the Ba Mangwata road they formed a landmark to test the correctness of our longitude. Our last night's track through the fly country had been about 13 miles, and during the afternoon and evening we made about 10 more. The night was dark and cloudy, preventing any observation for latitude, but affording us additional security against the insect pest.

On Saturday, the 4th, by early dawn we were again fleeing for the lives of our cattle, and making about 13 miles and a furlong during the day outspanned just short of "De Schimmel Paard-pan," so named after an adventure of my former friend and fellow traveller Joseph Macabe, who refusing to believe that a ridiculous little fly could kill so large an animal, had outspanned by the pan and deliberately rode a valuable horse into the infested country. In a few hours after his return the steed was dead. I may as well explain that schimmel means mottled or dappled. Schimmel day is when the light clouds begin to be dappled with the tints of early dawn, but the word is generally used to imply the time of dawn, even though there are no clouds. A "blaauw schimmel paard" is a dappled grey, and others are distinguished as red or brown, according to their colour.

On Sunday, November 5th, we inspanned about half-past five, so as to get into the definite road before dark, and about seven we descended into a sandy tract with dense bush haunted by the tsetse. We made about seven miles and halted, the night being dark and cloudy and rain coming on towards morning. At dawn on Monday we trekked again, a steady shower protecting us as we laboured on through the infested district, and in ten miles and three furlongs we reached the west bank of the Maghaliquain or Fierce Crocodile river, called by the Boers the Nyl, because in the early days of the emigration some of them who found it flowing continually north thought it must certainly be the Nile, and would lead them to the land of Egypt, whence they might reach the promised land they read of every Sunday in their Bibles. They had found long ago, even as far south as the Cape Colony, heaps of stones which they thought had been thrown up by the children of Israel within forty years wanderings, but which in reality were heaped together by Kafir women clearing pieces of land, and remained to mark the spot long after the cultivator had passed away, and the corn field had again become part of the wilderness.

Our cattle would not eat the poor and scanty grass* but crossed the river to the better pasturage they saw on the other side, but unfortunately the "fly" was there and we had to drive them back again. We caught voetgangers or young wingless locusts, fried them with a little salt and found them better than nothing. After sunset on the 9th we crossed the river and trekked up its eastern bank for some distance and passing through the last patch of "fly" outspanned upon an open plain 9¼ miles from our last camp; the night was clear and I obtained an altitude of "a Eridani," 111·18·50; and "Canopus," 121·51·30; and latitude by both exactly the same, 23·31·33.

We had now cleared the infested parts between the Blauw Berg and the Hang Klip mountains, so called from their over-hanging cliffs, but for further security we made 4½ miles more before sunrise. We now travelled over a mimosa clad undulating country with limestone, sandstone, granite kopjies and quartzose indications, and again came within the habitat of the Springbok, one of which fell to Carl Lee's rifle.

On the 10th we halted opposite the hill on which are the villages of the chiefs La Kallakalla and young Makapan.† I went up to visit the latter, who spoke Dutch. I wanted to buy corn, but he had none, the late war with the Republic having exhausted his supply. Finding we were English he came down to the wagons, and with an apology for having no corn offered me two shillings, a mark of respect, as the first present is expected by the superior. I thanked him and declined it, telling him I was satisfied to see that his heart was right towards me.

---

* Drift of Maghaliquain, lat., 23·27·20; long., 28·51·40; 90 miles, 1 furlong, 64 yards, from the Limpopo.
† Makapan's Village lat., 24·9·25; long., 29·16·10; distance from Maghaliquain 62 miles, 6 furlongs, 144 yards.

Saturday we passed between the abandoned villages of Potgieters' Rust and the mission house and were sorry to find Mr. Beyers was absent. Jewell bought a pig for brass wire, and slaughtered it on the spot, as it was too unwieldy to be brought out of the village without demolishing several walls. At night we outspanned on the east side of Moordenaar's Drift * at the south end of Makapan's poort. The name " Murderer's Drift " is derived from the treacherous massacre of a party of Boers under circumstances of atrocious cruelty ; I believe by Makapan's father. I understand that he had a blood feud with the Republic, but no particular provocation from the individual victims. It was in the war following this that the tribe fortified themselves in caves, and the Boers adopted the effective but cruel expedient of bringing several hundred wagon loads of wood to the brow of the mountain, hurling them down to the foot of the cliffs in which the caves were, and then throwing fire upon the mass. These caves are said to be of wonderful extent, and many unsuspected passages lead up from them to daylight. Mynheer Potgieter was sitting on the edge of a deep cleft, little thinking it led down so far, when a Kafir, who from the obscurity of the cave beneath saw his figure clearly defined against the sky, fired up and killed him.

Here we lost our first ox, and at the time thought it might have been from eating the Makhanw, a poisonous plant with leaves two inches broad and 6 or 8 inches high. Gee found wormwood and gave a strong decoction, but in vain. Monday 13th we crossed the Maghaliquain or Mill Stroom at Moordenaar's drift and two more oxen were ill. Their loins were weak, which is a symptom of Mahanw poison as well as of the fly. We did not see the swelling of the gullet nor staring of the coat, and were therefore inclined to hope that it was not fly, but nevertheless gave them a dose of ammonia.

On Tuesday I mounted Jewell's white horse and rode on with my letters; I was kindly entertained by the Rev. Mr. and Mrs. Kobold at the Berlin Mission station of Modemolulu, Modemoiela, or Melie Fontein. I halted also at the farm of Theunis de Klerk, who told me they now knew where to ride their horses with safety between the patches of fly ; they also have safe or inoculated oxen and even ride their horses in ; they will not tell their medicine but charge an ox for making a horse safe ; they told me they thought the fly was a curse that was being removed from the land. At night I reached

---

* Moordenaar's Drift lat. 24·16·3; long. 29·16·3; distance from Makapan 11 miles, 1 furlong, 199 yards.

Nylstroom but found many of the houses deserted. Mr. De Wittan and Mr. James entertained me, but I could not get letters sent away. On Wednesday Mr. Van Nispen, the magistrate,* invited me to his house, and the kafirs having brought my sextant I found the latitude, 24·42·30, shewing that all this country is laid down 20 miles too far north on existing maps. Mr. Ver Doorn told me he saw some bricks from an old city near the Blaauw Berg mountains, but whether Portuguese or more ancient he could not tell. I had already heard of the party prospecting for gold on Mr. Button's farm at Eersteling. On Thursday I rode some distance west from the direct road and slept at Mynheer Swanepoel's, where I found the community agitated by the news that one of their ministers had resigned and accepted a secular office under government. They regarded this innovation with great alarm, and the hospitable farm house that evening gave me by no means a faint idea of the meetings for worship among the Scotch Covenanters in the times of persecution.

On Friday, 16th, I crossed the Springbok flats, slept at Mr. Vanderwalt's, who took me to see a quartz reef on his farm, and on Saturday reached Pretoria, the seat of Government of the Trans-Vaal Republic, where the hospitality of Mr. Brodrick, Mr. Leys, and other friends, hardly allowed me time to add a postscript to my letters ere I sent them away.

Tuesday, 20th, Mr. Biles and Jewell arrived with the wagons, the yellow ox was dead and three more were ill on the 26th. Mr. Frank, of the Government Gold Commission, shewed me 2 ounces of alluvial gold he had brought from Eersteling on the 25th; Jewell and I rode along the Magaliesberg to Mr. Hartley's, 47 miles about southwest, and found our friend as hospitable and glad to see

---

* Mr. Van Nispen's house at Nylstroom, lat., 24·42·36; long., 28·36. Mr. G. P. Moodie makes the long., 28·50.

Mr. A. Brodrick's house, Church Square, Pretoria, Seat of Government, Trans Vaal Republic, lat., 25·44·35; long., 28·25·20. Boiling point 204—4; Barometer, 26—62½; height above the sea, 4007 feet.

Population in 1868, 300, much increased now; situated about 4 miles north of the sources of the Apies river, which flows through Maghaliesberg to the Limpopo.

	Miles.	Fur.	Yds.
Pretoria to Moordenaar's drift	133	7	11
Pretoria to Lee's farm Mangrove, via Moordenaar's drift	479	7	3
Pretoria to Vaal river at Retief's drift	133	4	59
Pretoria to "Plough Hotel," Pieter Maritzburg, v a Retief's drift	359	7	16

us as before. I left Jewell with the wagons and oxen here, and the number that subsequently died—nine in all—the symptons they exhibited, and above all their long lingering sickness and the punctures found inside the skin after death, convinced us that the fly was the cause of the mortality.

Returning to Pretoria I made a trip to the Eersteling gold reef with Mr. William Leathern, and this journey will be found described in the part relating to the Trans-Vaal gold fields, which also contains a chapter devoted to the fly. My subsequent journey to Marthinus Wesselstroom, by a road not hitherto laid down on any map, is also separately described.

HUNTING ZEBRAS IN "THE VELDT." FROM A PAINTING BY MR. BAINES.

CHAPTER V.

THE GOLD FIELDS OF THE TRANS-VAAL REPUBLIC.

Maraba Stadt, Eersteling, Lydenburg, MacMac and Pilgrim's Rest.

I HAVE already stated that the existence of gold in considerable quantities in South-east Africa has been known from the earliest period of history. The early Dutch pioneers in times more recent brought back vague statements of its mineral wealth, and when, after the great migration of the Dutch colonists from the Cape Colony in 1836, from Natal in 1842-43, and from the Orange river Sovereignty, now the Orange Free State, in 1848, set toward the northern side of the Vaal river, these rumours gathered strength and acquired form, but yet were spoken of " with bated breath and whispering fearfulness " lest the fame thereof should get abroad, and the English Government should follow and take possession of the country. In 1850 I myself visited the then little village of Potchefstroom and heard of gold among the Slaamzyn (Islaams or Mahomedans) Kafirs, achter (beyond) Zoutpansberg. In those days, however, my friend Joseph Macabe was fined 400 rix dollars for having written an itinerary of one of his journeys, and I had the honour of being made "Vogel Vrie" *i. e.* "Free as a bird" *(for any one to shoot at)* for the crime of possessing, and being able to use, a sextant. In 1852 their independence was acknowledged, and one of their first acts was to repeal a former resolution of the Volksraad, fixing their southern boundary at the twenty-fifth degree of south latitude "because the Volksraad has no means of determining where the said degree of south latitude is."

My sentence of outlawry, however, must I suppose, be effaced by lapse of time, for in 1869 I enjoyed a jovial glass of grog with the very officer who nineteen years before had been sent to take or shoot me. Civilization made slow progress. Not many years ago their own surveyor general was mobbed for using a theodolite in the streets of Potchefstroom instead of stepping off the distance like the Veld-Valkt meester of the good old times. It is not more than four years since a Boer found a small quantity of metal, probably nickel, and made rings for his pipe sling of it, when immediately the Raad passed a law forbidding any one to work this metal, or even to reveal the locality in which it was found, under a penalty of 600 rix dollars, lest the English should hear of it and take the country.

In 1868 the eminent German explorer, Carl Mauch, made his pedestrian journey from Pretoria to Lydenburg, and thence northward into Matabililand, and marked a spot in lat. 24·10, and long. 31·50 approximate, and about seventy miles north-north-east of Lydenburg, as a profitable gold field. It is well known that to the westward of the Hangklip* mountains there is a small rivulet called gold spruit flowing into the Pollsela river, while native reports pointed to that place, to the Marico district in the west or inland border of the Republic, to Maraba's country near the centre, and to many others, as spots where the precious metal could be found, while patriarchal Boers, almost aboriginal Doppers,† complained, with rueful faces, that sundry "verdomde Engelsche kerels" had come to their places, looking for white stones, and had taken them away by wagon chests full, with all the mysterious treasures they might contain. Others lamented that, in their days of inexperience, they had found crystals, bigger than hen's eggs, which must certainly have been diamonds, and unheard of quantities of yellow metal, which just as infallibly must have been gold, and had recklessly thrown away their good fortune, for want of knowing when it was in their hands. And now the English, with their cunning, were going to reap the profit which belonged, of right, to those who had explored and pioneered the way, and had

---

* Not Hanglip but Hangklip, the overhanging rock or cliff.
† Equivalent to English Baptists.

"schoongemaakt" (cleared or made clean) the land. I had the pleasure of knowing one right hospitable Boer, near Hoe Fontein, who was greatly exercised in mind because an Englishman had found a diamond on his farm. He thought himself excessively liberal in foregoing any claim to the diamond on condition that he was shewn the exact spot where it was picked up; but the answer of the finder was—"If I know it is quite enough for me." Another living near the Eye, or fountain head of the Mooi River, told me he had been asked by an Englishman for permission to seek diamonds on his farm, but he refused at once, "No, no, decidedly not! I will not have diamonds found on my farm—where shall I get grazing, or corn land, or garden ground, if the diamond diggers come and overrun my land?"

Nevertheless a few diamonds were found, one of them on a small ridge near the Limpopo, north of the Marico, but the finder, in his ignorance of the fragility of a diamond, resolved to test it by its hardness, and either struck it on the wagon wheel, or let the wheel run over it; of course it went to pieces. He picked up some of the fragments, lost a few more, and ultimately sold the few bits he saved for £30.

Meanwhile rumours of the discovery of gold were gathering strength. Travellers, whether Dutch or English, who could gain the confidence of the natives were daily shewn, or told of spots where gold might be found, sometimes in coarse grains as large as wheat or peas; but the revealers always begged the person informed never to betray them to the resentment of their countrymen, and sometimes in a more suspicious mood denied the information they had given in moments of greater confidence, for the prevalent idea was that war would be at once made upon them, and they would be expelled from their country for the sake of the gold it contained. I need not say now, except for the information of our friends at home, that they are finding the presence of the diggers, who buy their produce, and pay them for their labour, an advantage instead of a detriment.*

---

* Yet, this being understood, it may not be amiss to illustrate the idea of justice to the native, which is held by, I hope, only a few among us. I was speaking to a friend respecting the new discoveries, and we both agreed that it would be very wrong to make war upon the natives and take the gold fields away from them. "But," said my friend, "I would work with voorzegtigheid," (foresight). "I would send cattle farmers to graze their herds near the borders, and the kafirs would be sure to steal them; but if not, the owners could come away, and he could even withdraw his herds.

It will now be as well to give a brief resumé of the principal explorations in search of gold, and then to summarize the yield of the various reefs or fields, and treat as briefly and comprehensively as possible of the facilities (or want of them) for living and working in the country, and its natural features and geographical character.

I have already mentioned the journey of Carl Mauch and the indication of a probable gold field by him, and although not immediately connected with the search for gold I ought not to pass over the establishment of the settlement by Mr. McCorkindale of

NEW SCOTLAND

on the highlands of the Drakensberg or Quathlamba mountains, in latitude between 25°30 and 26°, and longitude between 30° and 31°, lying on the eastern border of the Trans-Vaal Republic, 130 miles east of Pretoria, and 110 miles west of Delagoa Bay, which is reached by a gradual ascent, the former part of the distance being a gradual rise from 4,000 to about 5,000 feet, and the latter a descent of 3,000 feet in twenty or thirty miles, with a plateau of about 2,000 feet leading to the secondary ridge of the Lebomba mountains, between which and Delagoa Bay is about eighteen miles of low and unhealthy fever country; but Mr. McCorkindale proposed to bring small vessels into the Umsuti river, entering Delagoa bay from the south, which river carries three fathoms for full ten miles up, and water enough for boats more than twenty miles further. I regret to add that the spirited projector died on the 1st of May, 1871, on the island of Inyack, at the entrance of Delagoa bay, and is buried there; but the settlement of New Scotland is now well established and its prosperity seems increasing.

Mr. Edward Button's Journeys.—First—1869.

In July of the above year Mr. E. Button, the son of a well-known Natalian colonist, having traversed the Trans-Vaal Republic, arrived at the village of Lydenburg, or New Origstadt, founded about the year 1849 or 1850, in consequence of the unhealthiness of the old village, a fault which I believe has been completely remedied in the choice of a new site. The position of Lydenburg is yet but imperfectly known. Mr. G. Moodie places it in lat. 25°11 S., and

---

man, and let them run day and night, then the kafirs could not resist the temptation. We could go in and claim the stolen cattle, and if the kafirs resisted, and made war, of course they would lose their country." I have never heard, however, of my friend's diplomacy being carried into execution, and am happy to say the occupation of the gold fields is being carried on without the necessity for any policy that is not fair to both sides.

long., 30·30 east, while Mr. Jeppe lays it down in 24·40 south, and 31·5 east; Mr. Forssman, the Surveyor-General, in 25·4 south, and 31·35 east; and Mr. St. Vincent Erskine gives its latitude as 25·4 south, and its longitude east as 31·30. A somewhat uncertain point of departure it must be confessed; but colonists have a particular aptitude for finding their way about the wilderness although they may not be able always to fix upon the map correctly the places they have visited.

Mr. Button, accompanied by Mr. Sutherland, a miner, who had travelled for twenty years in California, New Zealand, and Australia, and by Mr. Parsons, who had been employed prospecting at the Umtwalumi River in Natal, proceeded north, finding a little gold in two streams, which they crossed before reaching Triegardts farm, twenty-five or thirty miles from Lydenburg, where Mr. McLachlan joined them. As the oxen were poor and the season not fit to travel, they left their wagons, and in an hour and a half on foot reached the edge of the Quathlamba mountains, whence they had a magnificent view of the low forest clad country, through which the Olifants river or Lipalula meandered. Two hours more brought them to the river, and the mountains they had left rising in successive cliffs of shale and sandstone, 2000 feet above the riverine plains, shewed grandly in the warm glow of the setting sun. The Lepalula at the ford was 100 yards from bank to bank, and the water three or four feet deep, it would be quite impassable when in flood, but at that season they were able to prospect, and found fine gold in the crevices of the bed rock of the river.

Their path led three days under the Quathlamba or Drakensberg, being cliffs passing over granite with occasional argillaceous slate, and then turning North-east they found chloritic slate with talc, but did not find gold. In two days more they reached the Salati river, on the bed rock of which they found gold, and had similar success in a gully half a day beyond the river, but were obliged to push on without bestowing on this place the examination it merited, and in a week they joined the wagon in charge of Mr. A. R. Ash, at the Spelonke (or cave) near Zoutpansberg.

A little further west stood the wagons of Mr. Walker, the surveyor from Pretoria, one of whose horses was standing apart suffering from the "dikop" form of horse sickness, and another hundred yards more west Mr. Ash with a gang of Kafirs was engaged in breaking out quartz from the reef on which he holds claims in partnership with Mr. Button. The hole was already 18 or

20 feet long from west to east, the direction of the reef being nearly from south-west by west to north-east by east. It was six feet or more in width, and about hip deep; most of the casing or capping had been removed within these limits, and lay in heaps showing very favourably as specks of gold were easily discernable with the naked eye, contrasting with the red and yellow oxides of iron prevalent among the stones. In one piece which Mr. Ash gave me it was very conspicious standing out like a coarse net work over the stone, and I supposed one fragment as large as a pigeons egg which accidentally broke off, contained half a sovereign's worth of gold. The solid rock lay beneath, and in pieces of this as they were laboriously removed, specks of gold were frequently visible.

Mr. Button was anxious, in case of my company sending me a machine, that I should not take it up to Matabililand, but halt it here and crush for the diggers, and I offered, if favourable terms were given me, to advise the company to send out a second machine for the Trans-Vaal.

Thence they trekked to the country of Sekundo an Amatonga chief, whose mountain, south of the Limpopo, forms part of the boundary between the Republic and the territory of the Portuguese. Crossing a sandstone hill, with a spur stretching to the eastward, adorned with fine specimens of the *encephalartos* or kafir bread, and then descending the valley of the Limpopo, they passed over metamorphic limestone and gneiss, the latter rising in cliffs of 600 feet on the south of the river, but sloping gradually on the north. The banks were covered with verdant and golden blossomed acacias, many of them with yellow bark, probably the sweet gum which is looked upon as indicating the presence of the Tsetse fly. They encamped near a gigantic baobab tree fifty feet in circumference, and procured a welcome supply of excellent meat by shooting a Zee Koe (hippopotamus) in the river.

On the north of the river the gneiss gave place to sandstone, the latter prevailing nearly to the river Bubya. Most of the rivulets were dry except at occasional brackish pools, whence the few natives extracted salt. The Bubya runs through a level country, its course being indicated by a fringe of darkgreen trees. In the dry season it ceases to flow, but water may be found in places by digging in the sand. Groves of fan palm and mimosas, with stems forty feet to the lower branches were met with, and the farthest northern point attained was the kraal of Matabili, a chief of the A'Banyal, subject to the Matabili.

Messrs. Button and Sutherland returned to the wagon at Sekumdo's and then would have made a detour to the east, but the difficulty of obtaining natives was great, and the season far advanced; they therefore made straight across country for their wagons at Triegardts, passing on their way the tribe of Sabulaan, who were busy making iron picks, the ore being plentiful and good. They crossed a range of metamorphic rocks running W. S. W. to E. N. E. and found a little gold, but could not stay to prospect as they were short of food. Though the formation seemed extensive, the ranges stretching E. N. E. as far as they could see, the strike of the rocks was in the same direction, and chloritic and talcose slates interstratified and interjected with veins of ferruginous quartz were noticed, as also dykes of trap.

Then passing granite gneiss and trap they crossed the rivers Utabani and Utabi, and in a few miles more reached an enormous vein of quartz in chloritic slate and gneiss; its width was 150 feet, and its height above the plain about 600 feet. It had been conspicuously in sight for several days, and from its magnitude they named it Mountain Reef. Water was scarce, and Mr. Button while seeking some came upon a fine pair of lions, but being armed only with a fowling piece did not molest them. Game was plentiful. Still farther south among the Mosheshiman hills of porphyritic granite, with occasional chloritic slate, they found natives working copper, but were not allowed to see any of the mines.

Crossing the river Salate, and emerging from the hills to the west, they came upon talc schist with bands of steatite and dykes of trap, while crystalline quartz nearly translucent was plentiful; but, as it showed no traces of iron, they were not encouraged to prospect. Between the rivers Makutyi and Lipalula they found groups of conical hills, composed of loose blocks of granite, with a single mass upon the top. After crossing the latter river they came to chloritic slate and gneiss, which continued to the foot of the Quathlamba. They ascended the mountain, reached their wagon, and started for Lydenburg on the 8th October.

Second trip.

On the first of June 1870, Messrs. Button and Sutherland started from Lydenburg and descended the Quathlamba through a chasm formed by a great dyke of trap, 15 miles east of the pass used in 1869, and amid scenery grand beyond description. They returned to the white quartz, found the year before (and marked on Mauch's map as a probable gold field), but did not succeed in getting even a colour. Iron which seems so generally to accompany gold being entirely absent. They then pushed on for the range of which "mountain-reef" forms a part, and shortly after crossing the Salate river came upon the desired formation, and finding it of great promise they named the hills Murchison range, after the late great geologist who had shortly before predicted that the Limpopo country would prove auriferous. Those mountains near Sabulaans they called "Sutherland range" after the surveyor-general of Natal.

They found gold in a gully named Wildebeeste gully from the herds of those animals frequenting it, and Sutherland thought it would pay well if a head of water for sluicing could be brought to bear on the deposit.

The Murchison ranges consist of two lines of hills about 600 feet high, running parallel from W. S. W. to E. N.E. with a valley six miles in width between them; the S. E. range is of chloritic talcose slate in a highly crystalline state; the N. W. of argillaceous of a deep red colour, owing to the presence of iron which is strong enough to prevent the action of the compass. In the main valley are smaller hills with large quartz veins running through their centres, and one which seems to be the oxide of the *vein* system is of considerable size. The ranges intersect the Quathlamba at right angles, where the mountain is much broken, the valleys are covered with immense beds of rich red alluvium.

In the N. W. range a native named Maniman lives in a gorge near a small spring and at the head of the valley into which fountain gorge opens. There is a flat topped or table mountain on the other side of this. They found auriferous quartz in three distinct veins, testing it by crushing the quartz between two stones, and washing the gold out with a diggers' dish. One of the reefs is about ten feet across, and another three feet; a third a few inches, but parallel to one forty feet wide capped with cellular quartz full of a red oxide; there are many traces of copper near this reef. In consequence of these discoveries Mr. Button named the place Mineral valley; they sunk a shaft and obtained a little gold, and before leaving they ascended mount Eureka and had a fine view of the snow white top of mountain reef far away to the North-east. In fact four days distant, judging from the slope of the hills, there is a favourable spot to sink for the main gutter of the mineral valley opposite mount Eureka; the expense of deep sinking would be little, there being no water to contend with No timber is required for the sides of the shaft; native labour is abundant and cheap, the greatest outlay would be for tools. The months of March, April, and May are considered unhealthy, and it would not be safe to enter till the dry season has set in and then water is scarce, but there would be no difficulty in securing a supply if dams were made in the beginning of October, during the first rains. The clay is well adapted for holding water and large reservoirs could be made without much labour. Game was abundant and several buffaloes were killed, but a native hunter lost his life and Mr. Button wounded himself accidentally and had to lie up for three weeks.

They descended the Lebomba mountains and proceeded on foot down the Limpopo some distance beyond the confluence of the Lepalula or Olifants river, and returned to their wagons on the 9th of September. They brought out specimens of auriferous quartz which were sent from Natal to the South African Gold fields Exploration company for assize, and they believed that on the Eastern side of the Lebombo mountains, where it intersects Murchison and Sutherland ranges, great deposits of auriferous drift must occur, similar to the Terhartz gold drifts of Australia. They thought it probable that the gold fields of Sofala must be due to these auriferous belts, as if they extend to the east coast their direction would bring them out not far south of that district.

About the close of January, 1871, I returned to Natal from the Northern Gold Fields, and finding the quartz sent down by Mr. Button lying at Dr. Sutherland's I offered to send it home to the S. A. G. F. Co. in London to be tested, and he agreed, but we have not yet heard the result. Rumours, however, were rife of the discovery of other auriferous localities in various parts of the Trans-Vaal, and I was requested by Mr. MacFarlane, at that time I believe speaker of the legislative council, to go out of my way a little and visit the reported gold fields on my way up. The kind assistance of many gentlemen in Natal greatly facilitated the re-equipment of my expedition, but the season was so far advanced that I was obliged to proceed without delay to Matabililand where the King Lo Bengula confirmed most fully the concession he had already made me in the Northern Gold Fields, and gave me liberty to come out of his country by a more direct road, southward through the Tsetse Fly country into the Trans-Vaal. This might be considered no great boon, as cattle once "stuck" by the fly are doomed to almost certain death. But the Tsetse, though occupying large tracts of country, does not completely overspread it, but leaves parts which are known to various hunters, and which serve as channels by which a course may be steered with some chance of escape from the deadly pest. Unfortunately I could not obtain a skilful pilot, and came in contact with one patch of fly, by whose stings I lost nine oxen, but having a pound of carbonate of ammonia I dissolved it in a bucket of warm water and washed all the horses. I am not prepared to affirm that this was the actual saving remedy ; but none of them died, and I think the presumption is in favour of the ammonia.

While passing Makapan Poort I heard that gold seekers were at work to the eastward, and on reaching Pretoria I found that Mr. Edward Button had discovered a reef, some portions of which at least were richly auriferous, while alluvial gold was supposed to exist not far from it.

A commission consisting of Magnus Forssman, the Surveyor-General of the Trans Vaal, and two other gentlemen, were still away at the fields, and about the end of November 1871 they returned bringing with them about two ounces of alluvial gold which had been washed from the soil near Mr. Button's reef. Here I had the pleasure of meeting Mr. William Leathern of Natal, who being about to start on a visit to Eersteling invited me to accompany him. At midnight on the 2nd December we started from Mr. A. Brodrick's house in Church-square, in a light open cart with four horses, rattling at a good pace along tolerable level roads till we passed through the Derde (or third) Poort, in the Magaliesberg, about seven and three-quarter miles north-east. We then turned north over extensive undulating plains, with the Apies river at some distance on our left, but on testing the trochiameter against the results obtained on my previous journey I found that it showed less than the truth. I am obliged to protect it against bushes, &c., by placing it in a small box between the spokes of the wheel at ten or twelve inches from the nave, and the rapidity with which our light cart skims over the ground causes the instrument to acquire a centrifugal motion, coinciding with the revolution of the wheel, and makes it register less than the truth. We stopped at Mynheer Willem Prinsloo's ; then again opposite the Soul's Kraal, Berlin Mission station ; then leaving Apies river we crossed Pienaar's river, both flowing to our left to join the Limpopo. Let the horses have another rest at Klip Fontein, known also as Enkelde boom (or single tree) fountain, on the Springbok flats, and finally unharnessed for the night among the mimosa groves at Sand Fontein ; our only guide in the darkness being the croaking of the frogs, by which we guessed that there was water near us. We heard from a farmer we met during the day that Andreas Duvenage (commonly called Devenaar) knows of a safe road through the fly, between Blauw-berg and Zoutpansberg. We also heard that when Mr. Franks showed an Australian digger the two ounces of alluvial gold, and told him he could not yet give a positive opinion as to the payable nature of the fields till the report of the Commission was made up the digger asked, " Do you know that this gold was found in this country ?" Answer : " Yes." " Did you see it got out ?" " Yes." Can you tell me where it came from ?" " Yes." "Then," courteously replied the digger, " may angels in their softest whispers breathe blessings on the invaluable documentary evidence you graciously design for us, but in the interim the precious metal you have deigned to exhibit more than suffices for your devoted and humble servant." [P.S.—I have some suspicion that the digger used other words, and that ears polite would not thank me for recording them too faithfully.] We also heard that gold had been found on a farm called Biltong Fontein, between Makapan's Poort and Matlalas hill. On the 4th we reached Zacharias de Beer's farm, and breakfasted with a friend of Mr. Leathern's, when Mr. Dyason agreed to bring down a wagon load of the quartz to Pretoria for £12. As we rode on, with the Waterberg on our left, I asked Mr. Leathern how he proposed to send the quartz home, and finding him in doubt I offered to send it to our Company, requesting them to have it assayed by Johnson and Mattheys, of London, so that we might have a chance of estimating the wealth that lies hid under the rugged hills of South Africa.

Passing through Oesterhuyscus poort, we turned to the left from the direct road, crossed the Klein Nylstroom, or little Nile, and reached the town of Nylstroom before sunset. Another mile and three quarters brought us to the hospitable house of Mr. Verdoorn, where we spent the night, and found the latitude 24°40′51 S., that of Nylstroom at Mr. Van Nispin's house being 24°42′30 S. Mr. Verdoorn told us that from the top of Krantz Kop we might see Moselekatze's Nek, Hang Klip, and Wakkerstroom hill, and it would well repay the trouble of the ascent to get so extensive a set of bearings. The skeleton of a rhinoceros still remains on the top, these animals, like the elephant, being able to climb any path that a man can.

He says the ruins of an old town, perhaps Portuguese, are 100 miles from Marabastadt, and about east-north-east or due east from Duvenage's. He has been near, but not quite to the place, and brought away three bricks pitched out by the Kafirs. It is said the Kafirs used likewise bricks themselves, but this seems at variance with the superstitious awe they are said to entertain for the place. The Rev. Mr. Merensky had an intention of visiting it, but had not yet succeeded. He pointed out the interest that would attach to the discovery of the church or any public buildings, and any treasure or relic that might be found in the ruins. The chance of finding such relics would of course be greatly affected by the degree of haste with which the inhabitants abandoned their town. If they removed leisurely they would take nearly everything with them, while in a fright like that of the "Noche Triste" valuables of all kinds would be lost and left. When I was in Jette, in 1859 I saw the font, the holy water cistern, the images and furniture of the deserted church at Zumbo, and these are still carefully preserved and used in processions on Good Friday, Easter, and other holidays. I may add that I look with great interest to the rediscovery of the sites of the old Portuguese trading stations, for we know that they dealt rather largely in gold collected by the natives, and all the native evidence we possess goes to prove that stations or houses were built wherever the natives could most easily collect gold, whether crushed out from the quartz by hand labour or gathered from alluvial deposits.

On the 4th we turned more east and reached Zacharias de Beer's surnamed "pure gyft," or rank poison, on account of the quantity of Makhonw or cattle poison that grows on his farm, and also to distinguish him from "Zakrees." On the other side Nylstroom, one of the family very obligingly offered to accompany us to Krantz Kop. Three of our cart horses were equipped with borrowed saddles. We rode to the foot of the hill, tied them to a tree, and climbed by one of the few passes to the top, 250 feet by aneroid from where we left the horses, and 350 feet above the level of the house. The long range of the Magaliesberg was visible in the red light of the setting sun, and what we took for Derde poort bore 223 degrees from north and Moselekatses' Nek 233 (variation 25 west). Heavy clouds came on as we returned, but I* obtained an observation of one star, which gave the latitude of the house 24·32·37 S. The family took great interest in the mechanism of the trochiameter, the sextant, and other instruments, and seemed liberally free from the prejudice frequently

---

* My compass is marked with degrees all round from zero or north to 360; thus east is 90, south 180, west 270, and north is zero or 360, and it is much handier than counting by points. Suppose for instance I wished to note W.N.W. ¾ W., double the amount of writing is required if letters are used, to say nothing of the risk of mistaking afterwards the hastily written W for an N.

entertained against observations. They were also anxious for the success of the gold fields, and very wisely considered that the Boer's source of wealth was in his corn and grazing lands, and that his share of the good fortune must be the profit on such produce as he could sell to the diggers, as it has proved to be in the diamond fields. On the 6th we rode along the Maghaliquain or "Fierce Crocodile" river, which has acquired the name of Nylstroom, or the River Nile, in a somewhat singular manner. It is well known that in the earliest migrations of the Dutch Boers from the Cape Colony they entertained hopes of being able to reach the Beloofte land, *i. e.* the promised land or Canaan. The heaps of stones, collected by the Kafir women when they clear a field for cultivation, and which remain long after that field has reverted to its primitive condition as part of the wilderness were supposed to be monuments piled up by the children of Israel, who, if this evidence is to be received, must be supposed to have come as far south as the frontier of Albany during their forty years wanderings. And when the avowed Jerusalem trekkers or pilgrims came to the Maghaliquain and found it flowing north, they at once christened it the Nile, and fondly hoped it would lead them down into Egypt, whence they could easily reach the Belooftcland. We crossed the Nile at Moord or Moordenaar's drift, and outspanned near the market tree, in latitude 24·16·23 ; long. approx, 30·16·0. We turned to the right of my former road, and about 7.45 P.M. reached the first house in the village of Pieter Potgieter's Rust, deserted rather more than two years before in consequence of wars with the natives. We turned the horses loose, and, as it rained, took possession of the house to cook our coffee for supper, but spread our blankets and slept outside for fear of fleas. The house which belonged to the late Carl Smidt (drowned in Pienaars river) was rather tastefully decorated (one of the inhabitants having been a painter), but it looked rather out of keeping to see granite pillars and arches painted on mud walls already crumbling to decay ; the lat. came out 24·11·35, probably nearer 24·12. Next morning we had a delicious feed off all the figs we could find in the garden, no other fruit being yet ripe. Just before the house were the foundations of a church, never yet completed, and the ruins of a red brick fort, with bastions and loop-holes quite sufficient as a defence against musketry. But, however bravely farmers might be willing to defend their town, the impossibility of guarding large herds of cattle from being driven off by savages from *

---

* This constantly happened during the Colonial Kafir Wars.

their wide-spread grazing veldt, compels them to retreat when soldiers with no property to look after would defend themselves.

Makapan's village is about two miles north-west upon a rugged hill, and a Kafir armed with a gun came from it and told us he was in charge of the houses. We asked him why, in that case, he had allowed them to be burned, and their doors and fittings destroyed, till not one except that which we occupied was covered with a roof. We passed through the main street bordered by perhaps ten or a dozen roofless ruined houses, and then turned more east through the mountains, and again north-east up a branch of the rivulet that runs past the town and saw that the Kafirs had destroyed the water furrow that irrigated the gardens.

While passing up the mountain valley of this rivulet we began to observe strata of clay slate and reefs of quartz in the mountain sides. And one sharp peak and then another which we concluded to be those of the Yzerberg or Iron mountain appeared before us on the right of the valley. As we passed beneath them they assumed the appearance of a long camel backed ridge, but again became sharp peaks when we could look back and see them end on. The mountain as its name implies is an immense mass of iron ore which the natives have quarried for ages past, and the holes they have dug are visible as dark spots upon its sides, the Surveyors say it affects the compass for a radius of fully ten miles. Button hill on the west side of Eersteling, Mr. Button's farm where the gold diggers are, became visible to the south as we passed out of the point, and Marabas mountain was seen to the North-east right ahead. We passed a deserted house on the Farm Turf Fontein (which also is now stated to be auriferous), and leaving the mountain on our right reached Marabastad, a long street with some five or six white houses, some thatched and flat roofed on one side of it. A heavy shower came on and in the absence of the owner we took shelter in the house of Mr. Goodwin, the duties of hospitality being well attended to by his servant. Du Venage lives 18 miles to the north and has the best known road through the Tsetse; he crosses the Limpopo at Commando drift, meeting only one patch of fly which he rides through in the night. The night was very cloudy and I had great difficulty in getting observations of two stars which gave latitude as under.

"A Tauri Aldebaran" observed altitude, 90°37'0; lat., 23°58'59;
"A Orionis Betelgnese" observed altitude, 117°21'30; lat., 23°58'2;
Index error 2' minus; mean latitude, 23°58'15; we found speculation rife as to the existence of payable gold, and the consequent

effect on the value of land; even now farms which might have been bought six months before for two oxen have been taken up by speculators for £15 hard cash (British sterling),* and are now valued by hundreds or thousands of pounds, in fact, if nothing whatever is known respecting the auriferous properties of a farm the very uncertainty causes the owner to place a higher and fictitious value on it, because it may be worth any money.

We left a little before nine on the 8th, keeping south, and rounding the southern end of Marabas Hill, where Mr. Leathern halted the cart a little while. I climbed two or three of the spurs and found quartz ore indications pretty well marked in several places; then turning west south-west over a beautiful undulating country, studded here and there with mimosa groves, and shewing glimpses of white quartz reefs shining through the verdant herbage, we reached Mr. Button's house on his farm Eersteling, about eleven. We were kindly welcomed by him and Mrs. Button, and were fortunate in being just in time to see some very beautiful specimens of gold quartz, which were already packed to be sent to the diamond fields; some of these were very rich, and a few, collected by Mrs. Button, exceedingly so. A regular network of gold standing out in high relief all over the stones, and looking like a filagree of gold thread, rather than a natural production. In fact, I believe, Mrs. Button had selected a few pieces to set as a brooch and pendants just as they came from the reef, and besides these, there was an ounce of alluvial gold purchased from one of the diggers.

After breakfast—such as a well stocked up country farm can produce, and a hungry traveller can do ample justice to—we went to see the working.

Close to the house, in a deep gully of rich brown soil, with a small rill dammed up to contain the water, were two cradles, and across another branch of the rivulet, in a broad grassy valley, were half-a-dozen holes side by side like newly made graves; they were eight or nine feet deep, heaps of soil lay near them ready for washing, and from these the two ounces of gold I saw in Pretoria had been extracted.

On Saturday, the 9th, a committee meeting of the diggers, with Mr. Button as gold commissioner, was held, for the purpose of

---

* N.B.—No person will take a promissory note except it is specially stated that payment is to be made in British sterling, because the debtor would probably pay in Blue backs, and call them the sterling of the Trans-Vaal.

framing regulations for the general guidance, and the following series of resolutions was passed :—

1st.—That all business and correspondence be conducted in English.

2nd.—That the section of the law prohibiting a digger to transfer his claim without giving notice to the commissioner be rescinded.

3rd.—That dry claims, *i.e.*, claims situated at a distance from gullies or water-courses, be thirty feet square.

4th.—That not more than four adjoining claims be held by one company.

5th.—Prospecting claims to be increased in size by distance from any known company—viz., half mile, double; one mile, treble; over four miles, quadruple.

On Saturday, 9th, a committee meeting of the diggers, with Mr. Button as gold commissioner, in the chair, was held, for the purpose of framing requisitions for the general guidance. It was decided that not more than four adjacent claims should be held by any one company, and that no claim should be more than 100 feet along the reef, and 100 feet on each side, *i.e.* 100 feet x. 200.

Sunday, 10th, we walked out a few miles south towards Riet Fontein, passing several reefs and outcroppings of quartz—the diggers all seemed hopeful, but considered it too soon yet to say positively that they had found a payable field—meaning by this, a field on which an individual digger, without capital, could reckon, with confidence, on earning good wages. On Monday Mr. Dyason arrived with his wagon, and we loaded up more than a ton of quartz. No selection was made, more than would have been considered proper if we had been sending the quartz to a crushing machine upon the spot, in fact, the only care taken was to choose quartz presenting, at first sight, a tolerably good appearance, that which was most deeply coloured red or yellow ferruginous tints having the preference. There was no time to examine whether each piece contained gold, though we saw specks in several as they were passed into the wagon. I wished to pack it in skin bags, but no skins were obtainable. Mr. Button promised to send me, at Pretoria, a hundred weight of selected quartz, to be forwarded to England for assay. He named the reef Natalia; and was employed most of the day in levelling ground, and placing sluice boxes to carry water from a dam in the western spruit to a gold cradle;. there was a long tom at work in the rivulet, just below the dam and cascade, formed by a moss of clay slate, tilted up at an angle

ARRIVAL AT PRETORIA.   87

of forty-five degrees. One of the alluvial diggers found an egg shaped nugget, about an inch long.

We had another very pleasant musical evening; and the latitude of the house, by three good stellar observations, came out, as under :—

"A Eridani, Achernar," alt.. 112·28·10 ; lat., 24·6·21
"A Tauri, Aldebaran,"   „   99·19·50 ; „   24·7· 4
"A Orionis, Betelgnese," „   117· 3·50 ; „   24·6·52

                                           3] 72·20·17
Index error 2, minus.   ——————
                 Mean latitude south   24·6·51

On Tuesday morning Mr. Button, as gold commissioner, gave me a letter referring to the laws already passed, and offering to submit to the Government any proposal I might have to make, and to recommend them to favour the introduction of capital into their country by the establishment of such companies as ours. At three P.M. we put our horses to, and while Mr. Leathern rode to Marabastadt Mr. McHattie Woodhouse and I drove over by a short cut, and took possession of the deserted house. It was destitute of doors or windows, but some of our own countrymen had already been showing their superiority to the aboriginal Boers by adorning the walls with specimens of caligraphy, not remarkable for refinement or delicacy. I spent a spare half hour in sketching the remarkable peaks of the Yzerberg or iron mountain, where Maraba was killed by a party of kaal (or naked) Kafirs some years back. Mr. Leathern arrived late, and about noon on Wednesday we met at Peter Potgieter's Rust several diggers on foot, and others with wagons bound for the gold fields. The rough roads and rapid motion affected the trochiameter, and I therefore adopted the plan of counting the revolutions of the wheel per minute, which, by an easy calculation, gives the rate in miles per hour. At night a succession of heavy showers flooded the country and drenched us to the skin. On Thursday we reached Zacharias (pronounced Zakrees) de Beer's, called "onde boetthie" (old brother) to distinguish him from Zakrees Puregyft, and Mr. Scott invited me to his farm to meet the brothers Main and a Californian miner, who had been prospecting and had found satisfactory evidence of mineral riches in the country, but had not as yet made a pile for themselves. The next day we reached Pretoria, and in due time the quartz followed, and was duly handed over at the house of our hospitable friend, A. Brodrick.

At Pretoria we learned that Capt. F. Elton and some other gentlemen, deputed by merchants in Natal, had passed to the north-east, taking what is commonly called the "Pan route," because travellers depend for their supply of water on a number of shallow pans which are filled during the rains, but become very scanty in the dry season.

A few days later Mr. Leathern received from Mr. W. H. Evans of D'Urban, a letter, containing a series of questions respecting th gold fields, and as this form of interrogation compelled me to put my information into a more practical form than that of a journal, I think it advisable to give the questions here—each followed by its respective answer.

D'Urban, Dec. 9, 1871.

W. LEATHERN, Esq., Pretoria.

SIR,—After Nov. 4th, I finished assaying 20 lb. weight of the quartz that came down from Mr. J. D. Kock to Messrs. Snell and Co. The yield was an average of 6 oz. 5 dwt. 1 gr. to the ton of quartz, a capital per centage, which, if borne out by larger quantities, will be the making of the Trans-Vaal. Four oz. of the quartz (selected) gave 6½ grs., or equal to 122 oz. to the ton, but 3 to 6 ozs. would pay well enough.

Now, as to alluvial gold, we are very much in the dark here, and I will tell you what we want to know immediately. What is the kind of climate? Is the fly there? Is it a fever country?

ANSWER.

The climate is tolerably good, the farm being high up on the slope of the mountains, forming the watershed between the Waterberg and Zoutpansberg districts. Some of the higher parts have almost the appearance of Zuurveldt, but I cannot class them so. because, as far as I have been, mimosas grow and horses are said to thrive. Eersteling seems to be on the boundary between the two, where a patch of Zuurveldt may be converted into sweet by keeping cattle on it, while if neglected it may revert to its original condition. It is well known that sweet veldt oxen suffer if taken to the coarse rank grass of the Zuurveldt, while Zuurveldt oxen will live almost anywhere. I cannot tell exactly how high Eersteling is, having no spirit for my boiling point apparatus, but my little aneroid stood at 26·45, which, allowing for its general rate, I believe to be equal to about 3,800 feet. I had no thermometer, but I guessed the temperature at 80° or 85° at noon, and

50° or 60° at night, which is a very healthy range for December, or the South African midsummer. In the winter I should think the minimum would often be down to 27° about daybreak.

There is no fly. Probably the country is clear for forty or sixty miles north—say nearly to the Limpopo—and perhaps forty miles east, but persons travelling must seek for the *latest* information on this point when approaching the borders of a Tsetse country.

A hunter, named Andries Du Venage (pronounced Devenaar) knows a safe road to the northward, where the belt of fly country is so narrow that it may be crossed in two hours of night travelling. The fly leaves a country if the game is driven out or the bush cut away, but returns if the conditions again become favourable to its existence.

Fever.—I do not think there is much danger at Eersteling, but lower down the river, where I should look for alluvial gold, there is undoubtedly more risk, especially in the summer months. I should say it is not safe to go lower than 2,000 feet above the sea before the end of May, or to remain there later than the middle of September. A broken country at a low level will, however, be less dangerous than a flat one at a higher, because there is a chance of living on the heights above the pestiferous exhalations which fill the valleys.

In all cases new comers are in more danger than seasoned travellers, and stout persons of a full habit of body, even though strong and accustomed to labour, are in greater peril than those who are thin and wiry. In the dry season, or winter, the country is tolerably safe; but in the summer rains never camp in hollows or close by rivers, in nice little groves of palm or mimosa. Get up on bleak barren stony hillocks, where the water runs off, and the wind whistles freely round you.

Watch in the early morning for the line of white mist that lies in the river bed, and always sleep above it—all poisonous malaria is heavier than common air and lies low in the hollows. The Portuguese on the Zambesi know this so well that they always build on an elevation, and use the basement of their houses only as store rooms. In some cases the elevation of a few feet may save a man from fever.

Take quinine and opening medicine, and never neglect the first headache or roughness of the tongue. The Rev. Mr. Allison told me to give Kafirs five or six grains of tartar emetic as soon as they complained of headache or of nausea, and put them off work for the day, and I have followed his advice with good results.

People of delicate constitution should wear flannel next the skin, and never remain at rest for any length of time with the clothes damp, or with wet boots or socks. It will do a man no harm to work with wet feet, but to sleep without changing wet socks or garments is another matter.

Is there abundance of water for alluvial washing and for household and agricultural purposes?

This question is rather hard to answer. The country *is well watered* for household and agricultural purposes; but supposing that any large alluvial deposits should be found some thousands of diggers would make very heavy demands on each rivulet. In the rainy season, from November till May or June, there will be plenty of water all over the country, then the supply will decrease, but will never fail, except in some very dry localities. If an extra demand is anticipated much of the water could be saved by dams in various places, where strata of clay slate, tilted at different angles, or dykes of granite, run across the bed of the rivulets.

Zeekoe gaten (hippopotamus pools) form naturally in level reaches, and clever engineers might be able to make imitations of them. The Boers lead out water to irrigate their land in furrows of great length; there is one at Mooi river two miles long. Hermanus Ras, or Slim Hermanus, at Roode Kop, Krokodil drift, has a dam which raises the water of the Limpopo sixteen feet, and leads the water out in a viaduct over two deep gullies to irrigate his farm. Some of the rivulets seem to have subterraneous outlets, and dams will only raise them to a certain level. Some rivers are subterranean for many miles, as those in the limestone caverns of Wonder Fontein, which is believed to flow to the Mooi river.

Is there plenty of timber for building purposes, &c., to be cut up by steam power into planks?

About the level of Eersteling, and perhaps two or three hundred feet above it, there is a very fair sprinkling of mimosa of good size, also marnea trees, and boeken hout below it. There will be kameel doorn, and various kinds of acacia and mimosa, haak doorn, wagh-een-bietje, and knopjes doorn. The latter excessively hard and tough—all good for different kinds of wagon work. But real large timber must be sought in Hout Bosch Berg, about thirty-six miles north by west. Mr. Leathern speaks of fine large forests, with all kinds of wood for building and wagon making, thirty or forty miles away. Most of the Boers keep plank enough in their houses to make their coffins; and I once unintentionally offended a portly Baas by offering to buy, for boat building, the plank he was saving for his *dood kist*.

Is the country corn producing? Would a mill be required?

The country can produce the finest quality of corn in abundance. At such an elevation above the sea the climate is cool enough for all the English cereals, and most of our fruits ; while at lower levels all kinds of sub-tropical delicacies can be raised. If a large population come in, new tracts will be laid under cultivation. The Diamond Fields have already stimulated the farmers, and much new ground is put under the plough. A Boer does not like to enlarge the fields he has once fenced in, indeed, very often natural obstacles prevent this, but he will break ground in a new place, and if he cannot cultivate both, will sell the first, or give it to a son or relative. At present there are water-mills enough, and Boer's meal, in plenty, can be supplied at Marabastad. A sudden rush of diggers causes a demand to which the regular supply is unequal, and prices rise very high, but when they depart the old standard prevails again. A permanent increase of population will make more mills necessary. Peaches, apples, pumpkins, onions, &c., are dried by the Boers, and are a very convenient provision for travellers. Tobacco of tolerable quality is grown plentifully.

What is the nature of the soil at the alluvial diggings at Eersteling?

The soil is soft, and of a dark red, or rich brown colour, with quartz and other pebbles ; the rivulets during the rainy season cut ravines ten or twenty feet deep. I believe the bed rock is clay slate, and Mr. Button considers the hills around to be of metamorphic slate ; the Yzerberg being five or six miles away, is, as its name implies, of iron, the natives quarry it for ore, and the surveyors say it affects the compass for ten or twelve miles, as we before observed. Below Eersteling the soil is said to be sharper, and more sand and gravel is mixed with it.

Are the alluvial diggings easy of access; open, or down deep declivities, rocks, &c. ?

The alluvial diggings are in a small spruit, or rivulet, which has cut a ravine ten or twenty feet deep for itself, about a hundred yards westward of the house ; in this ravine a sudden flood might cause the diggers to suspend operations for a day or two, but in the open valley the work need not be interrupted ; there is not the slightest difficulty of access.

What is the probable extent of these alluvial deposits?

At the time I was there they were known to extend about three miles down Eersteling rivulet. In the ravine of the little streamlet next the house there were two cradles, and I believe they never worked without finding something, a few grains or pennyweights in the day, two or three small nuggets about three quarters of an inch long were found during our stay. On the morning I made a sketch of the cradles, gold was obtained ; other men were prospecting with the pan, looking out their claims rather than actually working. It was then about the end of the dry season, and the stream had to be dammed back for a day or two to collect water. Across the stream west of the house are the pits, from which the two ounces of gold shown in Pretoria were extracted. There were six or eight side by side, each about three feet wide, eight long and eight or ten deep, with heaps of rich brown alluvial soil lying by them ready to be washed. They are in a broad grassy valley coming from the west, and forming a " Nek " over low hills. Natalia reef crosses the rivulet hardly 100 yards north of them. Somewhat more to the westward Mr. Button's party were working on the reef, and still further on we found the main rivulet to be a tolerably strong stream. Mr. Button had made a dam, and was pulling in sluice boxes to wash the soil from the pits. I was sorry we could not stay to see the result. The alluvial deposit is found to be rather thin, and to practical diggers the gold and soil in which it is found has not the appearance of alluvium carried from a great distance and waterworn in transit, but has probably been disintegrated from the Natalia reef close at hand.

Further down the river the nature of the soil changes. At Venters gold was found in the latest alluvial deposit of sand, gravel, and quartz or other pebbles at about two feet deep. At Dupree's farm a sinking of about 20 feet was made, the soil being dark clay sandstone mica schist, and alluvial water worn gravel with particles of quartz, sandstone, clay slate, and pipe clay in mixed clays. On bed rocks of hard sandstone or granite gold was found in small quantities at every prospect. The diggers seemed to think that this (say three miles below Eersteling) held out fair hope of the discovery of a payable "true alluvial" deposit when the district should be properly prospected.

At the time of my visit there were probably thirty persons on or near Eersteling, of whom about twenty might be classed as miners more or less skilful. Among these the party near the house found about ten ounces of gold ; the others found some, but I am not able to state the quantity. My friend Mr. Biles, an elephant hunter had joined a party of Australians ; they described to him the indications he ought to look for, and he being well accustomed to scour large tracts of country, rode out day by day " to seek his fortune." Most of the diggers, however, were men of little or no capital, and could not afford the time and expense necessary for prospecting so extensive a country ; and the diamond fields offering greater and more-immediate advantages, most of them returned thither, and the alluvial fields that may exist in the vicinity of Eersteling or Marabastadt are as yet undeveloped. Besides these few really hard-working men, a number of others with neither the skill to seek gold, nor the energy to work for it, arrived from time to time, and not finding the precious metal spangling the earth at their very feet returned disgusted and disappointed, after doing the smallest possible amount of work. The following extracts are from a letter, quite a gem in its way :—

"*Sept.* 19, 1872.

"DEAR ——, I arrived on the 15th and struck work yesterday. There is simply nothing—it is an abominable swindle. In a short time there will be a serious war with the natives ; therefore I shall try and hurry on to Pretoria."

The letter needs no comment. The intelligent reader will see at once that the man who loses heart after working part of three days and hurries off to Pretoria for fear of a war which has not happened to this day, must belong to the class of persons who are not fit to take part in prospecting a wild country, inhabited by jealous and suspicious natives. Other men more fortunate or persevering have found gold in dust, and nuggets of several pennyweights, and though Eersteling cannot *yet* be called a payable alluvial field, there is good reason to believe that when the rivers (which flow both north and south from a country studded with auriferous quartz reefs) are thoroughly searched it will be found better entitled to that name.

What is the nature and kind of rock in which the quartz reefs are found?

The reef "Natalia," on Mr. Button's farm, Eersteling, is in close proximity to clay slate, and appears to be cased with talcose schist and decomposed sandstone and slate ; its direction is from about S. W. by W. to N. E. by E. (true bearing) with a dip to the north-west. It runs across the gully in which the gold was found, north-west of the house, and re-appears in the same line on the hill to the east. From what I saw I should think it extended the best part of a mile. The only part I saw actually worked was between the two branches of the rivulet, 200 or 300 yards west of the house where Mr. Ash and a gang of Kafirs had taken off the rock capping of disintegrated ferruginous quartz, plentifully specked or filagreed with gold for about twenty feet in length. The reef was about three feet wide (in some places it is four), and at about three feet depth they had reached the solid stone. Captain Elton, who had visited it some days after me, had no doubt of its being a main reef, and that opinion was held by most of the diggers, although some thought it might be a mere "blow off" from a rock reef yet to be found. And here, for the sake of conciseness, I may as well trace the history of this reef to the present time, returning afterwards to the chronological succession of events which it may be proper to lay before the reader.

Shortly after I had left Mr. Button resigned his office of gold commissioner, and arrived in Pretoria, *en route* for England, with a wagon load of rich quartz, of which he very generously gave me 100 lbs., as a sample for the information of our company. Some other samples were shewn to Mr. August Greite, the well known Swedish miner of the Tati, who was then at Potchefstroom, and the letter in which he expressed his opinion of them is so terse and to the point that it can hardly be abbreviated.

"*Potchefstroom*, 20*th December*, 1871.

"DEAR SIR,—At your request I have carefully examined the ore or quartz which came from the new gold fields, and it is certainly the best sample that I have seen in South Africa. It is as good as some of the best I have seen in Australia, where I have had many years experience. I am quite certain it has been taken from the out croppings (gossings) or from the cap of a very rich reef on or near the surface.

"The ore contains a great deal of iron, and is rich in gold. The latter is of a very good quality, and is running through the ore in all shapes and angles; it is not confined to any particular part of the ore. I have known this kind of quartz give a much better return than even men of experience expected.

"The alluvial gold, of which I have seen about $1\frac{1}{2}$oz., is also of a very good quality, somewhat honey combed, and it is quite certain the gold has been deposited in the alluvium through the decomposition of rich quartz reefs near the place. The alluvial gold does not indicate much of a golden lead, but rich quartz mines.

"As I have not been on the place I cannot tell whether the surrounding formation indicates a rich alluvial gold field, but my intention is to visit it.—I am, &c., AUG. GREITE."

During Mr. Button's absence Mr. Ash and Mr. Pigg were left working the reef, and one great advantage they had was that it had never been stripped in old times by Mashonas, but the whole capping of rich friable disintegrated quartz laden with its gold was left to be easily quarried by them with the simple tools they possessed and a few Kafir labourers, and on the 30th March, 1872, Mr. Ash wrote :—

"We commenced sinking two or three deep shafts adjacent to the reef for the purpose of examining it below, but after getting down about 30 feet water came in, and having no pump we were compelled most unwillingly to desist.

"The rich lead discovered by Mr. Button on the western extremity of the reef, a portion of which he has with him, continues, but the excavation on the surface whenever the stone is taken is also full of water, so that it cannot be worked at present.

"I believe the whole of the stone on the reef, from end to end, taken as it comes, will pay for crushing, without taking into consideration the rich beds which are occasionally met with.

"Mr. Pigg has discovered a good bed which continued near the eastern outcrop, and will probably yield several ounces to the ton.

"I have found near the reef, and running parrallel with it, about 300 yards west of the gully, a large quantity of stone with lots of gold in. I thought at first it was another reef, but I am inclined to think it is loose stone dislodged from the Natalia. We intend stripping the cap off the reef, and feel certain of lighting on something very rich.

"Next post I purpose sending to Mr. Button twenty or thirty ozs. of reef gold. Nearly half of which have been obtained by grinding the quartz with a hand stone on a slab, as Kafirs grind their snuff. This is a very slow and tedious process, and the Kafirs do not like it, as it hurts their hands; they can grind from 100 to 150 lbs of stone in a week. This shews by what primitive means we are able to get gold. Mr. Pigg has mounted a large boulder, but it is unwieldy, and he gets on badly. A tree is bolted across the top, and two Kafirs ride see-saw on it, while he feeds it with small pieces of quartz, and another man brushes the fragments under the stone to be crushed finer. What we want is machinery,

"I compute the yield of the 2,000 lbs. of quartz, Mr. Button has taken with him, at 120 to 150 oz."

Mr. Button arrived in Pieter Maritzburg about March, 1872, and shortly after sailed for England, leaving 130 lbs. of refuse quartz with his father-in-law, Mr. Marshall, who succeeded, with very rude appliances, in extracting five ozs. of pure gold from it; being roughly at the rate of above seventy-five ozs. to the ton, and this coincided most remarkably with the assays made in London, for when letters arrived from Mr. Button, the following certificate of assay was furnished us :—

Assay Office and Laboratories,
Basinghall Street, London, E.C.
July 20th, 1872.

Certificate of product of two parcels of gold quartz—
1 case marked B. S. Gross 1 0 13
                  Tare   0   1   8
                  Nett   0   3   5—produced metallic gold 3.260 oz.
Quality of gold—gold, 900 ; silver, 076 ; equal to fine gold, 73 oz. 6 dwts. 21 grs. to the ton of 20 cwt.
1 marked P. taken from case marked B. 18 Gross 1 0 6
                                        Tare   0   9   0
                                        Nett   3 25   0 — produced metallic gold, 3.175 oz.

Quality of gold—gold, 912 ; silver, 080 ; equal to fine gold, 59 oz. 10 dwt. 2 grs. in the ton of 20 cwt.

(Signed) JOHNSON & SONS,
Assayers to the Bank of England, H. M.'s Mint, and
Council of India.

We were also glad to learn that Mr. Button had succeeded in forming a company, which was duly registered as—" The Transvaal Gold Mining Company, Limited, with a capital of £50,000, in 5,000 shares of £10 each ; its object being to acquire by purchase an estate called Eersteling, in the district of Zoutpansberg, in the South African Republic, with the gold reefs mines and buildings belonging thereto. The subscribers who take ten shares each are—

Messrs. H Sewell, 14, Copthall Court ; Mr. H. Syrall, Alverstoke; Hants ; H. E. Montgomerie, 17, Gracechurch-street, ship owner ; A. R. Roche, 31, Palmerston Buildings ; F. A. Weatherley, 16, Lewes Crescent, Brighton ; J. Griffiths, 5, Royal Exchange Avenue; E. J. Burgess, Pitville House, St. James's Road, Brixton.

Early in November, being then on my way to Port Elizabeth, I had the pleasure of meeting off East London, Mr. Button, who was returning to Natal with a powerful 12 stamp battery and suitable steam engine, and on my return in May 1873 one of my fellow voyagers was Mr. Hambley, a mining engineer of considerable experience in South America, who was following him with a smaller crushing apparatus on the pneumatic principle.

A disease called red water, prevalent among our cattle, rendered it difficult to obtain transport, but somewhat later in the year the whole was transported and erected at Eersteling, where I believe it is now nearly ready to commence operations.

The question of the extent of reef that might be held by one company had been seriously discussed in the Volks Raad of the Trans Vaal. The alluvial grounds which could be worked by men possessing only a few tools were at once thrown open, and there was a disposition to do the same as far as practicable with reefs, but as quartz crushing demands a large amount of capital for introduction of machinery it was evidently necessary to allow a company to hold a larger extent of reef, and in the case of Mr. Button, who left the country and formed a company in England on the understanding that the whole of the farm belonged to him and his coadjutors, they conceded to the company the right to the whole reef, for it would have been an evident injustice if Mr. Button, who had pioneered the way to the fortune of the Trans-Vaal, by first finding the gold and then introducing capital and machinery to work it, had been deprived of any of the rights which were actually his when he entered into the agreement with his company. I trust before long we shall hear that his machinery is at work, and that the rich promise held out by the assay already mentioned is being fulfilled by the Natalia Reef.

Other Reefs.

I have already mentioned that I saw other reefs on the farm, Riet Fontein, south of Eersteling, and also at Marabastad hills, to the north-east. Prospectors, singly or in small companies, were scattered abroad over the land, and several reefs of good promise were found, but for want of capital to carry on vigorous operations the unaided efforts of the miners were insufficient to lead to any profitable result. A couple of enterprising young men, Messrs. Cunningham and Lazenby, went up with two wagons and a set of machinery, constructed in Natal, but after a short trip returned, disheartened, it is said, as much by the suspicious and jealousy of the natives, as from any other cause.

Another company was formed in D'Urban, my friend Leathern taking a leading part in superintending the details of the outfit, and two or three of its members, led by Mr. Wood, an Australian miner, left D'Urban about the end of September, 1872, reaching Pretoria on the 18th October. In April, 1873, "the Leathern Young" gold company heard that Mr. Wood had found the lead in four places on the Marais' reef, Marabastad; that he had sunk in two places to the depth of thirty-five feet ; that at the lowest calculation he estimates that the quartz would yield ten ozs. to the ton, and that he had then, on the surface, quartz in which he considered there was gold to the value of at least £800 ; the directors had it in contemplation to send up a quartz crusher.

Reefs in considerable numbers are known to exist in the Waterberg, Zoutpansberg, and Lydenburg districts, but until they are tested and proved auriferous, they do not call for special notice. A gold bearing reef is reported on the farm Waterfall, and the Griqualand West Mining Company are said to entertain good hope of a reef near MacMac.

How did you get the quartz you are sending down? From one place, or several distant from each other? Did you select the quartz shewing gold, or take it good and bad as it came?

We took it from the heap out of the then only working of the Natalia reef, and from a depth of not more than three feet, some of it capping and some solid stone. The only care taken was to send tolerably good looking quartz. The wagon was loaded in less than three quarters of an hour, so that there was no time to inspect the pieces, though we saw gold in several. Hardly so much care was taken as would have been exercised in sending it to a crushing mill on the spot. It is a fair average sample of the quartz then worked out of the reef. Of course rubbish would be rejected even in sending the quartz to the stampers, when they come into operation.

Would it be necessary at first to take up from here slight wooden buildings for stores or dwelling houses, as is now being done to the Diamond Fields?

When alluvial diggings of any great extent are discovered, it would be well for persons who can afford it and desire to have a dwelling without delay, to take up such houses. Galvanised iron would be more burglar proof; but slight frame houses are never comfortable either in hot or cold weather or rain. Good tents are sufficient for the prospector, and are more handy to move; and when he requires a more substantial residence it is generally easy enough to cut poles and build a wattle and daub house with a thatched roof. Two hundred feet of galvanised iron would roof a room ten feet square, and allow projecting eaves enough to give a good shadow. If tolerably straight poles were chosen for the ridge pole and wall plates, the roof could be put up at once, and the walls wattled or filled up with reeds or small poles at leisure.

Is it necessary to take up provisions—say for twelve months' supply —or can they be got at Pretoria or nearer the fields?

Provisions of every kind may be bought at the stores in Pretoria, but it would be well for prospectors to take up groceries of every kind—sugar, tea, coffee, salt, pepper, mustard, vinegar, &c. All farm produce—such as corn, Boer's meal, salt pork, dried fruit, figs, apricots, peaches, Boer tobacco, peach brandy, vegetables, &c., can be bought from the farmers; but if a rush of diggers go in among a few farmers, the demand is greater than the supply, and prices go up alarmingly; meat especially becomes very scarce and dear.

Would it be advisable to take up a small steam-engine, a pair of mill stones for grinding corn, &c.?

Such an engine, with circular saw and mill stones, might be useful; but is not absolutely necessary till population increases. A portable forge with carpenters', smiths', and miners' tools would be always useful.

Would there be any difficulty with the natives? Can they be induced to work for wages, and at what rate?

There are always rumours to alarm the timid; but I do not apprehend any real difficulty with the natives. A fair-dealing man especially, if known to be English, can usually hire as many as he wants. Some of them will engage for money, some for beads, goats, or other articles. They mostly ask to work for guns, but it is against the Trans-Vaal law to give them any.

Are the roads in condition to allow machinery to be carried over them, or how soon will they be fit?

During the rainy season, say from November till the end of February, some parts of the roads are swampy, and the long turf flats are soft and unable to bear heavily laden wagons. In the dry season they are better; wagons with 8,000 or 10,000 lbs. of wool or more pass over them, and a cargo of machinery need not be heavier.

Would there be any difficulty in people finding their way? It is said a prospector lost himself for four days!

It is easy enough to point out the road, but impossible to overcome the propensity of our countrymen to lose it. The "Dommigheid" (stupidity) of "e'en Engelscheman" is proverbial among the Boers. Wherever diggings are established or even a number of persons are prospecting, vehicles pass to and fro and soon make a visible road. Kafirs are employed to carry the mails, and signs of traffic are soon visible. There is little or no danger to life by natives ; but most of them will give trouble by begging or pilfering. A firm straightforward bearing, with moderate liberality, will generally secure their friendship and assistance.

The remainder of the questions in Mr. Evans's letter have been answered under the foregoing heads ; but I may add a word of advice as to the kind of persons who are required to assist in the developement of our gold fields ; and first I must class men who have already a practical knowledge of either quartz or alluvial gold diggings, health, strength, and perseverance to carry on their work, and a little money to support them while engaged in prospecting ; and secondly, men who are willing to learn, not afraid to work, and capable of turning to other industrial pursuits, should they fail at gold digging. The blacksmith, the carpenter, and most other tradesmen in our colonies and the adjacent Republic and Free State, have in their own skill a source of wealth, perhaps not quite so rich, but certainly less precarious than the fortune that may attend them at the gold diggings.

To all who are in regular and remunerative employment I would say—count well the cost before you quit a certainty for the hard work, hard fare, and many privations of a gold digger's life ; there are dazzling prizes in the lottery, but there are many blanks. And lastly, to those who, from weakness of body, indolence, or other causes, are unfit for, or averse to, regular work at home, and who look upon the journey to the gold fields as an extended picnic, and sporting tour, where strange animals of all kinds are to come and be killed, and where, after luxuriating for a few weeks in *al fresco* enjoyment beneath the greenwood tree, some good fairy is to guide them to the spot where the glittering prize lies waiting to be released, I would mention that a friend of mine has to turn over perhaps a hundred boulders of all sizes, from a few pounds weight to half a ton, in the course of a day, and be thankful if he finds gold under some of them. To hawks, sharks, and vultures in human form, who have no intention of doing any honest work, but hope to drain off the profits of the real labourers by pandering to their lowest propensities, I have nothing to say, except to offer my best wishes for their unsuccessful journey and speedy return to some more honest calling. Messrs. Faro and Co. have already tried on their little game, but finding the diggers—for the present at least—like unto the deaf adder that stoppeth her ears, have retrograded somewhat faster than they progressed, asseverating that the gold fields are a sell, a delusion, and a snare ! Long may they find them so.

TROOP OF ZEBRAS, FROM A PAINTING BY MR. BAINES.

CHAPTER VI.
PROGRESS OF DISCOVERY.

The District of Lydenburg and its Gold Fields.—MacMac.—
Pilgrims' Rest.—The Saabi Valley.
Capability of the Country for Formation of Roads or Railways.—
Comparative Merits of Transport,—Vehicles and Animals.
Routes to Marabastadt, and Lydenburg.—Pretoria.—
Wakkerstroom.—Delagoa Bay, &c.

My own sojourn in the Trans-Vaal came to an end about the beginning of 1861. But ere I left I rode over to our friend Hartley, at Thorndale, to look up Jewell, and Gee, and get my wagon in order for the homeward journey, and there I had the pleasure of meeting Mr. Saunders, of Rockdale, who invited me to make a little detour southward, and visit the quartz reef on his place, on my way back to Pretoria. I found his house pleasantly situated in a sheltered valley, among the broken cliffs and ridges of the Witte-waters, round a range running parallel to, and southward of, the Magalies bergen, and its highest portions at an altitude of about 4,500 to 4,800 feet, forming the watershed between the sources of the Limpopo and the tributaries of the Vaal-river. He had worked unsuccessfully upon the reef near his house, but more to the south-west in a little gorge shut in by clay slate rocks it had a more promising appearance. Asbestos was found in small quantities on the farm, and I believe, may be obtained near Pretoria and Makapan's poort. Coal is brought from "Waterval" River, and commonly used for household and smithy purposes.

The covered cart was brought out, the horses put to, and striking to the eastward we reached Mynheer Grobler's Farm, and turned south to see the lead mine—or rather the crevises and fissures in the rock from which the lead ore had been excavated. The strata seemed altered and contorted by igneous action. We found some very fine specimens of galena and bluish slaty stone, also galena in which there was crystalline quartz, which easily broke into small fragments, besides these we saw traces of copper and small pieces of malachite. The works were on a very limited scale, and, I believe, enough had been done to prove that good useful lead could be procured when the young man who had charge of the works died.

Some of the lead ores from the Republic, when assayed at home gave 62 per cent. of lead, and 31 oz. 11 grs. of silver to the ton of ore.

A piece from E. Potgieter's, Groote Marico, assayed by Mr. Hubner, mining engineer and assayer, gave $9\frac{1}{2}$ oz. of silver to the ton of ore. And two other specimens sent to London were certified as under :—

Assay Offices and Laboratory,
Coleman Street, E.C.,
25th January, 1869.

To Messrs. G. F. NEAME & Co.

No. 1.—Small pieces of quartz in box ; fine gold 16 oz. 16 dwts. 6 grs. per ton of ore.

No. 2.—Two lumps of quartz with galena ; lead 31 per cent. ; silver 16 oz. 3 dwts. per ton of ore.

(Signed)   Pro. F. CLAUDET,
F. CHAMBERLAIN.

Keeping still a little southward of east with the Witte-waters' Raand (proper) on our left, and the watershed of the Limpopo on our right, we saw several quartz reefs, but with the little prospecting we could do, it was not likely we should find gold ; we slept at Mr. Forster's house, and saw a number of reefs and quartz ore indications, and next morning I parted with my friend at Klein Jeuk Skei Rivier, and continued my course to Pretoria, passing numerous other reefs on my way.

Mr. Bekker had promised to show me a place on the Palhalhah or Roodebok river, a tributary of the Limpopo, where rather coarse grains of alluvial gold had been found by natives ; but neither of us were at that time able to undertake the journey, and, pending the arrival of support from home, I accepted commissions for pictures of Pretoria and its vicinity, as my only means of supporting myself and party.

We were not entirely destitute of festivity in Pretoria. On New-Year's eve we formed a "cutting-out party," captured *the cannon* of the Trans-Vaal Republic, brought it into the Market Square, made cartridges, side-arms and faze, told off a crew to their several duties, and welcomed the new year with a royal salute. The commandant of the artillery woke up at the first discharge ; but when the second and third followed, he paid me the compliment of remarking : " Oh, its somebody that knows how to work a gun," and went off to sleep again. Songs and glasses round followed ; then bell-ringing ; and, lastly, the demolition of the Dutch and English belfries, in which, I am sorry to add, a distinguished member of the local government took a leading part. It is true that the belfries aforesaid were only wooden frames of no imposing order of architecture, and the churches did not suffer, as a subscription for the erection of new ones was forthwith raised among the delinquents.

The Trans-Vaal, after a long series of struggles, the history of which, with the exception of some dark and indelible stains, will yet command the admiration of the world, for the perseverance, the primitive manliness, and hardihood of its pioneers, was then beginning to emerge from its obscurity, and as a proof of its advancing prosperity its £1 notes had *risen* in value, till four were taken as equivalent to a sovereign, and several hundred pounds worth had been called in and publicly burned upon the market place ; the Boers and Doppers (adult baptists) crowding wrathfully around, and bitterly commenting on the wasteful folly of their government in wickedly destroying so much of the money of the Republic, while others of more advanced views discussed the means of raising them still further in value, and sagely remarked that because they had been printed in Holland the English would not take them, but if others were printed in London they would certainly be as good as a Bank of England note.

Mr. Frederick Jeppe, the enterprising Postmaster General, who has done so much to make known the geography of the country, sent to Holland for a set of postage stamps, and on receiving them forwarded specimens to other countries requesting exchanges. Shortly afterwards he observed a notice in an American paper that fictitious postage stamps were being sent about from an imaginary "Trans-Vaal Republic" which had no existence in the map of Africa,* and warning all postmasters to be on their guard against an impostor calling himself Frederick Jeppe, Postmaster General of that Republic.

Some amusing scenes took place now and then in the Volks Raad (equivalent to our House of Commons.) The progressive party wanted to pass some measure for the opening and improvement of the country, when the opponents finding themselves in a minority thought "to put the drag on" by bringing forward an old law that all members should sit attired in black cloth suits and white neckerchiefs. This had the immediate effect of disqualifying so many that the business of the house could not be legally conducted; but an English member who lived next door slipped out, donned his Sunday best with a collar and tie worthy of a Christy minstrel, sent his coadjutors to his house to be rigged out in the same style, and resumed the sitting with an array that completely dismayed the anti-progressionists.

A well known medical friend of ours, who prides himself on his knowledge of thirteen or fourteen different languages, was interpreting into Dutch, for an Englishman, when some dispute arose.

"Oh!" said he, "it is impossible to translate your barbarous idioms—Try me with some piece of pure English?" The witness immediately gave :—

"She never told her love,
But let concealment, like a worm in the bud,
Feed on her damask cheek."

The interpreter got on very well till he came to the last line, which he rendered thus :—

"Vreet op haar Verdomde Wang."

"I did not say damned cheek," interposed the witness, "the word is damask."

"Oh!" said the interpreter "'damaged,' then it must be rendered thus :—

"Vreet op haar Vernielan Wang."

To say that the court was convulsed with laughter would be superfluous.

---

* The date of the map not given. Probably it was one of those on which "unexplored country" was written—from the Cape of Good Hope to the Mediterranean.

SCENE IN THE INTERIOR.—FROM A PAINTING BY MR. BAINES.

CHAPTER VII.

PROGRESS OF DISCOVERY.

Mr. George Pigott Moodie's journey to Delagoa Bay.

DURING my stay in Pretoria I became acquainted with several residents and travellers, who readily gave me every information and assistance in their power. I have already referred to Captain F. Elton's visit to Eersteling, and I think I have said that his opinion—like my own—was that the quartz reef would repay the introduction of machinery and skilful systematic labour, but that no warranty had hitherto been found on which the existence of a payable alluvial gold field could be proclaimed. I also had much pleasure in making the acquaintance of Mr. George Pigott Moodie, who had made two journeys down to Delagoa Bay, chiefly with the object of discovering a line of road which could be used as a highway for wagons to and from that seaport, and also for a railway, should the Republic be able to induce men of capital to invest in the construction of one. His most successful journey was undertaken about the end of 1871, and I had the gratification of meeting him on his return to Pretoria, about the end of February, 1872.

Starting from Pretoria in lat. 25·44·55 south, and approximate long., by my calculation, 28·25·30, and by Mr. Moodie's 28·37·00 east, and at an elevation, by boiling point thermometer, of 4,007 feet above the sea, he directed his course first to the east and north-east, along the broad high land which forms the watershed just between the sources of the Limpopo and the Vaal river, and further on, where it turns more northerly, between the sources of Olifants river, the largest tributary of the Limpopo, and the streams flowing by the Manice or King George's river, into Delagoa Bay. The strict line of watershed, however, was somewhat circuitous, while the more direct road intersected the various branches of the Limpopo, where they had already assumed the proportions of considerable streams, flowing often in deep broad valleys, bordered by mountains more or less precipitous or steep, and occupied mainly by Vee Boeren, or cattle farmers, whose vast flocks and herds, multiplying on the rich pastures, supported them in primeval and patriarchal plenty, relieving them of the necessity of helping to support themselves by more than the most primitive attempts at cultivation of the soil.

The town of Lydenburg, which was built about the year 1850 because the original settlement of Origstadt was liable to deadly visitations of fever, stands on a tributary of the Spekboom river, at a height of about 5,400 feet above the sea, on the inner or landward slope of the Drakensberg, which shelters it somewhat from the cutting easterly winds ; while its altitude ensures an atmosphere sufficiently cool to be at least tolerably healthy. Wheat and all kindred grains flourish in such a climate as they would in Europe, and, in fact, a sample of wheat sent from a Lydenburg farm bore off a prize at the recent exhibition in Paris. Lower down all sorts of sub-tropical, and even tropical, fruit can be grown including even coffee and the sugar cane ; but in these rich valleys the healthy bracing air of the highland is, of course, lost.

To the east of Lydenburg the ridge of the Drakensberg has to be crossed. Some of its peaks—as Manchsberg for instance—attaining an elevation of 7,000 or 8,000 feet ; though I believe Mr. Moodie did not pass it at so high a level, and the rugged and precipitous nature of this mountain, which is properly the sea face of the great interior highland, made the path so uneven as it turned south-east to Delagoa Bay, that construction would have been too expensive, and would even, when made, have been circuitous and steep in many places.

In 1870 Mr. Moodie made a second journey passing the mission station of Nazareth. Fifteen hours on horseback, or about ninety miles east by north from Pretoria, and then instead of turning north-east to Lydenburg, turned a little to the south of east along the watershed, between the "Krokodil Rivier" (not the Limpopo which is also called by that name), and the Um Komatie. The former river being on his right, the two uniting in longitude about 32·15, and being joined by the Saabi lower down. The three together forming the Manice or King George's river, and entering Delagoa Bay, ten or fifteen miles north-east of the Portuguese town, or Lorenzo Marques,* he turned south-east after descending the Drakensberg, crossed the Um Komatie river above the junction of its affluents, crossed the Lebomba Mountains, a secondary or foot range to the Drakensberg, and traversed the low and marshy country at its base, till he reached the fort and factory above named. This route was not only shorter, but in many respects superior to that by Lydenburg. Still Mr. Moodie thought that he could strike out a better; and, therefore, in December, 1871, he commenced his third and final journey; leaving Pretoria at a height (as already stated) of 4,007 feet, he directed his course, at first, nearly south-east, and leaving behind him the immediate tributaries of the Limpopo—gained the highland, out of which flow those of its great affluent the Olifant, then for more than a hundred miles steering about east-south-east, over this broad, bleak, gently undulating plateau, abounding in grass, but destitute of trees; and crossing the various streams, composing Olifants river, from thirty to forty miles below their source, he passed Klipstaple. From this place at an elevation of near 7,000 feet, flow the waters of the Vaal river, to make their way past the Diamond Fields, and thence united with the Orange river, to the Atlantic—those of the Olifants river to reach the Limpopo and the Indian ocean, and the spruits of the Um Komatie to flow over the Manice to Delagoa Bay—while but a short distance to the south-west of the second "Mont Aux Sources," rise tributaries of the Maputa, falling into the same bay, on the south or British side of the boundary, between us and the Portuguese, carrying three fathoms water for a dozen miles up from Tudor point, at its mouth, and capable of navigation by large boats for about twenty miles more.

About twenty miles east from Klipstaple, and 120 from Pretoria,

---

* I was told in 1850, by the survivor of an unfortunate fever stricken expedition, from Origstadt to Delagoa Bay, that small slavers go twenty or thirty miles up the King George or Manice river.

lies Hamilton, the residence, I believe, of Mr. Bell, and one of the principal stations in the little *Imperium in Imperio* (if an exotic colony in a Republic can be so called) of New Scotland, which occupies nearly 500,000 acres of the most elevated and healthy land in the Trans-Vaal, and which is indebted for its origin to the enterprise of the late Mr. McCorkindale, who died of fever at Inyack Island on the 1st May, 1871, while endeavouring to bring to perfection a place for the formation of a port at the mouth of the Maputa river, for the use of his little colony. Up to this point as has been already mentioned, the country was so level as to offer no engineering difficulties to the formation of either roads or railways, capable of supplying almost unlimited pasture, as the vast herds and flocks of the neighbouring farmers testified, and though bare of trees yet abundantly supplied with coal, which was commonly used as fuel.

To the eastward of Hamilton the country falls gradually, sometimes by inclines and sometimes by a series of steppes, to a lower level; the road following the course of the Umpolosi river for twenty or thirty miles, winding along Eland's ridge by Dumbarton, and then passing by Batabela's Baatem, Hillgate, and several native villages to the Nabomba flat, and to Dedeen or Lotito, the residence of a powerful chief of the Ama-Swazi, named Sonthaan. Here it may be considered that the descent of the Drakensberg proper has been completed, and the lower ranges of the Makondshwa and Lobomba have to be crossed. The road, however, passing through by a tolerably level poort or valley south of the Umbolosi or Dundar river, and immediately after passing the last range, the Tsetse fly, fatal to domestic cattle, and the fever, no less deadly to man, await the traveller. Fortunately there is only about forty miles of this unhealthy country; but the fact should be known, in order that the risk may be guarded against by pushing through it as rapidly as possible, and at night or during a cold day, when the fly is dormant.

I ought to have mentioned that about forty miles east of Hamilton the country begins to be wooded, and groves and forests capable of supplying unlimited quantities of wood for fuel or railway purposes, clothe the lower slopes. The timber of course is various; but the Kameel Doorn, *Acacia Giraffe*, would probably be the most valuable, as it is an exceedingly hard close grained wood, and we are able to use it unseasoned and green as cut for axles and other wagon work when repairs are needed in the bush. It is unfortunately liable to be attacked by white ants, but before being laid down as sleepers it might be tarred, charred on the outside, or laid down with a thin sprinkling of salts in the earth all round it. If *mopani*, an almost equally hard wood, can be procured, its own resinous gum enables it to defy the ravages of the white ant.

From New Scotland to the Lebomba the soil was for the most part gravel or sand and free from marshes and such like obstacles, and Mr. Moodie considered that a good road for heavy wagons from Hamilton to the coast might be made for £3,000.

It must be remembered, however, on the other hand, that from the Lebomba mountains to the port, a distance of 30 or 40 miles, lies the track of low country from which Delagoa Bay derived its not undeserved reputation for unhealthiness. A considerable portion of this strip is infested by the Tsetse fly, and a point to be yet proved is whether this belt of fly is sufficiently narrow to be passed through in one night, while with regard to the deadly influence of the malaria rising from the Mattol and other marshes we hear daily evidence, for by the mail which arrived while I am writing these pages we learn that five young men who went up recently from Natal *via* Delagoa Bay, are dangerously ill, while the *Gold News* of 14th February stated that three persons have died of the Delagoa Bay fever.

With regard to the formation of a railroad from Delagoa Bay to Pretoria, Mr. Moodie feels sanguine of success.* He believes that easy gradients may be secured from the Bay up to New Scotland, while from that point to Pretoria the country may be regarded as a slightly undulating inclined plane dipping from a level of 7,000 feet at the former to one of 4,000 at the latter place, or 3,000 feet in 130 miles, the distance from the Bay to New Scotland being 110 miles, or 240 miles in all.

It may not be improper, in connection with this subject, to state the actual boundary between the Trans-Vaal and the Portuguese, as agreed on in the Treaty of 1869.

The boundary between the possessions of the Crown of Portugal, in South Africa, and those of the Trans-Vaal, or South African Republic, according to the treaty of 1869, made between the Chevalier Alfredo Du Prat, Consul-General and Plenipotentiary of Portugal, and Marthinus Wessels Pretorius, President of the Republic :—

---

* Arrangements have since been made by the President of the Trans-Vaal Republic with the Portuguese Government, and a railway is to be constructed immediately.

In the districts of the Bay of Lorenzo Marques, which is called Delagoa Bay in the English sea charts, is the southernmost portion of the settlements of Portugal, which are bounded on the south by a line drawn from a point on the coast in 26 30 south latitude; due west to the Lebomba mountains, and thence along the highest ridge of the Lebomba, to the middle of the lowest poort of Comatie, whence that river breaks through the Lebomba; thence in a north by east direction to Pokionies Kop, on the north side of Olifants river where it goes through the range; north-west by north to the nearest point of the mountain of Stricundo, on the Um-Voobo river; and from there in a right line to the junction of the Paforie with the Limpopo river.

The map I send home with this M.S. shews the above boundary line, as laid down by my friend Magnus Forssman, Surveyor-General of the Republic. I may remark, however, that this treaty places the southern boundary of the Portuguese possessions at 26·30 south, thus claiming the whole of Delagoa Bay, while we have always understood that the boundary between the British and Portuguese on the east-coast was the 26th degree, crossing the island of Inyack, at the northern extremity of Cape Colatto, the southern headland of the bay, and giving us a right to the southern half of its waters, and to the entrance of the Mapoota river.* One of our coasting schooners, the "William Shaw," entered the river some year or two ago, supposing that she was in British waters; but the Portuguese seized her, and, I believe, the matter is yet under adjudication. It is well known, however, that though the Portuguese claims in Africa are extensive, their real power extends but a few miles from their forts and the coast or the Zambesi.

---

* According to the decision of Marshal McMahon, who was appointed Arbitrator; Portugal now owns all the territory on the shores of Delagoa Bay.

GROUP OF NATIVES, FROM A PAINTING BY MR. BAINES.

CHAPTER VIII.

PROGRESS OF DISCOVERY.

My own Journey from Pretoria to Natal via Marthinus-Wessel-Stroom and Utrecht.

IN the beginning of 1872, having completed all the exploration my resources allowed in the vicinity of Pretoria, and being assured that quartz crushing machinery would shortly be sent to Natal from England by the company, I began to prepare for my journey. I had found such ready hospitality among my friends in and around Pretoria that my personal expenses had been very small, and three views of the town under different effects of light, and other artistic employment had furnished me with a couple of stout oxen to recruit our span and other necessaries for the road, and before leaving I received a pressing invitation to try the new road south-east to Marthinus-Wessel-Stroom, partly for the sake of testing the hospitality of my friends there, and partly to make measurements and observations, as it had never yet been laid down on any map.

I had already taken care to fix the position of my starting point Pretoria as nearly as possible. The observations for latitude by four stars were as under. The index error was 2 subtractive :—

Star.	Observed altitude.	Latitude.
Alpha Eridani	115·47·58	25·45·58
,, Tauri	96· 5·40	25·44·11
,, Orionis	113·50· 0	25·43·48
,, Argo	126·20·10	25·46· 1
	Total	4] 179·58
	Mean latitude south	25·44·59

The longitude as deduced by dead reckoning from the fixed longitude of Potchefstroom, I make 28·25·20 east, but Mr. Moodie places it more easterly in 28·37. The boiling point was 204 degs.—4/10ths equal to 4007 feet. My position by observations taken at Mr. A. Brodrik's house, Church Square, Pretoria, is therefore—Latitude South, 25·44·59 ; longitude East, 28·25·20 ; height above the sea level, 4007 feet.

On the 14th February, 1872, I finished loading up and sent the wagons out of town with colours flying, our friends of the "Royal" also shewing the British flag. I had taken leave of my friends, and was about to follow, when Jewell, going into the stable for his horse, received a severe kick, which sent him reeling backward out of the door with the lobe of the right nostril cut completely through, and with bruises wherever the horses feet had struck him. Brodrick and other friends carried him in and made a bed for him. We closed and strapped up the wound with adhesive plaster, and the majority of the inhabitants kindly came to inquire after his welfare. Next morning Brodrick and Leathern harnessed a spring cart and took him out to the wagon and I followed. The wound though painful was not dangerous, and healed in about a week.

From the first outspan we turned south-east along a fairly level road, over gently undulating hills, rising gradually till we reached Rademeyer's, nine miles, five furlongs, 180 yards from town, and about 4,600 feet high. Here we purchased a good supply of dried peaches, apples, &c., from the well-stocked orchard, sheltered by the hill side from the cutting blast, and left it open to be used freely by all hands as long as it would last. I noticed that the cactus of prickly pear grew freely at this elevation, and Jenny, the baboon, luxuriated in its ripe fruit, avoiding or plucking off the large thorns, and utterly ignoring the fine tufts of thorny down which causes us such lasting irritation.

From this we rode gradually to a grassy highland destitute of trees, the outline of the rounded heights barely varied here and there by a few blocks of granite and greenstone. And again descending slightly, outspanned at Kafir Spruit, at a height of 4,757 feet, having risen 150 feet in 7¼ miles since leaving Rademeyers. In the evening, still travelling over gently undulating grassy highlands where the eye might wander for miles without resting on a bush of any kind, we reached Maraison, a little rivulet 6 miles 169 yards from our last outspan, and 4,864 feet above the sea.

On the morning of the 15th, we passed over the level country with the firm red soil or gravel road, with occasional flinty quartzite, and reefs of bluish quartz on either side of the road, till we reached Mynheer Joachim Prinslos' (familiarly called Kort Joachim), where again a slight hollow and protecting walls, enabled the owner to battle against nature for the existence of a few fruit trees. We bought some fruit and mealies, or Indian corn, and biltong, and the hospitable dame, added, with no stinted hand, a liberal supply over and above the measure. We had travelled seven miles, five furlongs, and attained an altitude of 4,882 feet. At Oesterhuy's, four miles, six furlongs further, our height was 4,810 feet, and when we outspanned for the night, seven and a quarter miles onward, our height was 4,864 feet.

On the 17th, we breakfasted at Witte Klip, so called from a great quartz rock, that looms like a wagon tilt in the distance, and at noon halted by a reedy pool, having made eight miles, six furlongs, 134 yards, and still keeping at nearly the same level, *i.e.*, 4,842 feet. In the afternoon we reached Daniel Kruygers—on the banks of the Stein Kool spruit, a tributary (like most of the streams we had passed) of the Olifants river. The family was using coal as their only fuel. These bleak heights being so absolutely destitute of wood, that we had been obliged to keep our Kafirs on the watch to pick up any cakes of partially dry cattle dung they might find along the road, to cook our meals, and keep them warm at night. I went about half a mile up the spruit, and saw where the coal cropped out under a krantz on one side, and from a sloping bank on the other. They told me that it extends far along the stream, and blocks three feet square were got out at "Brock band," *i.e.*, "Waist" deep. It looked tolerably well—black, with a moderate gloss, and clean fracture, and reminded me of the drier kinds of our own "Wallsend"—one could hardly expect bituminous quality so near the surface. The supply is supposed to be unlimited; and, indeed, when I consider that I have seen coal at several points, from Natal to Zambesi, a distance of 1,500 miles, I am almost inclined to subscribe to this opinion.

These facts, combined with the level character and the remarkable straightness of the road, seemed to me to offer extraordinary facilities for the formation of a railroad, which might very easily be connected with that which the Natalians propose making to Newcastle in the northernmost part of their colony. We went on a couple of miles, making 9¼ for the afternoons work, and spanned out 4,703 feet above the sea. We saw daily a few herds of wildebeestes, but they were exceedingly wild and shy and difficult to approach. The Boers here have abandoned their great clumsy roers and now shoot with "Westley Richards" and other rifles, vieing with each other for the possession of the gun capable of killing at the longest range. Beside this they make up great battues and drive the game into rivers, where they are drowned or shot in crowds for the sake of their skins, many thousands of which are sent down to Natal, affording an acceptable item of income to many a family in the Trans-Vaal, though it is evident from the wasteful manner in which the slaughter is carried on that this source of revenue must soon greatly diminish if not altogether cease. Gee and I went out daily to try to get one or two bucks for meat. We wounded some but could not secure any, and the country was so soft that it would have been cruel to ride Jewell's horse (our only steed) in chase of them.

On the 18th we travelled over undulating hills, grassy but bare of bush as before, and from frequent soft places in little rivulets made only 9 miles 4 furlongs 211 yards. Our height was 4,918 feet, and our latitude 26°22′12. On the 19th we made 16 miles, 4 furlongs, 50 yards, passing heights of 4,972 feet, 5,187 feet, 5,250 feet, from which altitude we descended to 5,187 feet, and 5,000 feet near the farm of Hendrik Lievenhuys in latitude 26°29′25 S. On the 20th we passed Treechard's, Grobler's, and Bouwers, all living on small streams which ran northward to the Olifants river, and outspanned during heavy rain, having made 11 miles 4 furlgs., and 47 yards, the levels of our halting places being 5,079 feet, and the immediate ridges a few feet higher.

On the 21st we left the sources of the Olifants river in latitude about 26°22, the clouds having prevented any stellar observation; and in two or three miles passed from the waters flowing to the Indian ocean to those which make their way past the Diamond Fields to the Atlantic—the first of the latter being a rivulet which runs to Blesbok Spruit, and by that into Vaal river. At night we crossed Knobkeerie Spruit, and unyoked on the hill side, our day's work being sixteen miles, seven furlongs, 212 yards; and levels 4,864 and 4,810 feet.

On the 22nd we travelled over a few small intermediate heights, to the north-east of the Blaauw kopjies, halting at 4,810 feet, and crossing the Vaal river at Retiefs' drift, fifteen miles, six furlongs, 152 yards from Knobkeerie Spruit, and at an altitude of 4,703 feet above the sea. On the lower parts of the Vaal river we are accustomed to see its banks bordered by dense fringes of magnificent willows and other trees, but here they were grassy and destitute of bush. An orchard, however, and two or three stray trees in a sheltered hollow near Retief's house, above the drift, refreshed the eye a little after dwelling so long upon the bleak bare hills we had passed over. A short ascent of one mile and 136 yards restored us to a level of 4,912 feet. And on the 23rd—leaving on our left the village and church of Amerspoort, and crossing the road from Newcastle to Lydenburg, near Gert Van der Merwes'—we halted at a height of 5,133 feet, after a day's work of twenty-seven miles thirty-eight yards. Here it became apparent that our level road was about to cease. The ridges of the Drakensberg, dim and distant during the morning, had been gradually changing from a misty æriel blue to a deeper and deeper grey, and, as the sun declined, shewed warmer local tints, revealing the grassy slopes; the cliffs and precipices catching the mellow light, and the dark kloofs, whose depths assumed almost a purple tint as the shades of evening closed over their recesses; while the higher peaks seemed to glitter more brilliantly by contrast as they alone reflected the last beams of departing day. Right in our path rose the rugged masses of the Wakkerstroom hills, and it seemed evident that if the long and level highland we had traversed were ever to be utilised as the continuation of the future colonial railways, we had now reached, or probably passed by a few miles, the point where the line must diverge to the south-west, in order to connect itself with the Natal line at Newcastle, about fifty miles distant.

On the 24th, fifteen miles, five furlongs, and eighty-five yards, over rough and mountainous country, brought us to the point of Wakkerstroom hill, at a height of 5,727 feet, and in latitude 27°17'49, as I ascertained by two good stellar observations during the clear cold night. And here again it appeared that we were on a ridge that might well be named "The Divider of Waters." We had left behind us the spruits flowing to Vaal river. On our right or south-west were streams running to the Umzinyati, or Buffalo, the boundary between the Trans-Vaal Republic and Natal; while to the north-east were the sources of the Umkonto or Assegai, and beyond the town to the south-east those of the Pongola, sweeping round to the east and north to flow as the "Mapoota," navigable for ten or a dozen miles up into Delagoa Bay.

On the 25th five miles, 53 yards brought us down to the Wakkerstroom river, which we crossed at a height of 5,349 feet, and four and a half furlongs more, on the 26th, placed us alongside the church in Marthinus Wesselstroom, and not far from the hospitable residence of Major A. A. O'Reilly, the Landrost, or magistrate, — latitude, 27·22·8 ; height, 5,800 feet. Here I had the gratification of learning that I had been named in London, as one to whom the command of an expedition for the relief of Dr. Livingstone might be entrusted, and our friend believed that the appointment was on its way to me from the Royal Geographical Society, but the newspaper in which this was mentioned could not be found, and I was left in suspense until my return to Natal. I can only say that if this had proved to be the case I would, after making such arrangements as should enable the company to spare me without loss, at once have undertaken the service, and would have spared no exertion to convey relief to the great traveller.

From Marthinus Wessel Stroom (named after the late president of the Trans Vaal Marthinus Wessel Pretorius, and incorrectly named on our maps as N. W. Stroom), a rugged journey of 35¾ miles over mountain ridges, and under the south-west face of the Belclasberg, which for two days frowned like an immense battlement above our path, brought us opposite the town of Utrecht, in a valley scantily clad with mimosas, and still further relieved by the orchards and ornamental trees which embowered the few houses dotted over the extensive lands laid out for the township. In one of the abutments of the mountain, a couple of miles or so north, crops out a seam of coal seven feet in thickness, easy of access and of good quality, at least so far as the experience of the village blacksmith went. I saw it burning in his forge, showing little or no evidence of the presence of sulphur, and he was turning out very good work with it.

Late in the night of March 2nd, fifteen miles one furlong from Utrecht, we halted at a house, the owner of which, Mr. Brayhirst, rose with alacrity from his bed to welcome us, and bestirred himself to set before us such refreshment as came to hand, a noticeable feature of which was a liberal outpouring of spirit from a cask into a hand basin, from which we were invited to bale out with our pannikins *ad libitum*, and not content with this when I sat up during the small hours of the morning to observe the stars, he turned out again and had coffee made to refresh me. The latitude by four good observations came out 27·49·33, the height above the sea being 3,686 feet.

Mr. Brayhirst proposed, if I would stay two or three days, to ride with me to visit his wife and daughter, and promised to supply me with necessaries as far as Grey town; he sent to the next farm and bought two sheep for a sovereign "hard cash," giving me the greater part of the meat besides wheat for the Kafirs, as mealies, or Kafir corn, could not be had. He sent to Utrecht for a man to take charge of his store, but could not obtain one, and much to my regret was unable to accompany me. The reader will pardon my being a trifle prolix, but kindness such as this demands some attempt to discharge the debt of gratitude, so far at least as thanks will do it, until our company enables me to pay in more sterling coin.

On the 5th of March, we parted from our worthy host, and late at night reached the Buffalo river, which we crossed next morning—nineteen-and-a-half miles from Mr. Brayhirsts, and 3,260 feet above the sea—and duly informed our Kafirs that we were now standing on British ground, in the Colony of Natal. Beyond the little Um Zinyati, or sand spruit, we found the store of Mr. John Agnew, who not only supplied us liberally, but resorted to tricks in weighing off, insisting that I wanted four pounds of sugar instead of three—allowing a *Seven* pound weight to remain in the scale—refusing any payment, and after treating me to coffee and a glass of spirit, riding three or four miles out to shew me the best road. At night we were kindly received by Mr. Wade at his farm Gowrie, on the Biggarsberg. Next day Mr. Wade lent me a driver, as Gee had strained his foot, and we reached De Waar, where Mrs. and Miss Brayhirst, Miss Rourke, and Mr. Wade entertained us during the rest of the day. We had a very pleasant musical evening, and in the morning were again sped forward with supplies for the road. We made about 24 miles, and slept at Hulp Makaar (Hulp Malkanderen, or help each other), a name which sufficiently indicates the difficulty of the pass—and here our Kafirs for the first time saw a regularly made road, cut out and built up the mountain side, with great rocks blasted by gunpowder. We halted at 4,435 feet, but the top of the hill was perhaps 150 feet higher. Night cold and no firewood.

Saturday 9th.—Descending all day into "The Thorns," the valley oppressively warm, and thickly clad with mimosas, euphorbias, aloes, and other vegetation.

At night we reached the Tugela river ; height, 1,461 feet, latitude 28·45·15. The drift was flooded, and utterly impassable ; but there is a flying ferry, and the charge is only 10s. for a loaded wagon. Mr. Rogan, the punt master, was very civil and obliging, and we sent our food down to his house, and messed in common.

Monday, 11th.—The river had fallen slightly, and a Dutchman succeeded in crossing the drift, but the water rose over the back plank of his wagon, and as our Kafirs were utterly unused to water, and would have been quite helpless had anything gone wrong, I determined to cross in the punt, as we should otherwise certainly wet our gear, fatigue our oxen, and perhaps damage cargo to more than the value of 10s.

The punt is worked with a hawser, stretched as taut as possible across the river, and supported by a ladder-like frame on each bank, to keep it high enough above the surface. On this runs a block with a large sheave, from which a stout warp leads to the bow of the punt. Now, as the river runs to the east, and we were to cross to the south, the wagon, with two oxen, was got on board, and the warp brought to the starboard bow. The force of the stream, then infringing on the starboard or northern side, drove her over to the southward. The rest of the oxen which had been driven over the drift were brought and hooked on, and the wagon was drawn ashore ; then commenced a long up-hill pull to a height of 3,154 feet, without water, and a descent to 1,935 feet at Mooi river, where we slept.

The quartz reefs prospected by Messrs. Marshall, Button, Parsons, Hill, Antonia, and others, are on the Tugela south side, ten or twelve miles below the punt.

Tuesday I called, *en passant*, on my friend Mr. Thomas Meikle, of Olive Fontein, and overtook the wagon just in time to shelter myself from the heaviest storm of wind, hail, rain, thunder, and lightning I have known for a long time.

Wednesday, 13th. I rode forward to the pretty village of Greytown, well sheltered by dense groves of Australian gum trees, and unexpectedly met a former friend, Mr. Handley, who supplied me with bacon, butter, &c., and kindly forced a sovereign upon me for refreshments on the road. The trochiameter reading at the corner of his store gave 115½ miles as the distance from Utrecht. A few miles beyond town I left the wagon and rode forward through continuous steady rain, till I found shelter at Mr. Garbutt's inn, and on the 14th, halted for tiffin at Cremers, near the beautiful lower falls of the Umgeni, I reached "The Plough" at Pietermaritzburg, forty-five and a half miles from Mr. Handley's store in Greytown, and fifty-four miles, by Colonial measurement, from Durban, which is in turn two miles from the Custom house of Port Natal.

Jewell and Gee arrived with the wagons in due course; and in May, 1872, our new company sent me the first instalment of machinery, and my time has since then been spent in efforts to get this transported to its work in Matabililand, or to complete a smaller set, the cost of transport for which will be more in accordance with the funds which my work as an artist may provide for me.

The following is the summary of distances on the above journey:—

	Mls.	fur.	yds.	ft.	in.
Mr. Brodrick's, Church Square, Pretoria to Cross Vaal River at Retief's drift	133	4	59	0	11
Church Marthinus Wesselstroom	49	4	169	2	0
Opposite Utrecht	35	6	71	2	0
Mr. Handley's store, Greytown	115	4	18	1	11
Plough Hotel, Pietermaritzburg	45	3	201	0	4
	379	7	80	1	2

VIEW OF THE ZAMBESI FALLS.—FROM A PAINTING BY MR. BAINES.

CHAPTER IX.
PROGRESS OF DISCOVERY.

The Lydenburg Gold Fields.—MacMac or Macamac and Pilgrims Rest, Quartz Reefs and Alluvial Diggings.

It would be impossible to indite a record of the discovery and developement of any of the gold fields of South East Africa without awarding the place of honour to the talented and enterprising German explorer the Herr Carl Mauch, whose vivid and glowing descriptions, highly tinted by the rainbow hues of hope, attracted to our shores a host of adventurers from well nigh exhausted auriferous regions in California, Australia, and New Zealand, when a more sober and realistic statement might have failed to elicit more than a theoretic and impractical assent to facts already known, and our gold fields might, as heretofore, have been traversed only by the elephant hunter, the emigrant boer, and the solitary traveller; while the legends of their former richness, told by patriarchal survivors of the Mashona tribes would have continued merely to beguile the tedium of the long evenings spent in social converse round the camp fires.

Sorely disappointed indeed were many of these early pioneers when on their arrival they found that technical terms descriptive of the richness of a gold field had been used here, in a loose and unrestricted manner, by writers who reckoned not upon the strict and literal sense in which they would be understood by miners in already established gold fields. In no instance was this more obvious than in that of the word "payable," which often was freely used to designate a field in which the quartz appeared sufficiently rich to pay when it should be properly worked, while the miners understood it to apply only to one on which all the preliminary explorations had been made, and which was already being worked and paying those who had claims upon it.

Numbers returned in disgust, but others, with or without colonial aid, made efforts, and so far sixty-one succeeded as to shew that the quartz reefs were really and richly auriferous—but the effectual working of these reefs was beyond the power of individuals, or even of companies with small capital and unprovided with machinery. Others more fortunate have at last been rewarded for their continued and persevering labours, by the discovery of alluvial diggings, where they are now verifying the predictions of the Herr Mauch in the most practical manner, by each man making his own pile, and letting the surplus gold they occasionally dispose of spread abroad the proof of richness in the place it came from.

Although Mauch visited Lydenburg in 1858, he appears not to have come across the present alluvial diggings, but marked a spot as a probable goldfield in 24·10 south, and about seventy miles north-north-east of the town, which, according to Mr. Moodie, lies in latitude 25·11 south, while Mr. St. Vincent Erskine places it in 25·4, the longitude being variously stated at from 30·10 to 31·30 east—its true position being probably 30·40 or 30·50 east. During the year 1868, Karl Mauch crossed the Limpopo and travelled north-west to the southern borders of Matabililand, where he was detained by Umtigaan the chief of that district, until leave was granted him to proceed to Inyati mission station. In 1871 he passed Marabastadt, apparently without touching at Eersteling, and proceeding north-east, achieved his crowning feat in the discovery of the long sought ruins of Zimbaoe, Zimbabye, or Mazimbaoe, in latitude 20·15·34 south, longitude 31·37·45 east, and 4,200 feet above the level of the sea. Here he found that the natives had been long accustomed to work for alluvial gold, and he himself, after finding some, expressed his hope of being able to work out enough to keep himself from want during the journey. He reported the goldfield as only half-an-hour north from Pikes Kraal, and the people as likely to engage in gold washing at some future time. The ruins are eleven miles east of the Kraal; they are extensive, and one collection covers a considerable portion of a gentle rise, while another—apparently a fort—stands upon a bold granite hill. The walls are still thirty feet in height, and are built of granite *hewn into small blocks about the size of our bricks*, and put together without mortar. The most remarkable of these walls is situated on the very edge of a precipitous cliff, and is in perfect preservation to a height of thirty feet; the walls are about ten feet thick at the base and seven or eight at the top. In many places there remain beams of stone eight or ten feet in length projecting from the walls, in which they must be inserted to a depth of several feet, for they can scarcely be stirred. At the most they are eight inches broad by three inches in thickness, and consist of a very compact stone, with a metallic ring and greenish black colour. On one stone, ellipsoid in section and eight feet in length, ornaments are engraved; consisting of lozenge-shaped figures one within another, separated by horizontal bands of diagonal lines. Under a great mass of rock Mauch found a broken vessel (shaped like a wooden Kafir basin) of talcose gneiss, extremely soft, eighteen inches in diameter and three inches in depth, one-and-a-half inches in thickness at the edges, and half-an-inch thick in the bottom.* The dense bush and gigantic nettle plants, the jealousy of the natives, and want of means, prevented further investigation.

Whether indeed this locality was the "Ophir" of gold is of course still open to discussion. A solitary traveller barely able to carry beads and calico to pay the expenses of himself and native servants could not be expected to dig for relics and inscriptions, but I may mention that these are not the only collections of such ruins known to exist. My friend the Hon. G. C. Dawnay saw and sketched a mass of similar masonry about 80 miles north-north-west of Tati, and others are reported in the Trans Vaal several days journey east from Nylstroom.

Brief as our space is I cannot omit to mention the loss of one of our gold seekers, the only one to my knowledge who has yet met a violent death at the hands of the natives. Mr. Charles Muller and Mr. George Anderson left Marabastadt in May for the

---

* The worn out slabs on which the women grind meal, with a large pebble used as a muller or hand stone, assume exactly this shape.

"RUINS AT ZIMBAOE, IN THE LAND OF OPHIR."

These Ruins are on a granite hill. The walls are of the same stone, and are 12 feet thick at the base, 5 feet at the top, and in some places are still 30 feet high. They are built of small hewn blocks. From the inner sides of the walls projected several beams of close-grained, dark coloured stone, about 20 feet long; but half their length was built into the walls to give them firmness. They probably supported a gallery. Zigzag and lozenge-shaped figures were carved on them, but no other ornament or inscription has yet been found.

purpose of prospecting and trading, and travelling in the direction of Herr Mauch's latest discoveries. They were attended by twenty-two Kafir servants. On the 8th of June they camped in the Veldt, Anderson and Muller sleeping in a scherm, or slight shelter of cut branches, and the Kafirs at their fires. In the dead of night they were attacked by numbers of strange Kafirs. Muller as he started up saw Anderson struck through the chest with an assegai, and he himself immediately received a severe wound on the head from a battle axe. He escaped, however, into the bush, and at daylight ventured out and found nothing but the dead bodies of Anderson and two Kafir servants. The attacking party, which seemed to have been numerous, had taken away everything. Muller managed to bury his friend, as well as the Kafirs, and then started for Adam Kinders, a hunter further north, but found that he and Carl Mauch had left for Sofala (about six days distant) some time before the murder took place—250 or 300 miles north of Zoutpansberg—and no suspicion rests upon the native servants, who evidently fled for their lives.

The remarkable escape of my friend Mr. William Leathern will serve to illustrate another danger to which the solitary prospector is more frequently exposed than to that last mentioned. In the beginning of May 1872 Mr. Leathern was on his way from Lydenberg to Marabastadt and off saddled. Man and horses being wearied out near Crocodile-heavel on the north bank of the Olifant river, he tied the halter of one horse to the tail of the other to prevent them separating, made a fire and arranged his bed under a small and solitary tree. Towards morning, when the rain had killed his fire, he heard the noise of a rush and struggle and the crying of a horse in agony. He saw that a lion had seized it by the neck, and at the same instant the other horse dashed passed closely followed by another lion. Armed only with a little toy revolver he rose and approached the lion, which leaving the dying horse sprang at him. Instinctively he threw up his left arm to defend his face, and the lion perhaps springing short seized it in his jaws. Throwing back his head as far as possible he pointed the revolver at the lions throat and fired two or three times, when providentially the lion left him and sprang to the horse again. Leathern fired the remaining barrels, and the lion dragged away the carcase down a declivity. Although severely wounded in the arm and clawed on the cheek, breast, and shoulder, he tried by moving his finger to ascertain whether the arm was broken, and concluding that it was not laid himself down in the rain and prayed earnestly for the appearance of the morning star. He tore up his linen to make bandages, slung his wounded arm, packed some bread in his leggings and hung them round his neck, wrote a statement of the accident and the course he meant to take in a book which he left with his saddle, and through rain above and mud below walked 80 miles that day, reaching a Kafir Kraal where the people from superstition refused to help a man wounded by a lion, and mocked his sufferings, one woman only relenting so far as to assist in bathing his arm with hot water, laughing at his pain as she did so. On Sunday he hired a man to carry his things and walked twenty-five miles, his attendant (a Makati) kindly helping him, till worn out he made his bed in heavy rain under a bush. On Monday he struggled on five or six miles and reached the wagon of Mr. Courtenay, a gold prospector, who at once took him to Eersteling, where Mr. and Mrs. Pigg did all that kindness could suggest till the return of the Rev. Dr. Dalzell, whose unremitting care saved him, although he has never perfectly recovered the use of his arm.

I am compelled to pass lightly over the labours of many other deserving but less fortunate explorers, but I cannot omit to mention Mr. C. F. Osborne, who about 1872 traversed the country from Pretoria to Delagoa Bay, finding " the colour " in several places, but weary and footsore, unprovided with means or implements, and weakened by incessant fever, was unable to prosecute his researches to a successful result. Nevertheless his opinion was* on the eastern slope of the Drakensberg (near Lydenburg) gold exists over a considerable extent of country, but its matrix is usually in low valleys overlaid by shales and sandstones, hence denudation has not been sufficiently extensive to form payable alluvial ground except to a very limited extent, which may also be generally said of all the districts to the south. On the Tugela river, in Natal, gold bearing veins have been discovered and a considerable amount of work done, but the result was small. Excellent specimens of galena and copper were found with manganese and cinnabar, and it seems probable that Natal is the southern boundary of that great field which extends north to the Limpopo and Matabililand. Hitherto though an immense amount of prospecting has been done, and " the colour " obtained over thousands of miles, no payable alluvial gold field has been discovered, a fact which goes far to prove that Africa is to be a reefing country. It is a notable

---

* It must be borne in mind this opinion was formed previous to the discovery of the Lydenburg alluvial gold fields, but taken in connexion with that discovery it points to very extensive fields.

South African Native Kraal—Zululand, Oham, and Inwedu.—The Royal Brothers receiving the Advanced Guard of a Regiment on its return from an Expedition. The Author was an eye-witness to this scene.

fact that where the schists and other gold producing rocks occur they are nearly always exposed in a very limited manner, generally resting unconformably upon granite and overlaid by sandstone shales and occasional limestone. Apparently the beds are of no great thickness, and owe their appearance solely to the action of intrusive rocks which in many places have burst through and formed the higher hills in the great valleys, throwing the prodigious superincumbent strata into those enormous ridges whose escarpments are so characteristic of the Drakensberg districts, and showing the schistose rocks in narrow beds between. The schists appear only in the lower valleys and gorges, and have experienced but little denudation, hence the paucity of anything beyond "colour" in alluvial gold.

It is difficult, if not almost impossible, for anyone not resident upon the spot and thoroughly conversant with all the incidents, to award rightly the merit of the actual discovery of what we may now term with some confidence, the payable alluvial gold fields of Lydenburg, but it seems probable that our fellow colonists, Mr. E. Buttons, Mr. Parsons, and Mr. McLachlan were among those who gave the earliest impulse to the tide of research, which taken at the flood has led to fortune in many cases, and will we hope in many more. Mr. Button sunk a shaft near Lydenburg and found gold in small quantity, but his good genius led him to the reef at Eersteling, where according to the latest accounts (April 1874) he has now about 3,000 tons of rich quartz upon the surface and probably has his machinery ready to commence crushing.

From Lydenburg various reports calculated to excite or depress the public hopes continued to arrive, till in February, 1875, news was received officially in Pretoria that Messrs. Parsons, McLaughlin, and Valentine, had given notice to the Landdrost of Lydenburg, that they had discovered alluvial gold, six hours on horseback east of Lydenburg, and, that in case it should turn out payable, they claimed the amount provided by the law. To understand the position of the new gold field with tolerable accuracy, it must be understood that the interior of Southern Africa is a vast table land, say roughly about 5,000 feet high in the central regions, and of this the Drakensberg, running nearly parallel with the coast, and from 100 to 150 miles inland, forms its south-eastern edge, presenting a succession of steep slopes, and secondary plateaux towards the sea, while landward it is but one or two thousand feet higher than the plains of the interior, and slopes towards them so gradually that the difference of level is scarcely perceptible, except by the change in temperature, and in vegetation. In consequence of this the Vaal and Orange rivers, rising in the Drakensberg, flow westward across the continent and find a passage to the Atlantic through chasms in the range which on that side answer to the Drakensberg. The rivers, such as the Tugela and others in Natal and Zululand, rising in the eastern face rush with comparatively short courses to the Indian Ocean ; but about the parallel of 26°, or in the latitude of New Scotland, a rounded elevation called Klipstaple, 6,328 feet above the sea, and perhaps thirty miles inland from the edge of the Berg, is the highest point, and from this Hill of fountains flow waters to join the Vaal-river and the Olifants river, a branch of the Limpopo to the west, while others hastening south-east to flow by the Dundar river into Delagoa Bay, and north-east to reach the same goal by the Umkomatic, Manice, or King George's river, break through the ridge by deep clefts and rush in torrents down gorges in its sides, until they reach the comparatively level country intervening between the Drakensberg and its secondary ridge, the Lebomba, forty or fifty miles from the coast. The Limpopo itself rises about 240 miles from the east coast ; but instead of flowing to the Atlantic sweeps round by north and east, breaks through the Drakensberg in about 22·30 south, and joined by the Olifants river under the Berg, and turning south through a vast extent of alluvial country, formed in a great measure by sand and *debris* brought down by this and other rivers, it enters the sea at Inhampura, in latitude, according to Mr. St. Vincent Erskine, 25·15·9 south, longitude, 33·40 east. South of the great bend thus formed, and fifteen or twenty miles west of Mauchberg, a peak 8,725 feet high, on the Drakensberg ridge, the town of Lydenburg, or New Origstadt, nestles in a valley 5,825 feet above the sea, on one of the spruits of the Spekboom river, which flows north to join the Olifant. The old town of Origstadt, abandoned about 1850 in consequence of its liability to fever, being about forty miles below Lydenburg on the same river.

From Lydenburg two roads lead over the ridge ; one taking a north and east course by Kruyger's Post, and John Miller's, to Pilgrim's rest, on the Blyde river, flowing north to the Olifants river, and the other going south-east past Mauchsberg over a series of hills, called most descriptively the " Devil's Knuckles," to the Spitz kop, a peak of 100 feet in height, and then turning north across the valley of the Umsaabi or Sabia river, passing the Sabia waterfall 150 feet high, the Picnic falls 250 feet in height on Badenhoff spruit, also a branch of the Umsaabi, and then ascending to McLachlans' farm, Geelhoutboom, on which are the gold fields and township of Macamac or MacMac, near a waterfall about 50 feet high of the same name.

I have only to add that MacMac, or Geelhoutboom (the yellow wood tree) is about 4,750 feet high (by Mr. Bellville's measurement), that the Saabi flowing eastward breaks through a poort in the Lebomba and turns south to join the Umkomati, or King George; that to the south of Lydenburg the Umgwainza or Krokodil river rising in groote Zuiterboschkop, breaks through the Drakensberg, and collecting a number of affluents on the eastern slopes joins the Umkomati before it reaches the Lebomba range, and I trust with the aid of the map which accompanies this work, that the reader will gain a tolerable idea of the geography of the Lydenburg gold fields, which are supposed to extend about 60 miles north and south along the sources of the Blyde river, the Umsaabi, the Krokodil, and the Umkomatie, and eastward perhaps 50 or 60 miles into the fly and fever country in the direction of Lebomba.

CHAPTER X.

THE PRODUCE OF THE LYDENBURG GOLD FIELDS.

For a long time, as is invariably the case between the first discovery and the announcement of the first decided success, the public were kept on the *qui vive*, elated beyond measure, when some fortunate fellow found a nugget, and as unduly depressed when others, who perhaps had worked hard for weeks or months and had found nothing, returned or sent letters describing their disappointments. On the 2nd April, 1873, Mr. Frederick Jeppe, Postmaster-General at Pretoria, received a letter from the Landrost of Lydenburg, together with two and a half ounces of alluvial gold, found by the Landrost himself, in six days, on the farm named Hendricksdale, five and a half hours (thirty-three miles) east of the town, and shortly after gold was discovered on the farm of Jan and Hendrick Muller. Small nuggets were found in the plaster of their houses, and gold dust in the water furrow flowing past the door of the former. The early incidents in the history of these gold fields are related so succinctly in a letter published in the *Trans-Vaal Advocate* that I cannot do better than give the translation :—

"In the bed of a spruit running through the farm (Hendricksdale), alluvial gold was found in sufficient quantity to justify the opinion that it was present in paying quantities, and this opinion was confirmed from day to day by the following facts :—

"1st.—Messrs. McLachlan, Palmer, and Valentine, with two kafirs, and without proper appliances, found in fourteen days the first sample of two ounces, among which is a nugget the size of a half sovereign, somewhat longer but more flattened.

" 2nd.—Mr. Valentine with two kafirs found, and sent to the cashier of the Standard Bank of Natal, a second sample of above two ounces, in which was a nugget as large as a middle sized bean.

" 3rd.—Messrs. James and Sekntte brought in a sample of three quarter ozs., found by two men and three kafirs in five days.

" 4th.—The same persons in similar time found gold which weighed six sovereigns.

" 5th.—Mr. Abel Erasmus brought in a sample in a very small medicine phial, which weighed fourteen sovereigns, bought by Mr. James for £8, found by one man and four kafirs in five days, on Mr. Erasmus's farm.

" 6th.—His son, eight years of age, found five shillings worth of gold in two days.

" 7th.—Mr. James casually visiting the fields found gold to the value of seven and sixpence in four hours.

" 8th.—Mr. De Sousa bought a nugget from Erasmus for ten shillings.

The gold district was at that time supposed by Mr. McLachlan to be about fifty miles long by eight broad, and six or eight farms were known to have gold upon them. The samples just mentioned were obtained with the most primitive appliances, and often by inexperienced people, who were incapable of saving anything but coarse heavy grains, besides which labour was scarce, provisions and accommodation the same, and the road extremely rough and mountainous, but this last-mentioned fact, combined with the elevation of the country above the sea, rendered it very healthy. The gold was found about three feet below the surface, the upper layer being red clay; then large gravel quartz in fragments, lime stone, and a cindery fused substance, like slag from a smelting furnace, but softer; below this is a soft black soil which when put in the box reminds one of a mixture of tar and oil, and with this a soft pipe clay is found. The quartz when pounded proved also to have gold in it, and so did the cinder layer, and the stones of which the cattle kraal was built contained gold. The best finds were usually under or between large boulders, as well as in the plaster of the house. A reef not far off showed signs of richness. The farm (Messrs. Erasmus and Muller's) was at that time hired for thirty years at £200 per annum. One of my friends describes the country as magnificent, and in fact it must resemble very nearly the up-country districts of Natal. To the west are the huge sandstone cliffs of the Drakensberg, broken here and there by deep kloofs and gorges for the passage of the larger rivers, while little rills and rivulets stream from the mountain sides, and find their way by various channels down grassy slopes or wooded hollows, or over precipitous leaps of from 10 to 200 feet. Among these hills are caves, in one of which one might travel underground for hours, and here, in olden time, the natives sheltered themselves and cattle in many an inter-tribal war. Skulls and bones of men and cattle are found, and tradition, whether justly or not, brands the occupiers as cannibals.* Near some of the southern sources of the Um Saabi, or Sabea (so called by the Boers in mistake for the real river of that name), is the Spitz Kop, 7,100 feet high, under which the first gold in the district was found. Of course exaggerated reports were rife both for and against the fields. One Boer wrote to say that he had four ounces, but it turned out that he had weighed in apothecary's scales, and had reckoned each separate weight as an ounce, the fact being that his whole find hardly amounted to an ounce in weight.

---

* It has long been known that tribes robbed of their cattle by stronger ones have been compelled to resort to human flesh for sustenance, and that they have continued the habit after their return to comparative plenty has relieved them from the necessity; but it has always been understood that under such circumstances the dying out of the practice was only a question of time.

A SOUTH AFRICAN BAY WITH NATIVES IN THE FOREGROUND.—FROM A PAINTING BY MR. BAINES.

CHAPTER XI.

THE WORKING OF THE GOLD FIELDS.

The Dawn of Prosperity.

MONTH after month the pioneers in the Lydenburg districts worked on, sometimes elated by success, which cheered their spirits, and brightened their prospects, as with a gleam of sunlight ; and at other times depressed by long, and almost fruitless labour, while their discomfort was enhanced by the high price and precarious supply even of the necessaries of life ; as well as by the impossibility of building permanent, or even tolerably comfortable, habitations, while no actually "payable field," on which it would answer a man's purpose to settle down to steady work, had yet been discovered. Meanwhile the unemployed, or the unfortunate at the diamond fields, watched their progress with breathless anxiety, for to the success of the Lydenburg diggers they looked, as to to their sole chance of salvation from ruin and helpless poverty.

In Natal attention was for some time divided by the Embassy of the Hon. Theophilus Shepstone, Secretary for Native Affairs, accompanied by 130 Colonial Volunteers, to Zululand, for the purpose of installing Ketchiwayo, as Chief of the Zulu

Nation, and successor to the late Supreme Chief Umpanda, and after this by the rebellion of the Chief Langalebalele, who, having been admitted as a fugitive into Natal, and located and sheltered for many years within the Colony, had at length thought himself strong enough to defy the Government that had so long protected him. But the diggings were not forgotten, and while we were away upon this duty, my friend, Mr. Alexander Maclean, had reached the gold fields, and was trying his fortune there. He left Pieter-Maritzburg on the 27th May, 1873, and reached Lydenburg in twenty-nine days, with the loss of only one ox by "red water," and a couple knocked up, an instance of somewhat singular good fortune compared with the mishaps of others, many of whom lost nearly all their oxen from disease, want of grass, and other causes. He found the road from Newcastle to Lydenburg heavy enough, but the thirty miles from Lydenburg to the Spitz Kop diggings baffled description. There had been a great number of persons at Spitz Kop, but only three parties (one of them a very strong one) remained. They had been working three weeks, and the amount they had done was considerable, but the result of their labour was not proportionate, and they had determined to remove.

After a week's initiatory digging at Spitz Kop, Mr. Maclean accompanied the last of the diggers to McLachlan's farm, twenty or twenty-five miles north, and found the creek occupied by promising diggings for about two miles of its length. The prospects were improving, and the claims were all taken up, but a friendly and kind-hearted fellow let him have half his claim (the full measure being fifteen feet along the stream by fifty on either side). He set to work without delay, and the first operation was to divide the stream that he might be able to work down to the bed rock or clay where most of the gold lies, but it was almost impossible to do this properly, because there was not fall enough to carry away the water, and the waste of one digger would sometimes keep the man above him working knee deep in water, and, therefore, unable to clear up from the bottom all the auriferous soil.

Some, however, who had a better fall, and were in consequence able to keep dry and work in comfort, were doing pretty well, that is to say, "occasionally getting their ounce, or two, or three, or even five ounces in one day," but these bore a smaller proportion to the mass of diggers. It is difficult to learn the finds per diem, but Mr. McLachlan guessed the average at five or six penny weights. In his own case, after sluicing for three weeks, from sunrise to sunset, with the help of four Kafirs, his gold weighed hardly three ounces. Even the most experienced, and fortunate, were of opinion that something better must turn up before the fields could be proclaimed as payable. But it had been sufficiently proved that there was gold all over the country, and every one hoped that a rich spot would soon be found.

Mr. Maclean wrote in the highest terms of "The beautiful country, and delicious climate; the happy medium between heat and cold, such as he had nowhere else experienced." Fine rains had fallen during the early part of August, and the grass was already so forward that it was beginning to be possible to travel. Some were already on the move to prospect new localities. The number of diggers at work, on the 10th of March, was about 180, and the writer thought that in another month or two the claims would be worked out and deserted—the creek being only two miles long; he adds, " Gold digging is thoroughly established and will be carried on in other fields, but at present I do not advise my friends to come up. The Trans-Vaal Government takes no notice of the diggings, but we have a *pro. tem.* Commission, and Committee of Diggers, who settle disputes."

Mr. Maclean's anticipation of the exhaustion of the creek has not been realised, but with regard to its speedy desertion, he was right, for in September, Mr. William Trafford, a miner, who had been prospecting twelve or fourteen miles north, on the sources of the Blyde river, reported the discovery of payable gold in a valley on one of the head waters which he named " Pilgrim's Rest," and this he duly notified in the " Commissioners'" camp, asserting his right to a " Discovery Claim," *i.e.*, a choice piece of ground, from double to quadruple the size of common claims, according to the distance from any established gold field at which the new diggings are found.

The new diggings at Pilgrim's Rest were, I believe, so named from the similitude of a prospecting journey to a pilgrimage, and of the likeness of the fortunate discovery to the arrival at the Shrine. They were situated on a farm, bought in April, by Mr. Guzman, of Pretoria, and extended about five miles along Pilgrim's Creek, a tributary of the Blyde (Blythe or Joyful) River, so called because in the early days of the Dutch emigration from the Cape Colony, say about 1840, two parties of Boers, travelling about with their flocks, their herds, and their families, rejoined, after having missed each other at Trewe Rivier, or the River of Weeping, a few miles more east. Blyde River runs north to the

Olifants river, or Lipalulah, which in turn empties itself into the Limpopo.

In the early part of September, although little mining was done, excellent prospects of coarse gold had been found from higher lands in the vicinity, but the richness of the creek had yet to be ascertained. There was plenty of water with immense boulders of iron stone, granite and quartz. The Gold Commissioner visited the place and issued licences, and the Commissioner of Police established a force there. Provisions were very scarce and no meal of any kind was in camp. The few Boers in the vicinity being unprovided for so sudden an increase in the demand for farm produce, while those at a distance had not yet cogitated long enough over the probable advantage of getting their wagons under weigh to carry bread stuffs to the newly assembled diggers.

The old diggings still continued to yield a steady reward to those who stuck to their claims, instead of deserting them at the first rumour of fresh fields and pastures new, and they began to find that gold extended into the banks and terraces instead of being confined to the bed of the creeks. The revenue of the camps was still good, and gold was sufficiently plentiful to be recognised as a circulating medium, and was taken for goods at the rate of £3 15s. per ounce. On the 22nd September there were not twenty-five lbs. of meal in the camp.

His Honor, the President of the Republic (Mr. Burgers), visited the fields, and sanctioned the general name of New Caledonia, while at the original diggings on MacLachlan's farm, or Geelhoutboom, he authorized the establishment of a township to be called McMc, MacMac, or Macamac. The first orthography being most clearly indicative of its origin, and the last of its general pronunciation among the Boers and natives, though, I believe, the latter, from the apparent fact that both are "diggings," call the gold fields the "New Diamond." The President authorised a grant of £1,000 for the construction of a road to Delagoa Bay.

The Big Nuggets.

In the course of September it was reported that Mr. Honeyman found a nugget weighing ten ozs., and that several others of considerable size had been found. The "Emma Nugget," weighing sixteen and a half ozs., was described as an irregular square of two and a quarter inches, and the "Adeliza Nugget," of twenty-two ozs. seventeen and a half dwts., as a somewhat kidney shaped mass three and five-eighth inches long by one and three-quarter broad—photographs of their natural size were published in the Colony—and others of twenty ozs., thirty ozs., and four lbs., and eight lbs. weight, respectively, were reported, but I cannot state positively that the latter received confirmation.

Some of these nuggets (I think the Emma and Adeliza), were taken by His Honor, the President to Pretoria, and their genuineness having been questioned, two experienced Australian diggers, John Williams and William Grosser, examined them, and publicly recorded their verdict in favour of the nuggets. These men were on their way to the fields with a party, and had hired a wagon, at an expense of £5 per head, with a right to carry 200 lbs. of luggage each; they were well supplied and were expected to prove an acquisition to the community.

The nuggets already mentioned were, however, doomed to fade into comparative insignificance by the reported find of another, whose weight was variously stated at from fifteen to twenty-five lbs.; but was confidently supposed to be not less than two lbs. Speculation was rife, and every one was eager for proofs. The latest arrivals at Pretoria were closely questioned, but they could only say they knew men who had seen it, and begged that the names even of these eye witnesses might not be mentioned, as great reticence, for obvious reasons, was observed by the diggers, and no man liked to be suspected of bruiting abroad the secrets of another. A movement was immediately set on foot to form a company for the purpose of buying this nugget and exhibiting it at the Diamond Fields, Port Elizabeth and Cape Town; while Mr. Parker, of Parker, Wood and Co., Durban, and Mr. Leathern, who were then starting from Pretoria for Lydenburg, hoped to purchase and bring it down to Natal. A P.S. to a letter written on the 7th November stated that it had actually arrived in Pretoria, but this was never confirmed, and gradually this "nugget of the brain, this false creation," faded and vanished from the letters of occasionals and specials, and was subsequently said to be a bundle of kafir's picks coroded and rusted into one mass, which some one had humourously christened a nugget. Another nugget of sixteen lbs. was talked of, but this was presented to the fortunate digger by his wife, who declared it to be the most precious little thing that mortal ever set eyes on. [N.B.—Mamma would not accept £3 15s. per oz. for it, even had a dealer been liberal enough to make the offer.]

To balance this disappointment, however, it was stated that Mr. De Villiers arrived, bringing fifteen pounds weight of gold, which was freely shown in Pretoria, and Mr. Piet Kirsten "arrived this morning" (7th November) with twenty-one pounds.

About the same date a writer from Pilgrim's Rest says :—" The finds at this creek give general satisfaction. The only grumbling we hear is about the numerous unwieldy boulders. We were told yesterday of one digger who had collected seventeen ounces there in one week. The creek at Macamac is still producing very nice samples, and there is plenty of ground there which will repay working."

"A gentleman arrived from England in exactly two months. He reached the Cape per steam ship "Windsor Castle," stayed six days in Cape Town, five in Port Elizabeth, six in Durban, and three in Delagoa Bay, finishing his journey on foot to Macamac, making only forty-two days of actual travel."

The gold fields, as will be seen from the last extract, were by this time beginning to excite attention, not only in South Africa, but in Europe, and it was considered advisable to push forward to completion the road that some years before had been projected from Lydenburg to Delagoa Bay, a distance of about 200 miles, by which it was reckoned that a saving of half the land carriage might be effected, the distance from Port Natal, viâ New Scotland being reckoned at 420 miles. Nevertheless, against this saving must be set the difficulties of the route, the low country between the fields and Delagoa Bay being infested for about forty miles by the deadly cattle pest, the Tsetse fly, and dangerous to human life, on account of the prevalence of fever from September to May—while during the same season the two principal rivers, the "Krokodil" and the "Comati," were rendered frequently impassable by the rains. On the 16th of November Mr. J. P. Ablett was at Macamac, having gone up from Delagoa on an experimental trip, but was of opinion that at that time transport was impracticable, he himself having been stopped, although so early in the season, by the rivers just mentioned. The weather was fearfully wet, and corn crops that had withstood frost, drought, locusts, and hail, at Comati and Krokodil rivers, were all destroyed, a sure omen of hard times in store both for farmers and diggers.

Nevertheless, successful finds kept up the spirit of the digging community, and encouraged them to battle on against hunger and discomfort. One of my friends wrote dating

"McMc, New Caledonia, Gold Fields,
"17th November, 1873.

"Well, here I am, settled in the most beautiful country I have ever seen, and what lends enchantment to the view is the consciousness of treading on ground that will, with ordinary intelligence and labour, yield to every one a living. Some reap a larger harvest than others, but none need starve. The sound of grumbling is rarely heard, and the majority of diggers are making something better than wages. I know personally of several diggers who have been enabled to lay aside from £500 to £700.

"I have a fourth share in one claim, and that alone would enable me to keep the wolf from the door. In short, let me tell you the payable gold fields here are a fact.

"On the creek here, from which the present nuggets were taken, the gold is not so heavy as that at the other camp.

"One man I met took out of his claim during three days last week, seven ounces, two ounces, and five and a half ounces, and these, I can assure you, are not the largest quantities that have been washed out of adjoining claims.

"When I arrived here, in August, kafir labour was scarce, now it is plentiful, large gangs having been brought from Delagoa Bay.

"The road from Delagoa Bay to the Lebomba mountains has been completed, and by the time you receive this letter that from the northern slope of the mountains to Lydenburg Dorp will have been finished. * * * *

"As many people are at a loss as to the name of this camp, let me inform you that, by desire of the President, it has been named McMc, and not Macamac."

In December my friends, Mr. Wm. Leathern and Mr. Parker, arrived in Durban. The latter gentleman brought down nine pounds of gold, which I and, in fact, all who wished, were allowed to see. The firm (Parker, Wood and Co.) decided at once on sending up goods, and establishing a store at the fields.

Mr. Leathern told me he considered the twenty-one pound nugget to be an exaggeration, but he believed in nuggets up to nine pounds. The diggers will not tell what amount of gold they have, in fact it is not etiquette for any man to ask, and the questioner would most likely get a rebuff less polished in diction than strong in sentiment. Naturally a digger with a good claim would not like to tell what amount of gold he had in his tent unguarded for many hours in the day, and stored perhaps in some old leather pouch or equally insufficient substitute for a strong box. Even when they knew Mr. Parker was a *bonâ fide* buyer they were extremely reticent, but Mr. Leathern knew one man who had fifty pounds weight of gold, and another (one of a party of three) had for his share 105 ounces, which he produced, being one-third of the whole find. Mr. L. saw one man washing who expected to get an ounce for his day's work, and in fact declared he would not work for less than an ounce a day. Another refused £28 per month wages; asserting that he could do better for himself. There was little or no grumbling, and Mr. Leathern believed £10,000 would not buy anything like the gold then on the fields at £3 15s. per oz.

Not long after this a find was reported which was deemed worthy to be the subject of a special certificate, and perhaps it will be better for me to follow the example of the *Volkstem* in copying the letters, so that the signatures may carry their own due weight, and the reader be satisfied that the statement is not made on private authority.

"Gold Commissioner's Office,
"Macamac, 3rd *December*, 1873.

"Sir,—I have the honour to introduce Mr. J. W. S. Barrington, one of the lucky finders of four large nuggets, with a quantity of smaller ones, amounting in all to some thirteen lbs. eight ozs. in one day. He is going to take them to your city, Pretoria, Potchefstroom, and the Diamond Fields, and from there to the principal towns in the Colonies for exhibition.

"I have known Messrs. Barrington, Osborne, and Farely, for some time; they are all among the number who have remained here from the early days of our fields, have been hard workers and deserve their luck.

"I have requested Mr. Barrington to call on you at once, on his arrival at Pretoria, to shew the find to the Government, before exhibiting it to private parties.

"Everything here looks prosperous, and the miners are going in to work with a will.

"Hoping to be able to send you still better accounts from New Caledonia soon.

"I have, &c.,
"The Hon. N. J. R. SWART,   "W. MACDONALD,
"State Secretary,   "Gold Commissioner.
"Pretoria."

Accompanying this is the following certificate :—

"Gold Commissioner's Office,
"New Caledonia Gold Fields, S. A. Republic,
"3rd *Decr.*, 1873.

"This is to certify that Messrs. Osborne, Barrington, and Farely, Gold Miners, at the diggings known as Pilgrim's Rest,

New Caledonia Gold Fields, South African Republic, did find (4) four large nuggets, with a quantity of smaller ones—in all about (13) thirteen pounds (8) eight ounces—in one day, and that the gold was brought to me for inspection. This being the largest known find on these gold fields, in the same space of time. This is to certify to its genuineness.

"W. MACDONALD,
"Gold Commissioner.
"Certified for true signature of the Gold Commissioner.
"SWART,
"State Secretary of the Government Office,
"Pretoria, S. A. Republic,
"12*th* Decr., 1873."

A letter published at the same time states that " Last week one man found seventeen ounces in one day, and several ounces on following days, another found nine ounces in three hours' work. Many are finding two and three ounces a day. One claim produced over a pound weight, three consecutive days.* As a rule, people do very fairly, and when I see and handle, which I have done, these amounts, and consider the strides which have been made in the five months I have been on the fields, I cannot but believe in the predictions, which mark out for this country a grand career."

By this time the gold itself began to be distributed, various parcels reached the Diamond Fields, Natal, Port Elizabeth, and Cape Town, bearing in the most substantial manner testimony to the truth of such reports as those already quoted.

In February, 1874, the R. M. S. "Basuto" took from Natal thirteen to fourteen lbs. of Lydenburg gold. A parcel of twenty-five lbs. eleven dwts., in which was one nugget of eight and a half ozs., was received in Cape Town. A nugget of, I think, one and a half lb. weight was exhibited, and in the market report for March, in Pieter Maritzburg, we find " 336 ozs. gold Lydenburg £3 12s. 6d. offered, not sold;" "five ozs. gold Macamac £3 13s. per oz. Roseveare." Mr. Roseveare also brought down with him from the fields twenty-eight lbs. weight of gold, and this I narrowly missed seeing, as I called at the "Royal Hotel," Durban, where he stayed, just two hours after it had been packed up for shipment by the "Florence."

---

* The meaning of this is open to doubt, but if it is only one pound in the three days, the run of luck was not bad.

Our summer, or rainy season, was now well advanced, and the incessant showers, and flooded condition of all the creeks greatly hindered work in the known gold fields, and almost entirely forbade prospecting. Nevertheless, under all difficulties, the work went on. On the 24th of February, the editor of the *Gold News* (I think in the first number) vouched for finds of eighty-five ounces, five ounces, and four ounces. Mr. West, an Australian digger of more than twenty years experience, reported that about 300 men were at work, and all finding more or less gold. Five claims were yielding two ounces per diem each, while some were not making wages. Another digger, writing from the spot, says:—" Some find from three to four dwts. per day, others as many ounces." McKinnon, an old digger working alone, got sixteen ounces from one-and-a-half loads of stuff. You often hear of similar strokes of good luck but some parties are making nothing. On the 24th February, Dr. Scoble, of Natal, found on the terrace a nine ounce nugget and three ounces of small gold, while a day or two before "young Steere, of Maritzburg, turned out a five pound nugget at Pilgrim's Rest. In March, about the 26th, the *Gold News* reports:—"A nugget of pure gold, weighing twenty ounces nine pennyweights, was found on Tuesday last by Mr. Da Costa in the claim of Dr. Thompson. It was found on the top stuff, and lay snugly underneath a large stone." On April the 18th a nineteen ounce nugget was found, and another of a pound weight, the result of a day's sluicing ; while in a private letter of the 13th, the writer who went up " in Evans's trap " says he visited Pilgrim's Rest creek and found most of the diggers satisfied. He mentions one who had averaged one and a half ounces for 100 days, but says that Steere denied having found the reported five pound nugget. One digger had worked two months without success, and then shifted ground, and found in a few days " a two and a half pound nugget and lots of smaller ones."

One person left the fields for a trip to England with fifty pounds of gold, leaving his claim to be worked by a party till his return. He states also, on information he believes to be reliable, that there are diggers on the fields who have in their possession from 1,000 to 1,300 ounces of gold, all of their own finding. He himself had started digging with a mate. His first week was successful, but the second was occupied in nothing but moving boulders. At the date of his letter he was doing well and was satisfied. He adds:—" A singular occurrence took place the other day. A piece of land, thought nothing of by the old hands who were working on the opposite side of the creek, was rushed by an adventurer, who found on the first day nine ounces, second day thirteen ounces, third day eleven ounces, and has done well each day since."

Claims were valued at from £40 to £300 each according to the nature of the ground.

Prospecting.

I have already mentioned that the setting in of the wet season almost entirely put a stop to effective prospecting; nevertheless, some adventurous parties braved the discomfort and the risk of fever, and succeeded in finding gold bearing localities. One of these was a creek eight or ten miles north of Pilgrim's Rest, and on the other side of the Blyde river. The "prospect" announced was a nugget of three dwts. and five dwts. of fine gold to a pan, and this being in the top stuff encouraged several diggers to gather there in hope of better results lower down. Old buildings—deserted huts and remains of orchards—showed what had previously been a farm or inhabited place of some importance, and from the number of peach trees remaining it was called "Peach Rush."

Others ventured about forty miles to the northward, down the Blyde river, and got into the vicinity of Origstadt. They found quartz with gold in it, and also found alluvial gold in quantities, probably payable, but their temerity exposed them to attacks of fever, from which it is stated one or two died, and the others returned much weakened.

Another auriferous locality was discovered at Waterfall creek, and early in March sixty-three diggers were at work, but only twenty or thirty were said to be making anything. On the 18th Mr. Nolan had found two nuggets weighing half an ounce, but no one had found heavy gold. A canteen had arrived, but no store had yet been opened. Mr. Nolan, the discoverer of the gold, reported his success to the commissioner. "Waterfall Creek Rush," was proclaimed a payable gold field, and the discoverer would be entitled to a claim—probably double the usual size—as Waterfall could hardly be so far distant from Pilgrim's rest as to entitle him to have his claim trebled or quadrupled.

Should the whole creek, about five miles long, from Waterfall to Blyde river, turn out payable, it was estimated that there would be room for 1,000 men to work, and the general complaint of want of room would cease, at all events for a time. Messrs. McKinnon and Thompson found a handsome prospect of eight ounces in one crevice about the falls. The only man who had really done any extensive work had found a fair return. The flooded state of the creek prevented a thorough search, but it was expected that when the summer had passed, and the water was down to winter level, there would be something interesting to chronicle about rushes and nuggets.

During the same month a party of merchants at Lydenburg subscribed to equip two experienced Australian diggers for a prospecting trip. On the very first day they found "colour" at a short distance, and on the second day they brought into Lydenburg gold which had been found actually upon the town lands.

And now, in submitting this brief summary of the condition and prospects of the gold fields up to date, I must bespeak the readers' indulgent consideration to the impossibility of keeping pace (in a work to be published in London) with the current of actual discovery; the winter season in which prospecting may be safely carried on is now commencing, and perhaps, as I post this manuscript for the mail of to-morrow (May 14th, 1874), I may hear of new discoveries.

Besides this the quartz from the vicinity of the Berlin mission station of Nazareth, in the Trans-Vaal, "rich in gold, in nickle, and in cobalt," and said to be worth at least £25 per ton in the rough, may already have reached England, and the result of the assay will be known in London long before I can hear of it.

The latest testimony I can give is that I saw thirty-one ounces of gold a day or two ago brought from McMc and Pilgrim's Rest, and that one of my friends not long ago sent 145 ounces home. But to me the most interesting specimen was a half ounce obtained from the country to the south-east of Matabililand, probably about half way between Hartley Hill and the ruins of Mazimboeye— Zimbaoe or Zimbabye—of Herr Mauch, in which direction I have reason to believe that alluvial fields as rich as, and more extensive than, those of Lydenburg await the coming of the explorer who shall unite to skill in prospecting, patience, perseverance, and tact in dealing with the various native tribes, whose friendship must be cultivated, and assistance gained, before the richest of all the districts of South-Eastern Africa shall be ready to surrender its treasures to the enterprise and industry of Europe.

CHAPTER XII.

THE GATHERING OF MINING COMMUNITIES.

General and Provisional Government.—Mode of Working.— Establishment of Townships.—Formation of Roads.—Locality and Season, as affecting Health.—The Tsetse Fly.—Routes and Distances.—Mining Laws.—Conclusion.

[NOTE.—Before posting the last chapter by the Royal Mail Steamer of to-day, May 14th, 1874, I mentioned the impossibility of concluding a record of the finds in Lydenburg district, when the season for traversing the lower country, without danger of fever, was just opening. And this morning my remark is justified by the arrival of the *Gold News*, of April 25th, with the following paragraph :—

"We know of one party up creek this week who found seventy-four ounces in three days. A number of old hands are out prospecting, the rainy season is now past, and they can camp out without the misery of lying on wet ground."]

THE wisdom of the injunction, "Despise not the day of small things," was never better illustrated than by the history of the last few years in Southern Africa.

The purchase by a trader of a glittering stone, with which a child was playing, in that country, once described in the British Parliament, as "The most barren and worthless desert on the earth's crust," was the beginning of that industry, which has planted a British Colony in that wilderness—has flooded the markets of the world with diamonds—and now bids fair to fertilise the desert itself, with the water that impedes the diggers, by collecting in the mines, during the rainy season, and saturating the surrounding earth.

A hunter was led upon the spoor of elephants across quartz reefs, and abandoned native workings. The ancient gold fields were brought to public notice. Steam power now sends home gold from Matabililand, and learned societies look (not despairingly) for the discovery of the scriptural Ophir.

A young Natalian travelled with one or two experienced miners in the Trans-Vaal. He has brought from England and erected powerful crushing machinery, which is probably by this time in profitable operation on the reef at Eersteling; while his fellow-travellers are now among the successful pioneers of the Lydenburg fields, where the increasing extent and richness of the alluvial finds are laying broad and deep the foundation of prosperity for the country.*

In 1871-2, several prospectors were attracted to Marabastadt and Eersteling. Claims were marked out and worked with occasional small success, buoying up the hopes, but never compensating the labours of the diggers.

The Trans-Vaal Government took but little action in the matter beyond proclaiming a reward of £500 for the discovery of a payable gold field, and demanding payment of £1 per licence from all diggers. The licence, however, was to be paid at once, and followed by a payment of ten shillings per month while working on a claim; but the reward was payable twelve months after the opening of the diggings, and then only if 3,000 licences of £1 each should have been paid upon them. The field also to be ten English miles square, with the spot on which the first sample was found in the centre, and at a distance of at least sixty miles from any other known gold field. Several instances might be quoted in which the reward has been claimed, but I am not aware of one in which all

* June 25th, The *Volkstein* reports:—" A private letter from Marabastadt says, 'the operations there are turning out better than the greatest well-wisher to the Republic could hope. The yield of gold in proportion to the quartz crushed is something enormous.'" The *Natal Mercury* adds— " Letters have been received in Durban from Eersteling, confirming the above. Mr. Button's machinery is reported to be at work, and some quartz, which was not expected to give much, if any, gold, has yielded surprisingly." This (there is no reason to doubt the thickness of the auriferous quartz reef) has yet to be ascertained. Last finds at Lydenburg for the week something like 120, 105, 84, and 65 ounces.

the conditions have been so exactly fulfilled, that payment of it has been made.

The country, with reservations against trespass on cultivated lands or homesteads, was thrown open to all prospectors holding a licence, and the Government, perhaps wisely, interfered as little as possible, merely appointing a gold commissioner, who, with a committee of the diggers, was empowered to frame bye-laws, to be afterwards confirmed by the Volksraad or Parliament of the Republic. The search for alluvial gold at Marabastadt and Eersteling was, however, not successful enough to induce a permanent settlement, and all but those interested in quartz mining dispersed or betook themselves to the reported auriferous country near Lydenburg.

On the 2nd of April, 1873, the first sample of two and a half ounces of gold from that locality was received in Pretoria, and on the 10th of March about 180 diggers were at work on Mr. MacLachlan's farm and its vicinity. Bye-laws, as in other cases, were enacted by a diggers' committee, the Landrost of the district being considered, *ex officio*, as gold commissioner. The Government proposed to fix the mining licence at £1 per month, because it was stated that claims were yielding monthly about £30 each, but if the number of unsuccessful diggers was taken into account, the average would probably not be so high. In one instance, when the Government sent a commissioner to proclaim a gold field payable, the diggers compelled him to sign a document declaring that it was not so. Nevertheless, it was at least sufficient inducement for them to remain on one or other of the various "rushes," which, for the time, happened to assert most prominently its claim to richness. None of the diggers, for most intelligible reasons, would tell of their successes, nor reveal the amount of gold hidden in some nook in their fragile and often unguarded tents, but the fields soon began to acquire the name of "Poor Man's Diggings," and the Australians were accused of being dissatisfied if they could not turn out £8 or £10 worth of gold in a day.

In May there were at Nazareth about 100 wagons, and twice that number of diggers, bound for the gold fields, some of these vehicles, of course, were carrying provisions, but the majority of the men were consumers, rather than producers. And although great numbers returned in disgust at finding the work harder, and the reward less certain than they had anticipated, yet constant accessions swelled the number of those who demanded food, and high prices prevailed. Meat was 6d. per lb., and often not to be had, Boer's meal £3 to £3 5s. and £3 15s. per muid of 180 lbs., sugar 7d. to 9d. per lb., coffee (raw) 1s. 6d. per lb., butter* 1s. 6d. per lb.

Plank and timber were procured from forests some thirty, and others sixty miles distant, the sawyers paying to the owners six planks out of every forty for permission to cut them. The planks sold on the fields for 15s. each.

Farms of course rose in price. Hardly three years since, in some districts of the Trans-Vaal, farms of 6,000 acres, were scarcely worth two oxen, and at the first rumour of gold discovery, £15 each were given for several upon speculation, hundreds of pounds being demanded for them shortly after. In the Lydenburg district £150 was a high price, but with the increasing confidence in the gold fields, this rose to £6,000 or £8,000. Two gold bearing farms were let for thirty-three years at £200 per annum each.

The question of roads was forced upon the consideration of the Government, and its attention was directed to the repair and improvement of the main line from Pretoria *viâ* Nazareth to Lydenburg—while shortly after £1,000 was voted for the completion of that from Lydenburg to Delagoa Bay—and working parties were put upon the most steep or rugged parts of those leading from Lydenburg to the diggings. Many of the adventurers who had been unfortunate, accepting, with commendable spirit, work upon the roads in preference to indolence, while waiting upon fortune.

In September the President of the Trans-Vaal Republic visited the township that had already sprung up upon the farm, Geelhoutboom (or yellow wood), McLachlan's, and named the gold fields "New Caledonia," and the township "McMc." He bought two nuggets, the "Emma," sixteen and a half ounces, and the "Adeliza," twenty-two ounces seventeen and a half pennyweights. He was received most cordially by the diggers, and a public meeting, a pic-nic, and a ball, were included in the marks of respect and attention that were shown him.

Of course, the projected railroad between Pretoria and Delagoa Bay was the frequent subject of discussion, but nothing could be done, as the success of this depended on the negociations now being conducted by Mr. Moodie in Portugal and England.

A police force was established, and a gaol provided, but it would seem that prolonged incarceration was rather optional than com-

---

* Some of these prices, for butter, meat, and milk especially, are at present not only equalled, but exceeded, both in Natal and Cape Town.

pulsory, and that in some cases the constables were more ready to "thank heaven they were rid of a rogue," than to effect a recapture. A case of shop-lifting was punished with a week's imprisonment, confinement in the stocks, and banishment. Popular feeling seemed decidedly in favour of summary ejectment from the fields rather than long imprisonment.

There is a story—though I do not vouch for it—of a prisoner, whose rations were not forthcoming at the proper time, persuading his jailor to let him go and dine at the hotel, and of the sturdy janitor refusing to admit him again to the prison he had depreciated and deserted. " If this gaol is not good enough for you, go and find a better." It was also remarked that if treadmills, or other appliances for hard labour, were wanting the prisoners were not always unemployed, for some were seen in fetters, carrying about, for sale, fowls belonging to the constables.

"Gold Fields—Judge Lynch!"—A correspondent at Pretoria under date 17th of July, writes :—

"I have received a letter this morning from one of my friends at Lydenburg, mentioning that Judge Lynch has arrived at the fields; that an Englishman who had stolen something, has received at the Court of diggers, twenty-five lashes, had his hair cut, and one side of his beard shaved off. The reports are very encouraging, but the people are anxious to see the President, to make better laws."

Matters, however, could not be allowed to remain long in this condition of primitive simplicity ; in the beginning of 1874 when the population of the fields was estimated at above 1,000 men— 326 of whom voted at the election of members for the Volksraad—when well stocked stores were established by merchants from Natal and other places, and thefts of goods, of gold dust, of money, and of horses, began to frighten McMc from its propriety, the necessity for a more vigorous administration of the law was felt ; an Attorney-General was appointed, and at a meeting, held on the 12th February, the first resolution—affirmed the necessity of a substantial prison, and efficient police force. The second—the equally urgent need for the proper repair of roads ; while others brought to the notice of the President the desirability of using the English language in cases where both litigants were of that nation ; the reduction of licences, and other duties, which pressed heavily on storekeepers, as well as diggers ; the need for increased postal service, as well as for the establishment of a regular mail *viâ* Newcastle to Natal ; the appointment of a District Surgeon, and of one English Justice of the Peace ; the better regulation and collection of municipal dues, and the propriety of the Government granting some aid in the erection of an English Church, for which object a piece of land, and various sums of money, had already been contributed by the inhabitants.

Hitherto postal and traffic communication with the gold fields, had been kept up chiefly *viâ* Pretoria, involving a considerable detour to the westward ; but various persons had been tracing nearer routes. Mr. McLean favoured that *viâ* Maritzburg, Colenso, Ladysmith, Newcastle, and Lake Chrissie, in New Scotland, while Mr. Leathern explored that from Lydenburg to Lake Chrissie, Marthinus Wesselstroom, Utrecht, Greytown, and Maritzburg, the result being that the whole distance from Durban to Lydenburg, by McLean's route, was computed at 420 miles, and, by Mr. Leathern's, at 419¾ miles.

By these routes the Drakensberg is scaled a little south of the 27th degree of latitude. New Scotland is traversed at a height of 5,000 or 6,000 feet, and the road at such an elevation cannot fail to be healthy at all seasons.

A small iron steamer, the "Adonis," had been brought from Europe and put together in Port Natal, and by the close of 1873 was fit for sea. Several persons took passage in her for Delagoa Bay, with the view of shortening the land journey, but the exposure to fever in the rains then prevalent, the detention and difficulty of procuring native carriers in Delagoa Bay, the entire absence of accommodation and consequent hardships, privations, and exposure, during a pedestrian journey of 178 miles, during which two large and several small rivers must be crossed, far more than countervailed the 240 miles saved in the distance.

A letter from Pilgrim's Rest, dated Feb. 16, 1874, records the death of three persons who had arrived, *viâ* Delagoa Bay, and states that hardly one had been exempted from attacks of fever ; while many narrowly escaped with their lives, and were compelled to abstain from work till the bracing air of the elevated regions should restore their health. The first who died at McMc was William Nye Nightingale, aged twenty-six or twenty-seven, believed to have come from Durban ; next, Thompson, aged twenty-seven or twenty-eight, formerly connected with a brewery in Cape Town. The third victim was named Stewart, aged about forty-seven. He was supposed to have come from Algoa Bay, was formerly an engineer in the service of the Peninsular and Oriental Steam Company, was a widower, and had left a daughter. The writer considerately gives these particulars to facilitate the identification of the unfortunate victims to a deadly climate, and adds that every attention was shown them during their illness by the ladies of Mr. MacLachlan's family, and they had such medical assistance as could be obtained on the fields. Somewhat later a Frenchman, named De Beker, died from the same cause at Waterfall Rush; he is supposed to have come from Port Elizabeth, and the following letter, written by a traveller, *en route*, gives a vivid picture of the hardships and distress to be encountered on the Delagoa Bay road during the unhealthy season :

" Dear Mr. MANSFIELD,

"Your kafir, Jim, met Mr. Sankey Kennedy and myself on the point of death, with forty-three kafirs. I have been prostrated and reduced to a skeleton. Sankey also has been in a fearful state; in fact, our sufferings on the road have been such as I cannot tell you on this scrap of paper. Poor Rockencamp died at some kafir houses. Wilkinson, who went down to Delagoa Bay with Wynn, drowned himself in the delirium of fever. Dr. Graham's Cape Town boy (driver), and his little *protegé*, are both dead. Marshall is missing. A Mr. Jenkins is stopped by fever at some kafir kraals; his life is despaired of. Pray don't blame Jim; he has, I fully believe, saved my life by his attentions to me when raving with the fever by the road side. I am better, and Jim leaves me to-day. We have reached Rockencamp's wagon with Wynn and Mr. Ressner, who is on his back with fever. I trust in a few days to see you."

Dr. Graham, who left Pilgrim's Rest on the 21st January, was a fortnight walking down to the Bay, and reached Durban on the 12th of March. No supplies of any kind were obtainable along the road, except here and there a fowl, or a little maize, sold by Kafirs, or offered as a present, in hope of a still more extravagant return; an accommodation house (or rather hut) had been started at Krokodil river, but owing, I believe, to the sickness, or death, of the proprietors, was in a broken down condition—tenanted by two Kafirs—and the remnant of its stock consisted of six empty bottles, and a tin dish. At Lorenzo Marques, they lodged in the leaky wreck of an adobe stable,* with a mud floor, when the whole party

---

* Since that time an inn has been established. Dr. Wilson very kindly gave me the distance, by triochiametar, amounting to 178¾ miles, from Pilgrim's rest, to Delagoa Bay; and Mr. Compton gave me a sketch map of the route.

suffered from fever, aggravated by want of proper food, or medicine, nor were they the only victims, for of twenty-four diggers, who had recently passed, not one had escaped fever; and three died on board the "Sea Nymph." The death of Mr. Gray, and Mr. Thompson, from the same disease, was also reported—almost every one in Delagoa was ill, the inhabitants suffering also from the continuous wet weather. The four oxen, used by the party, had passed through the fly country without actual loss, and were bought by Mr. Parsons, for the return journey, but the poison was only latent, and, when he was seen a few days later, two of them were already dead; and the cases of brandy, &c., of which the cart had been lightened, were strewed along the road side. Mr. Goddard succeeded in taking up some loads on donkeys—a native girl swimming the rivers and leading them, when the Kafirs refused. He himself saved his clothes to sleep in, by rolling them up tightly, and carrying them under his arm, while he marched unclad through the heavy showers.

It is unfortunate that the attempt to open the Delagoa Bay route should have been made at the commencement of the unhealthy season, or in October and November, entailing the loss of several lives, and prolonged sickness and misery to most of those who survived. With the return of the healthy season, about May, renewed efforts were made to take advantage of the route, and early in that month, thirty-five Kafirs, carrying ten bottles of ale, or ten of stonejar gin each, arrived on the fields, having performed the journey in fourteen days. Several persons had goods at Delagoa, and great efforts, on the part of the authorities, were being made to collect native carriers to take them up. The rate of payment was 10s. for the trip, and it is stated that they can carry seventy or eighty lbs. each. This would make the freight about £14 per ton; but it must be remembered that prices will rise with the demand for labour, and I should think fifty lbs. per man, for a continuous march, could be reckoned on.

The Portuguese Government has recently remitted all duties on goods passing from Delagoa Bay into the Trans-Vaal, and the harbour being accessable to vessels of considerable draught, there is no doubt but some mode of transport to meet the exigencies of the case will be devised. Packages may be made to the weight a man can carry on his head, or baskets will be slung on bamboos to be borne by two or more. Animals may be found to pass securely through the fly country, and of these none can be safer than our own elephant, buffalo, or quagga; whether they can be sufficiently tamed is a problem only partially solved at present. The donkey is known to be fly proof in the interior, but some doubt its exemption on the coast. The camel would be sorely tried among our mountains in the rainy season, when the roads are mere alternations of swamp and slippery clay ; and the Indian elephants and buffaloes—though the first were used with success in Abyssinia, and the latter near Zanzibar—are yet untried here.

It is far from my desire to lengthen this concluding chapter, but this deadly little pest which so impedes and harasses the traveller in southern Africa, cannot be passed by without a brief description and some suggestions, which may perhaps lead men of science to the consideration of some remedy for its subtle poison.

The Tsetse is little more than half-an-inch long, and rather more slender than a common house-fly. The abdomen is marked with transverse stripes of yellow and dark chesnut fading toward the centre of the back, so as to give the idea of a yellow stripe along it ; the belly livid white, the eyes are purplish brown, and the wings, of dusky glassy brown colour, slip one over the other, just as do the blades of a pair of scissors when closed—so that the Tsetse at rest on man or animal may infallibly be known by this one token.

No fly which rests with its wings half expanded, like the house fly, or closed together like a pent-house roof, can be the Tsetse, but if one is seen in which the wings exactly overlap—one lying flat upon the other—that is " the fly." It has six legs and tufts of hair over its body ; its proboscis of piercing apparatus is about one sixth of an inch long ; its sight and smell seem to be keen ; its flight straight and rapid. To speak either of its sting or its bite would convey an erroneous idea. The Dutch colonists say it " sticks," and this is certainly more correct, as it first pierces the skin with its lancet, and then injects a fluid (poisonous to oxen, horses, and dogs) to thin the blood before drinking it. Men, mules, donkeys, sheep, goats, and wild game, are believed to be unaffected by the virus. I, in common with other travellers, have been stuck time after time with impunity. Mules, partaking of the equine nature, are not always secure from dangers to which the horse is liable, and Mr. St. Vincent W. Erskine doubts the safety of the donkey on the south-east coast.

My friend, Mr. Henry Hartley, the well-known hunter and pioneer of the gold fields, has kindly summarized the symptoms exhibited by a fly-stuck ox as under—

1st.—The hanging of the ears, general languid appearance, sometimes watering at the eyes. 2nd.—Roughness of the coat, the hair rising on end. 3rd.—Feeding voraciously, even to repletion, without improving the condition, and standing panting in the heat of the day. 4th.—Occasional swelling at the gullet. 5th.—Continual wasting and pining away (but sometimes an ox may improve in condition, and show no symptom of having been stuck for two or three months, or till the first cold rain falls). 6th.—An ox slightly stuck goes on wasting till the skin sits fast on the backbone. After this there is no hope ; but if severely stuck he dies before it can take place. Mr. Hartley did not notice running at the nose or other unusual discharge. If the ox is worked he will show weakness in the loins. 7th.—When the beast is skinned after death the puncture of every fly can be seen on the inside of the skin, and on the flesh is a ring of yellow mucous, nearly as large as the palm of the hand, similar to the mark that surrounds the bite of a snake, but smaller.

A bullock belonging to Christian Harmoe was stuck in May ; he worked for 500 miles, then began to show symptoms, and died in September. Some of my own—stuck during the passage through the fly country in September, 1871—worked about 300 miles, and died at Mr. Hartley's in January of the next year.

Chapman says,—" The fly stuck ox refuses to fill itself, be the herbage never so luxuriant. After death the heart is encased in a yellowish glutinous substance, which might be mistaken for fat ; the flesh is full of small bladders of water, the blood is half water, and on cooling becomes yellow and glutinous ; the vitals are livid."

Mr. Hartley adds,—" Horses swell about the eyes, nostrils, and testicles, where generally the wounds are most numerous, they pine away, and their hair stands on end, or is reversed ; cold rain also hastens their death." My friend, the late Joseph Macabe, being incredulous, deliberately rode a valuable hunter right into an infested tract, and returned to the outspan where his steed died in a few hours, and the place is now called Schimmel Paard's Pan, or the pool of the dapple grey horse. Mr. Hartley's splendid grey elephant charger, " Camelbuck," died twenty days after he was stuck ; ammonia was applied, and he was led to stand in cold water, which is said to be sometimes effectual, but in vain. My own horse, "Vegtmann," stuck, I believe, in October, 1869, travelled more than 1,100 miles, and died early next year in Pieter Maritzburg. Dogs pine and waste as oxen do. We lost some, but one, a rough hairy bitch, seemed recovering, the new hair that grew on places where she had apparently been stuck, was coarser and grayer than before.

The fly is extremely local, and extensive districts in which it prevails may be passed through by the aid of guides, who know the "patches" of fly, just as a pilot knows the shoals of an estuary; but it shifts with the migration of game, and, therefore, the knowledge of the guide ought to be recent.

The hunters endeavour to keep it from their road, in Matabililand, by burning the dry grass, as they come out at the end of the season. And when the Boers made their celebrated "Commando path," they destroyed the bush for several hundred yards on either side as they approached the Limpopo. If a belt of fly cannot be avoided, it may be passed through, if not too wide, in the night, or on a cold rainy morning; but the last is a dangerous experiment, for should the sun break through the clouds it rouses the insects with increased vigour and activity from their torpor, and it is well known that on a hot day all poisonous creatures are more virulent and deadly.

For the benefit of intending travellers, I may mention that Andries Du Venage (pronounced Devenaar), and Mr. Scott, an English hunter in the Trans-Vaal, are acquainted with safe routes to a considerable distance inland, and native doctors belonging to Ramapulana and other chiefs, take small herds of cattle through with impunity. A chief named Elange Puma, or Sunrise, living to the south-west of Sofala, was able to send cattle across the Limpopo without loss.

I am not aware that any certain remedy is known. The native doctors inoculate oxen by giving them the fly itself, mixed with herbs. The poor beast suffers dreadfully, and is brought almost to the point of death, but when it recovers is believed to be Tsetse proof.

All young animals, while living on milk, are safe. Some of the tribes living on the borders drive the calves into the fly during the day, and bring them out to be suckled morning and night. This is supposed also to render them secure during the rest of their lives.

It would be a great boon if any composition capable of being sprinkled or syringed over the animals—innocuous to them, and disgusting to the fly—could be discovered; tar, ox dung mixed with milk, the kidneys of the meer kat, &c., have been recommended, but carbolic acid would perhaps be more effectual, diluted with water, and applied by a syringe or the rose of a watering-pot.

Mr. Hartley tried a decoction of the bark of the roots of the wittegaat boom, or motlopre, I believe, with some success; and there are Boers who profess to be able to cure an animal recently stuck. Their fee is one good ox for saving a horse.

While passing through the fly, in 1871, I mixed about a pound of ammonia with a bucket of warm water, and washed all four of our horses. We noticed that they flinched, probably as the liquid entered the punctures. None of them died; and though I would not affirm on one experiment that the ammonia saved them, I think it highly probable that such was the case.* Unfortunately I had not enough to wash the oxen with. We tried to restore tone to the blood with muriate of iron when I reached Mr. Hartley's farm, but it was then too late.

Mr. Saunders, of Maghaliesberg, saved a horse with Croft's tincture of life, which contained ammonia, and two oxen with Perry Davis's pain killer. They stood for three or four days with foam issuing from their mouth, as if the poisonous matter were being thus ejected. After this they began to eat voraciously, and recovered their condition. Perhaps if milk could be given to animals as soon as they are stuck they might recover.

Vegetable poisons exist in many parts of Africa,—the *tulp*, in the Cape Colony and Natal, and the *maghaow*, in the Trans-Vaal and the interior. The latter is a leaf six or eight inches long and one or two broad. Any Boer will point it out. The danger diminishes when the grass grows higher than the plant, but does not entirely cease. Patches are found between Nylstroom and Makopan's Poort.

The dangers, however, of the Delagoa Bay route would be more efficiently met by the construction of a good road, with the bush cleared away as far as possible on either side, in the fly country, leaving the unhealthy lowlands as soon as possible, and climbing any elevated ridge, the course of which (even at the cost of considerably increased distance) might be followed to the highlands, so that man and beast might be as little as possible exposed to fly or fever. And still more effectual than this would be the railway to Pretoria, projected by my friend Moodie, bringing passengers and goods to the heights of New Scotland, whence Lydenburg could be easily and safely reached.

---

* June 27, 1874. I hear that during last season a hunter, on entering the fly country, dosed or washed his horses continually with ammonia, and has brought them all out safe, but very weak, probably from the combined effects of the poison and its antidote.

DISTANCES TO THE GOLD FIELDS.

In the *Colonist* of June 19th we are informed that Mr. Isidore Alexandre has brought an ox wagon down from the gold fields to Delagoa Bay in nine days, and others are to follow. There has been no loss among the oxen. I would fain hope the best for Mr. Alexandre, but I shall watch with great interest the future history of these animals. We know that in cold weather the fly is less virulent, but it never ceases to be dangerous.

Meanwhile, so far as the requirements of the intending visitor are concerned, the difficulty is already solved by the establishment, not only of regular transport wagons, but also of mail and passenger coaches or covered vehicles, from the diamond fields, and from Natal to Lydenburg.

The diamond fields may be reached by a regular line of vehicles from Cape Town in 700 miles, or from Port Elizabeth, by Cobb and Company's coaches, in 428 miles, after which they travel 456 more in the Gold Fields Extension Transport Company's wagons, *viâ* Pretoria to Lydenburg, making from Cape Town 1,156, and from Port Elizabeth 884 miles of land journey—with thirty more to add for the distance to McMc—hitherto traversed only by occasional wagons, but now, I believe, to be regularly performed by mail carts like the rest.

From Natal the distance, by the Graytown route, from Durban to Lydenburg, is estimated at 419¾ miles, and by the Newcastle line at 420. There is a third route to the eastward of these, passing under the sea face of the Drakensberg, which would probably lead the prospector through a great extent of auriferous country, and, therefore, in winter, would be worthy the attention of skilled gold seekers, well supplied with necessaries for an exploring trip; but those whose object is to reach their destination as speedily as possible will take the Newcastle road, on which mail and passenger vehicles now run regularly.

The distances as given by Mr. McLean are :—

From Durban to Maritzburg	54 miles
Thence to Newcastle	159 ,,
,, to Robertsons (beyond Wakkerstroom)	57 ,,
,, to Lydenburg	150 ,,
	420
Lydenburg to McMc...	30 ,,
Total	450

The journey from Durban to Pieter Maritzburg, by omnibus, is performed in one day, costing £1; thence to Newcastle in three days, fare £5; thence viâ Marthinus Wesselstroom to Lydenburg in three days, fare £10. Time, seven days. Total fare £16.

From Durban the road gradually ascends, frequently winding along the summit of ridges, from which extensive and beautiful views of sea and land may be obtained, to Maritzburg, 2,080 feet above the level of the ocean, pleasantly situated in a broad valley, nearly surrounded with grassy hills, and ornamented by groves of Australian gum, and other trees. Then comes a short steep path of from five to seven miles up the town hill, which is reached at an altitude of 3,686 feet, by roads which I hope are in better order than when I last travelled them. At such an elevation the air is delightfully cool and bracing, and during the winter, snow may sometimes be seen on the Zwart Kop and other hills, or on the more distant Drakensberg. At Howick a few moments should be spared to view the Umgeni cataract, falling about 350 feet into a deep rocky basin. The Mooi river, at an elevation of 4,230 feet, is crossed by an iron bridge, as also is the Bushman's river, at Estcourt, 3,562 feet above the sea. At Colenso, 3,000 feet high, the Tugela is forded, or crossed in a punt, except when the summer floods render it for a time impassable; and thence the road turns from north-west to north, and with the lofty, and often snow clad, peaks of the Drakensberg on the west, passes by Lady Smith to Newcastle; then turning north-east, crosses the Buffalo river—the boundary between Natal and the Trans-Vaal Republic—and reaches the town of Marthinus Wesselstroom, in latitude, 27·22·8 south; longitude, about 30·22 east; and 5,300 feet above the sea. Hitherto hotels have been frequent, but from this point, as the traveller turns north, and crosses the Drakensberg, at a height of 5,727 feet, he comes to a country more thinly inhabited, but will still find accommodation at houses, which I understand, are being opened along the line. The Vaal river, or Likwa (river of cold or snow) is crossed. The little colony of New Scotland, passed through at an elevation of more than 6,000 feet, and north of this the road again dips to cross the valley of the Um Komati, the Krokodil, and their tributary streams, and reaches Lydenburg, pleasantly situated in a healthy valley, 5,825 feet above the sea, on one of the branches of the Spekboom river. Then turning east, across the Drakensberg ridge, with the Mauchberg 8,725 feet high, towering on the north, the Devil's Knuckles and the Spitz Kop are passed. Various branches of the Sabea, with waterfalls, some fifty and some 250 feet in height, are crossed, and the traveller reaches the township of McMc, where he may rest a-while and decide on which of the various "Rushes" he intends working.*

It is obviously beyond the province of a book like the present to give very elaborate instructions for gold seeking or gold working. Treatises on this subject, from shilling pamphlets to costly and profusely illustrated volumes, may be bought in London, and most important and useful may be the knowledge to be gleaned from them; but as no written instructions can make a man a swimmer, a cricketer, or a sportsman, so neither can they, without long and arduous experience in the wilderness, make him a successful gold seeker. Men even who have spent their lives in Australia and in California, confessed themselves at fault when they came to Africa, and though their experience in those countries stood them in good stead, they had to modify their ideas day by day as new conditions were revealed to them in Africa. Yet there are general rules which apply in most countries, and a few brief hints can do no harm, and may direct the new comer till the advice of practical men upon the spot can be obtained.†

"Clay slate formations (especially in the vicinity or at the foot of granite hills), traversed by iron-stained quartz dykes, are well worthy of investigation, as the quartz when exposed to atmospheric action, alternations of heat and cold, torrents of rain, with friction from waterworn pebbles, rocks or boulders, during the floods and subsequent dessication in the dry season, crumbles away, sometimes slowly, but in other cases with marvellous rapidity. The sand, the gravel, and fragments of rock, are washed to the nearest river-bed, and hurried down the mountain sides, till some projecting rock forms an impediment, under which the stream arrested in its headlong course, whirls round in eddies, and lets fall the heavier particles hitherto held in suspension, or at the foot of the slope the river may reach a flat, and its speed may be at once reduced from five or six miles an hour to one or two. Search well

---

* The *Gold News*, June 6th, says:—"Dr. Pearce and William Leathern have contracted to run a passenger cart between Lydenburg and Pilgrim's Rest, in common with the mail cart." So that the facilities for travel are now complete. One party found 111 ounces in a week, and 47 in one day; but some claims do not pay for the kafirs' porridge. Nineteen nights in succession had been frosty.

† See "Shifts and Expedients of Travel, by Campbell W. B. Lord and T. Baines." Horace Cox and Co., London. "Diamonds and Gold," W. B. Lord, and other works.

the spot where such diminution of speed is evident. Dig away boldly all the top deposit, till the bed-rock is reached. Rout out all the depressions, crevices, and holes, in this scooping up all the clay, gravel, and grit they may contain. Take this in convenient quantities in a broad shallow pan or dish (a kafir's wooden bowl if you cannot get a prospecting pan), pour water on it, rub and break the masses with the hand, pour off the dirty water, add more, and repeat the operation. Shake and rotate the pan, making the water sweep round it over the "dirt." Pick out all large pebbles or lumps of stone. If they are quartz examine them carefully, or put them aside to be broken with the hammer. Keep on adding water, rolling and tilting the dish, till nothing remains but clear clean heavy sand. A little clean water is then taken in the pan, and with a dexterous whirl, to be learnt only by practice, the sand is swept round in the circumference of the pan, the lighter particles leading off, followed by the heavier—probably black ferruginous fragments—and, lastly, by the gold, the "colour" of which, edging the dark sand, cheers the prospector, and incites him to renewed exertion. There is little fear of his being deceived here, for no other yellow substance is heavy enough to tail off last as gold does; besides which, most others glance or glitter instead of showing the soft pure lustre of real gold. Gold is soft; it can be cut with a sharp knife, or flattened like lead with a blow from the hammer. Sulphate of iron or mundic is crushed into powder by a blow, or turns the edge of a knife, and a piece of any size struck against steel gives out sulphurous fumes. Mundic—if placed on a shovel and made red hot—is attracted by the magnet; gold cannot be. Nitric acid does not affect gold, but it dissolves mundic with effervescence, and if gold is contained in it the particles settle freely in the bottom of the testing tubes.

Yellow mica can be at once distinguished by its want of weight. If placed on iron and heated to redness it falls into lustreless flakes; while gold is unaffected. Mica floats unaltered upon mercury, while gold is at once amalgamated.

Sulphuret of copper breaks freely under the hammer, but can be cut easily with the knife, breaking, however, into powder as chalk would, and not giving off a pliable chip like lead.

Alluvial tin is dark coloured, breaks into powder under the hammer, and is very heavy. Stream tin, if heated red hot and tried by the magnet, will not be attracted as iron is. A common horse-shoe magnet, value two or three shillings, is very useful in separating iron, which otherwise would be difficult to get clear of.

A diamond may be known by the file test. A fine watch maker's file is drawn firmly and evenly across it, and the diamond, only, will resist its edge, and show no cut. A bit of sapphire is a still better; that stone will scratch all others except a diamond, by which, only, it can in turn be scratched.

A small test-case, not larger than a sandwich box, can be obtained at small expense; it should contain,—glass-stoppered and capped bottles of nitric acid, hydrochloric acid, liquid ammonia, and quicksilver; and corked bottles—ferro cyanide of potassium, bichromate of potash, fused borax, and common salt. Small jointed blow-pipe, forceps, small scales fitted for taking specific gravities, and weights; a bit of flint glass, a piece of sapphire, a nest of half-a-dozen test-tubes, as many watch-glasses, and strips of window glass quarter of an inch wide, and five inches long; a piece of stout copper-wire, with a loop to hold the watch-glasses over the lamp or candle; a wire cigar-holder, to hold the test-tubes over the flame; a few narrow slips of well-burnt light charcoal, and a watch maker's small bright-faced hammer. The amount of analysis this equipment will effect is wonderful.

Take a little sand from brook or road, spread it out on clean paper, suppose it shows glittering yellow particles, black grains, and fragments of quartz, and other stones, when examined by the pocket lens, take up any grain you wish to test on the moistened point of a pin. If it looks like gold, place it on a hard substance, and strike it with the hammer, if it flattens, without breaking into powder, drop it into a test-tube, with a little nitric acid, and hold it in the flame till it boils; if it gives off a train of minute bubbles and dissolves, pour a little from the tube into two separate watch-glasses, side by side, adding a little water to each, put a little common salt into No. 1, and if it is silver, you will at once find a thick white precipitate chloride of silver, or let fall a few drops of liquor ammonia into No. 2, and if copper, you will see the distinct and beautiful blue of ammoniuret of copper. But should the particle have been crushed under the blow, it is most likely either sulphuret of iron or copper ore. To distinguish these, when minutely subdivided, proceed with the acid, as before, and try a small bit of ferro cyanide of potassium in one watch-glass, when sulphuret of iron, or mundic, will produce a dense cloud of prussian blue. Test the other with ammonia, and you will have the same blue ammoniuret of copper colour, as if the sample had been native copper.

Yet again, if the particle flattened under the hammer, and has resisted the action of the hot acid, and remained bright, there is no doubt this is gold.

Put the sand on a shovel or bit of sheet iron, hold it over the fire till the whole is red hot, then let it cool and take out all the iron with the magnet; then with a hammer or a pebble, crush all the rest fine upon the shovel; then, in a clean pool or quiet stream, or large tub, carefully wash away all but the heaviest particles, and you will soon distinguish the gold, if any. A few remaining fragments of mundic or copper ore, might deceive the inexperienced; therefore, dry the remaining powder over the fire, and put it in a small clean dry phial with a little quicksilver, shake it well, till all the particles come in contact with the mercury. The particles which are not absorbed are not gold. Put the mercury into a piece of chamois leather, squeeze it through, and if it leaves inside a soft amalgam, heat this upon the shovel (avoiding the fumes), and the mercury will be driven off, leaving the gold behind. Silver will also amalgamate with mercury, but it can always be distinguished by the nitric acid and salt test.

Lead ore is easily known by its colour. Cubic crystallization and gravity, a little powdered and mixed with borax fuses into ordinary lead on a charcoal slip before the blowpipe, the silver often associated with it can only be estimated by a regular assay.

Sulphuret of antimony, though lead coloured, leaves a thick rough deposit on the charcoal, and fuses in a brittle crystalline regulus, in no way resembling lead. Specimens of galena or lead ore should always be reserved for assay, as it is often rich in silver. Cinnabar, cobalt, nickel, and other metals, are found in quartz in many parts of the country.

To test the quality of gold have a bit of black terra-cotta, or hard black stone, not too highly polished, rub the piece of gold on this till it leaves a streak, then, with one of the glass rods, take a drop of nitric acid and let it fall on the mark. If the gold is pure it will remain unchanged, but if alloyed discolouration or removal of the baser metal will take place, leaving the mark fainter.

Generally, however, the professed gold seeker, the working man who seeks "a poor man's digging," to repay him for his toil, disregards all metals but actual gold, and has neither the means nor the ability to profit by other metals, should he ever find them. For him, therefore, I quote descriptions of the method of working adopted on the spot, with the rough and primitive means available to the earliest invaders of the wilderness.

"Geelhoutboom Gold Fields,
"Lydenburg, July 24th, 1873.

"The fields are neither a sell nor a swindle, but will eventually prove a source of wealth to those who work diligently and hopefully. Hitherto, the sole workings have been confined to the banks of a small stream, four or five miles long, and the work has been done in the simplest and rudest way. Sluice boxes are the fashion here; three planks are nailed together for the bottom and sides. In the trough thus formed moveable gratings of steps of wood are placed, a stream of water is turned into the trough, and the washing apparatus is complete. The earth supposed to contain gold is shovelled into the upper end of the box, and the seeker considers himself fairly at work. By this rude device a considerable quantity of gold is found, but a large proportion of the fine gold is carried again into the creek. For example—I worked at a place where the gold was very fine, but found by pan-washing from five to sixteen specks in every pan. I emptied these finds into the sluice box, and at the close of the day looked for the reward of my labour ; judge my disgust when I found the result was only three specks visible to the naked eye. I am quite inexperienced, but this is enough to show me how much fine gold is lost to the diggers, sufficient in fact to make the difference between paying and failing. Only that which is coarse enough to resist the flow of the water is saved.

"The Australians here thought it worth while to turn the course of the creek for a distance of about 1,200 yards, the cutting being in some places twenty-five feet deep. I have not heard the amount of their reward, but I hear they are not dissatisfied.

"Small erven or business sites in the main camp sold for £4 or £4 15s. each, and let at £1 per month each."—*Natal Mercury.*

"J. S."

"Pilgrim's Rest Gold Fields,
"Feb. 25th, 1874.

"My advice to everybody is, 'If you have got anything at all to do stay where you are ; if not, come and try your luck.'

"People at a distance have a very faint idea of the work and hardships of gold mining. It requires personal attendance, and is a trade in fact. No putting in a lot of kafirs, as on the diamond fields. Lots of diggers from the diamond fields come here, and when they see the work go back without putting a spade in the ground.

"This is the work. On taking up your claim you make a flood race, or trough, or sluit, to carry off the surplus water of the creek, then a tail race to carry off the water from your sluice box; then construct a dam, to keep back the water not wanted for your sluice box, and turn it into your flood race. You then set your sluice box, which is eighteen or twenty feet long, with little obstructing ripples in it, at intervals of one to two feet, to catch the gold. The spaces between these ripples are filled with stones, laid all along the bottom, leaving about nine inches of the height of the box, as a passage for the water. You turn in a sluice head of water to carry off the dirt and small stones, and then throw in stuff all day. At night you take your dish and pan off all that remains in your box, and the result may be a pennyweight, worth 3s. 6d. or 3s. 9d., or it may be one, two, or eight ozs., according to the quality of ground, as the gold is very patchy, and about half the claims, out of fifteen, pay little more than their expenses. Some, chiefly Australians, do well: three men, in six weeks, netted £300 or £400 each; but they had been working three months at McMc. finding little or nothing.

"If my letter deters any one who is not prepared to work and rough it, or who has not capital enough to carry on the work till good luck comes to him, I shall not have written in vain.

"Yours, &c.,
(Signed) "ALFRED BAKER."

In conclusion. What can I do better than endorse the above straightforward and sensible letter? It is sheer folly for men to leave the writer's desk, or the mechanic's bench, where some earn 12s. to 13s. per diem, and rush to this or that gold field on hearing of a splendid find—totally ignoring the lengthened search, the sore privation, the exhausting toil, and the heart-breaking disappointments the finders have endured before success rewarded them—and trusting in some vague manner to realize the same "good luck," without the skill, or, perhaps, even the intention to labour with the same energy and perseverance that commanded the success.

As reasonably might the prospector, who has spent his life in learning to decipher the signs that indicate the proximity of the great treasure-houses of the earth, at once abandon his profession and take the place of the carpenter, the watch-maker, or the clerk, expecting at once to earn the income they have thrown away.

CONCLUSION.

But to those who have made up their mind to work, who possess a trifle to keep them from poverty during their noviciate, and who, above all, possess the Englishman's inability to acknowledge himself beaten, I say—Come !—make your way to the gold diggings by this or any of the roads now open, and arriving there do not disdain to take advice from more experienced hands, but economise your own store by seeking employment from some skilful and successful gold finder, until you see an opening for the investment of your capital and labour on your own account. If, after all, gold digging does not suit your taste or pay you as it should, never despair, but look out for some of the many opportunities around you. Tradesmen of all kinds must be employed in working for the actual diggers :— carpenters, smiths, builders, tailors, shoe makers, clerks, storemen, and others, are wanted in the new townships that are rising in the wilderness. Farmers and graziers are required to provide food for the increasing population, and carriers and dealers to distribute it to them.

Therefore, if you are able and willing to work, hopefully and trustingly for success, to accept it thankfully when it comes, or to work on with cheerful manly Christian spirit till better fortune attends you,' I have only to say, Welcome, may success reward your labour.

"Durban, Natal,
"June 23rd, 1874.

"It is calculated that 3,000 ounces of gold have been shipped from Natal during the last twelve months, but it is impossible to ascertain the exact quantity as much of it is not reported at the Custom House."

[NOTE BY EDITOR.—I saw at the Cape Commercial Bank, Cape Town, last winter (July, 1875), two thousand pounds' worth of dust and nuggets received from Pilgrim's Rest.]

THE GOLD REGIONS
OF
SOUTH-EASTERN AFRICA.

DISTANCES AND ROUTES.

Tables of Distances by Trochcameter—-Latitudes and Longitudes (astronomical or computed)—Heights above the Sea Level, and other observations, from PORT NATAL to the GANYANA RIVER, *via* HARTLEY's, or the POTCHEFSTROOM, RUSTENBERG, and TATI Route, free from Tsetse Fly; and return Route through the Fly country, *via* MAGHOLIQUAIN RIVER and MAKAPAN's POORT.

During the Years 1869, 1870, 1871, & 1872.

BY

THOMAS BAINES, F.R.G.S.

Also Tables of Routes from CAPE TOWN, PORT ELIZABETH, and NATAL, to the Diamond and various Gold Fields; and Routes from PRETORIA and MARTHINUS WESSELSTROOM to the EERSTELING and LYDENBURG GOLD FIELDS and to DELAGOA BAY—contributed by Messrs. WM. LEATHERN, J. MCLEAN, A. BELLVILLE, F.R.G.S., Capt. FREDK. ELTON, G. P. MOODIE, Dr. R. WILSON, Dr. GRAHAM, L. COMPTON, and other Friends.

PORT ELIZABETH.

ROUTES TO THE DIAMOND-FIELDS, AND GENERAL INFORMATION.

The fact that Port Elizabeth is *the* chief port of the Orange Free State and the Diamond-fields is now clearly established. The bulk of the goods consumed in these regions is obtained from this place. Most mercantile firms here have branch establishments at the Fields, and the largest number of diamonds is exported from Port Elizabeth. Considerable increase in the trade statistics of this port is therefore observable.

The following is a detailed statement of the Cape Town, Natal, and Port Elizabeth routes.

No. 1.—THE CAPE TOWN ROUTE.

	Miles.	Altitudes
To Wellington (town)	45	—
Ceres (town), through Bain's Kloof and Mitchell's Pass	38	1,560 ft.
Karroopoort	31	2,460 ,,
Grootrivier (Great River)	36	—
Zoutkloof	45	—
Bloedrivier	48	—
Uitkyk	48	—
Beaufort West	37	2,930 ft.
Waaifontaen	46	—
Richmond	76	—
(Beaufort to Richmond *via* Murraysburg, 20 miles more)		—
Hanover	35	—
Phillipstown	42	—
Saltpan's Drift, Orange River	54	—
Jacobsdal (village)	54	3,200 ft.
Pniel Mission Station	36	—
Total	666	

This is undoubtedly the longest route. From Zoutkloof to Saltpan's Drift (386 miles) the road is over a Karroo desert, which in certain dry seasons of the year presents considerable difficulties to travellers.

No. 2.—THE NATAL ROUTE.

	Miles.
D'Urban to Pinetown (village)	12
Halfway-house	13
Camperdown Hotel	13
Maritzburg (city)	16
Mooi River	42
Bushman's River	20
Tugela River	24
Dodd's	18
Sandspruit	16
Here cross the Drakensberg Mountains to Harrismith (village)	35
Bethlehem	52
Winburg	80
Widow Vissagie's Drift, Vetrivier	45
Branch road on right to Bloemhof	54
Boshof	39
Upper Klipdrift	31
Total	510

To reach D'Urban necessitates travelling by sea 500 miles further than Port Elizabeth, and transport thence to the Fields is more difficult and expensive than from Algoa Bay.

No. 3.—THE PORT ELIZABETH ROUTES.

GREAT PASSENGER CART ROUTE FROM PORT ELIZABETH TO THE DIAMOND-FIELDS BY COBB & CO.'S COACHES.

	Miles.
From Port Elizabeth to Grahamstown	84
Graham's Town to Hellpoort	15
Hellpoort to Carlisle Bridge	12
Carlisle Bridge to Fish River Randt	14¼
Fish River Randt to Goba	16
Goba to Baviaan's River	12
Baviaan's River to Daggaboersnek	7½
Daggaboersnek to Blaauwkrantz	10
Blaauwkrantz to Cradock	21
Cradock to Mechau's	18
Mechau's to Collett's	14
Collett's to De Keur	12
De Keur to Schoengezigt	16
Schoengezigt to Maccassarsfontein	16
Macassarsfontein to Rietkuil	12
Rietkuil to Groenefontein	7
Groenefontein to Colesberg	15
Colesberg to Roos' pont (Orange River)	16
Roos' pont to Phillippolis	17
Phillippolis to Varkfontein	24
Varkfontein to Titsjespan	16
Titsjespan to Van Zyl's	15
Van Zyl's to Riet River	15
Riet River to Jacobsdal	14
Jacobsdal to Du Toit's Pan	25

Total distance by Cobb & Co.'s coaches from Port Elizabeth to the Diamond-fields... 444

No. 4.—Via PORT ELIZABETH, PAARDEPOORT & GRAAFF-REINET.

	Miles.
To Newland's accommodation-house and outspan	11
Uitenhage (town)	7
Sandfontein (chalybeate spring here)	6
Prentice Kraal (accommodation)	5
Centlivres (public outspan and hotel)	2
Blaauwkrantz do.	10
Roodewal do.	14
Koms (private outspan)	7¼
Paardepoort (hotel)	9
Witteklip (public outspan)	10¼
Driekoppen (hotel)	6
Sunday's River Drift (Noorsdoorn Plaats. When river is "down" inquire if fordable of neighbouring farmers)	11
Hubbard's (private accommodation)	6
Hobson's do.	7
Spence's Toegedacht hotel	6
Melk Rivier Drift	8
Kruidfontein (hotel and mineral baths)	15

Carried over... 141

ITINERARY. 167

	Miles.
Brought over	141
Sunday's River (two drifts. Should the river be full, there is a municipal road to the right, round the bend, into the town of Graaff-Reinet)	8
There is a free outspan on the town commonage, which extends to Pienaar's River—from Graaff-Reinet to top of Ondeberg, where there is an hotel, plenty of water, and a free outspan, is	11
Road forks to right beyond hotel	1
Left going to Murraysburg.	
Poortje (water)	
Riviertje (water and free outspan)	
Fick's Hotel do.	35
Zuurplaats (water)	
Nieuweberg do.	
Widow Echardt's (private accommodation)	6
Hanover (village)	41
Philipstown do.	41
Saltpan's Drift (on Orange River—store)	54
Jacobsdal (village)	54
Puiel Mission Station	36
Total	428

No. 5.—Via ZUURBERG & CRADOCK.

Port Elizabeth—

	Miles.
To Zwartkop's Bridge Hotel	8
Clark's Hotel and outspan, Coega Drift	7½
Brak River (free outspan)	2¼
Tunbridge's Hotel, Addo Drift, Sunday's River (blacksmiths and waggonmakers)	14
(Free outspans both sides of the river.)	
Koomie River	11
(Free outspan at Brakkloof)	
Stubbles' (free outspan)	6
Matthew's Hotel, top of Zuurberg	2
Boontjes River (free outspan)	2
Webster's Hotel, foot of Zuurberg	9
(Smith and waggonmaker here—left hand road to Somerset, via Beenleegte and Karreebosch, 48 miles.)	
Webster's to Barry's Hotel, Little Fish River	14
Moordenaarsgat (hotel and outspan)	11
Maskell's Hotel, Roodewal	15
Ferguson's Hotel, Cookhuis Bridge (outspan)	2
Daggaboersnek (hotel and outspan)	23
Blaauwkrantz	11
Cradock (town)	19
Colesberg (town)	108
Fauresmith do.	70
Jacobsdal do.	65
Puiel	36
Total	436

No. 6.—Via GRAHAM'S TOWN & QUEEN'S TOWN.

Port Elizabeth— Miles.
By passenger cart in one day to Graham's Town... 86

Graham's Town to Queen's Town, viá King William's Town, once a week, in two days.

  Miles.
1st day. Graham's Town to King William's Town, by Breakfast Vley and Debe Nek (good accommodation along the route) ... 70
2nd day. King William's Town to Queen's Town, by Frankfort, Grey Town, and Tylden (good accommodation) 100

Graham's Town to Queen's Town, viá Fort Beaufort, once a week.

1st day. To Fort Beaufort by Fort Brown and Koonap Bridge (good accommodation) 46
2nd day. To Queen's Town, by Balfour, Katberg, and Whittlesea (good accommodation) 75
Stage 1. Queen's Town to Burghersdorp... 80
Stage 2. Burghersdorp to Bethulie 40
Stage 3. Bethulie to Fauresmith 60
Stage 4. Fauresmith to Du Toit's Pan 70

The road is almost a perfect flat, consisting of grassy plains, with game abundant. From Du Toit's Pan to Pniel and Klipdrift run daily passenger carts.

Total distance—
  Queen's Town to Du Toit's Pan through permanent grass the whole way 250
Total distance—
  Port Elizabeth to Du Toit's Pan 457

Another route from Queen's Town proceeds through Dordrecht, Aliwa North, Smithfield, and Reddersburg, to Du Toit's Pan and Pniel.

A dispassionate examination of the subject proves undoubtedly that it is the interest of all travellers proceeding to the diamond country to come to Algoa Bay. Here they will find the most flourishing town of the South African continent. Every comfort and accommodation can be secured, as well as great facilities for passengers, by the excellent public conveyances of Cobb & Co., over routes passing through well-watered, civilized country, the first of which is *two hundred and thirty-eight miles shorter than that from Cape Town, and eighty-two miles shorter than that from Natal.* The fact that the Diamond-fields, the Free State, and the Northern Districts of the Cape Colony are supplied with nine-tenths of their imported goods from Port Elizabeth shows, first, that the route is the shortest and the best from the coast; and second, that it is the most travelled, and, therefore, the one on which the greatest facilities for the transport of passengers and goods must always be found.

It is a mistake for persons from Europe or America to burden themselves with articles which they may think necessary at the Fields, as they can all be purchased at moderate rates in the principal towns of the Colony and at the Fields.

The South African Gold-fields, which are specially referred to in a separate section, are reached from Port Elizabeth viá the Diamond-fields, whence they are regular conveyances. From Delagoa Bay they are distant 120 miles. The climate of Delagoa Bay is dangerous during the summer months.

ROUTE No. 7.

Distances from Port Elizabeth viâ Hope Town and the Diamond Fields to Tati —the Southern or Victoria and Albert Gold Fields.

	Miles.
Port Elizabeth to Hope Town—375 to 400 miles, viz.:—	375
Kruid Fontein	25
Backhouse	18
Campbell	18
Doncé	8
Pap Kuil	16
Daniels Kuil	16
Koning (water between Daniels Kuil and Koning	30
Kuruman, late the station of Rev. R. Moffatt (New Lattakoo)	22
Mathuarin	16
Takoon (3 waters between Mathuarin and Takoon)	19
Little Chuie	19
Loharon	20
Moritemo	18
Great Chuie	10
Sitlagole	18
Maritsani	16
Molopo	16
Mashuani	16
Letsa ya Motlopé	8
Malao Hills	8
Kange (Khanjie) Ba-Wangketso	18
Moshupa	16
Moshupa River	8
Sechelistown Ba-Kwena (they of the crocodile)	18
Kopong	19
Bomminigani	24
Bo-atlanami	21
Lepepe	16
Moshue	21
Kurubete	8
Ba-Mangwato	20
Molachue	24
Mitlue	6
Tanani	8
Chakani	10
Limunwie	10
Palachue	12
Seruli river	22
Gokwe	20
Lotlakani	6
Motlotsi (Macloutsie River)	14
Shasha (Great Shasa River)	20
Tati Settlement—Southern or Victoria and Albert Gold Fields	8
Ramoqueban river, N.E. boundary of Tati district	20
Total	1081

Port Elizabeth to Tati settlement, 1,061 miles.
From the observations of Messrs. J. E. H. Chapman and J. A. Bell.

ROUTE No. 8.

Summary of Distances, &c., from Port Natal to the Northern Gold Fields, Matabili Land, by Hartley's Road, via Ba-Mangwato and Tati (clear of Tsetse).

PLACE.	Trocheameter. Miles. Fur.		Latitude. Deg. Min.		Longitude. Deg. Min.		Height in feet above Sea Level.
Outer Anchorage, Natal Bay ...	—	—	29	53	31	4	—
Landed at Point, Port Natal ...	—	—	29	52	31	1	10
By rail to Durban ...	2	0	29	51	31	0	22
Pietermaritzburg by Welsh's bus	54	0	29	35	30	23	2,080
Harry Smith, Orange Free State	148	6	28	16	29	5	4,950
Cross Vaal River at Lause's Drift into Trans-Vaal	130	6	26	52	28	38	4,408
Top of Plaat Berg	—		—		—		6,019
Potschefstroom Mooi River (Coulson's)	85	4	26	43	27	33	3,900
One mile S.E. of Rustenburg ...	89	4	25	41	27	39	3,367
Cross Marico River at Junction with Limpopo	121	5	24	10	27	3	2,676
At Cross Roads, Ba-Mangwato Hills	95	6	23	6	26	58	2,750
Cross Tati River, near Limpopo Company's Store	156	3	21	28	27	51	2,623
Cross Sawpit Spruit of Mangwe River	59	4	20	44	28	13	3,470
Manyamis, outpost of Matabili ...	11	0	20	37	28	19	3,470
Inyati Mission Station, London Society	88	2	19	40	29	13	4,115
Cross Gwaito River, over S.W. boundary	54	7	19	11	29	50	3,792
Hartley Hill, between Um Vuli and Simbo Rivers	115	3	18	11	30	49	3,798
Ganyana River, S.W. side, our N.E. boundary	37	1	17	44	30	41	3,953
	1,251	6					
To Maghoondas, Mashona Village, approximate	35	0	17	33	30	17	
Total distance from Port Natal ...	1,286	0					

INDEPENDENT DISTANCES.

Hartley Hill to Umtigesi's Village	92	0	18	47	31	46	4,060
Hartley Hill to Willie's Grave ...	13	0	18	16	30	59	—
Hartley Hill down Um Vuli River	25	0	18	1	30	31	3,154
Hartley Hill to abandoned Gold Workings	21	0	18	0	30	36	—
Hartley Hill to Workings, resumed by Mashona, near Maghoonda's	60	0	17	31	30	22	—
Zumbo on North of Zambesi ...	180	0	15	37	30	32	1,440
Tette, Portuguese Town on Zambesi	236	0	16	9	33	28	—
Thence to Quillimane River mouth	270	0	18	0	37	0	—
Hartley Hill to Quillimane River mouth	506	0	—		—		—
Sofala River mouth	290	0	20	12	34	50	—

ROUTE No. 9.

Distances from Natal, via Greytown, Utrecht, Marthinus-Wesselstroom, Pretoria, Nylstroom, Makapan's poort, to the Marabastadt, the Eersteling, the Tati, and the Northern Gold Fields (with distance thence to Sofala), observed by T. BAINES, F.R.G.S.

PLACE.	Trochcameter. Miles. Fur.	Lat. Deg. Min.	Longitude. Deg. Min.	Height in feet.	REMARKS.
From Point-Port, Natal	0 0	29 52	31 1	10	The distance from Durban may be found by adding 5¼ miles to the distance from Pietermaritzburg.
To Durban by rail	2 0	29 52	31 0	22	Per Welsh's 'bus.
Pietermaritzburg, Plugh Hotel	54 0	29 35	30 23	2,080	Another road goes via Newcastle & Marthinus-Wesselstroom
Greytown, corner of M. Handley's Store	45 3	29 3	30 35	—	After crossing Buffalo River, first town in Trans-vaal Republic—Coal.
Utrecht (drift oppositre the town)	115 4	27 37	30 24	3,526	
Marthinus-Wessel-Stroom	35 6	27 22	30 22	5,300	On east side of Church—grassy highlands, no trees.
Vaal River, or Likwa Retief's Drift	49 6	26 51	29 58	4,703	A road goes north-north-west to Marabastadt, and one north-east to Lydenburg.
Pretoria, Mr. A. Brodrick's, Church Sq.	133 6	25 44	28 25	4,007	Seat of Government, Trans-vaal Republic.
Oosterhuysin's Poort, 3¼ m. S. of Nylstroom	86 1	24 46	28 38	—	Marabastadt, 159 miles, 4 furlongs, 234 yards. Eersteling 152 miles, 4 fathoms.
Moordenaars Drift, Nylstroom River	47 5	24 16	29 16	—	The town of Nylstroom is 3 miles, 6 furlongs, 80 yards, 2 feet 3 inches, N.N.E. Latitude, 24 deg., 42 min., 36 secs. At Mr. Van Nespen's house.
Makapan's Village, North of Poort	11 1	24 9	29 16	—	South of Makapan's Poort. Thorns near Polgieter's Rust, abandoned village.
Maghaliquain River, north-west side	62 6	23 27	28 54	—	The Tsetse fly extends from south-east of Maghaliquain to Shasha.
Limpopo River, south side	90 6	22 37	28 38	1,935	Granite quartz, palms, thorns, castor-oil plant, Tsetse fly.
Maeloutsie River, north bank	67 6	21 57	28 35	2,094	Broad sandy river, water in places.
Shasha River, south bank	28 2	21 38	28 39	2,359	Tati is 54 miles west-north-west.
Lee's House, Mangwe River	85 4	20 44	28 13	3,580	Here we join the main road north of the house. Tati is 59 miles, 4 furlongs, 115 feet S.S.W. Granite and quartz reefs, well wooded.
Mangamis, Outpost of Matabili	11 0	20 37	28 19	3,470	Granite kopjies, well wooded.

ROUTE No. 9.—Continued.

Inyati Mission, London Society ...	88	3	19 40 29 13	4,115	Highland—few thorns and proteas and other trees. English wheat grows.
Cross Gwailo R. Quartz Reefs, well wooded	51	7	19 11 20 50	3,792	South-west boundary of country given me by Lo Bengula for mining purposes.
Hartley Hill, my house ...	115	3	18 11 30 49	3,798	Between Um Vuli River and Sembo Rivulet.
Ganyana river, south-west side ...	37	1	17 44 30 41	3,953	North-east boundary of country given me by Lo Bengula for mining purposes. The whole of this country abounds in auriferous gold reefs and ancient gold diggings.
Port Natal to Ganyana River ...	1223	4	0 0 0 0	—	
To Maçhoonda's Mashona Village, approximate distance on horseback ...	35	0	17 33 30 17		From Durban to my house on Hartley Hill, 1,183 miles, 3 furlongs, 19 yards, 2 feet 6 inches.
Total from Port Natal ...	1257	4			

I think the longitude of Marthinus Wesselstroom will be found 30 deg. 14 min., the latitude is correct.
I think the latitude and the longitude of Utrecht will be found, latitude 27 deg. 40 min., longitude 30 deg. 22 min.

ROUTE No. 10.—MISCELLANEOUS ROUTES.

	Miles	Fur.
Mr. Goodwin's house, Marabastadt, is distant from Mr. A. Brodrick's house, Church Square, Pretoria ...	159	4
Kersteling is about 11 miles back, or from Pretoria, via Turf Fontein, to Mr. Buttor's house, Kersteling	153	4
Mr. St. Vincent Erskine calculates the distance from Sofala to the hills in Umzeilas county ...	133	0
And from Umzeilas to Lo Bengula's in Matabililand in a direct line ...	180	0
	313	0
	400	0

Or in all, allowing for winding of the road, not more than ... ...

Captain Elton gives the following distances, observed during his expedition from Tati down the Limpopo, to Lorenzo Marques.

	Miles	Fur.		Geographical miles direct	
Delagoa Bay:—From Tati, lat. 21 deg. 27 min., long. 27 deg. 40 min., to Limpopo, at the affluence of Shasha River	258	4		175	
Thence with boat down the Limpopo to falls of Azime, where boat was wrecked	85	0		60	
Thence on foot to affluence of Nuuetze	187	0		119	
Thence to affluence of Lipalula River, or Olifants River (called by St. Vincent W. Erskine "the meeting of the waters") ...	174	0		110	
Thence to Lorenzo Marques, the Portugueso settlement at Delagoa Bay ...	260	0		165	
Total miles travelled	964	4	Total geographical miles	629	

ROUTE No. 10a.

Approximate distances from Natal by the shortest route through the Gold Fields of Eersteling and Marábastadt, and through the Fly country to the Northern Gold Fields; the commencement of this line is also the usual route to Lydenburg, and the Gold Fields at McMc and Pilgrim's Rest.

	Miles.	Latitude. Deg. Min.	Longitude. Deg. Min.	Height.
Durban, by omnibus to		29 52	31 0	22
Pietermaritzburg, by mail and passenger-cart to	54	29 35	30 23	2,089
Newcastle (distance by Mr. Mc Lean, who states the distance from Newcastle to McMc as 237 miles, or from Durban to McMc as 450 miles)	159	27 47	29 52	3,800
Heights, a few miles north of the town	—	—	—	3,936
Leathern's Drift, between Staander's and Retief's Drift, in Vaal River	64	26 53	29 48	4,650
Cross Pretoria Road a little west of Nazareth	—	—	—	—
Berlin Mission Station, Rev. Marensky (Cobalt Mine)	95	25 22	29 40	4,750
Malute's Kraal	37	25 5	29 37	—
Eersteling, Natalia Reef, Mr. E. Button's Farm. The first quartz crushing machinery erected in the Trans-Vaal (viâ Stryd Poort)	68	24 6	29 31	3,800 or 4,000
Marabastadt (gold reefs in vicinity)	11	23 58	29 34	—
Pass between Blaauweberg and Zoutpansberg through Fly country, probably to Commando Drift, Limpopo River, enquire for safe road of Der Venage or other hunters	125	22 20	29 10	1,700 or 1,800
Junction of Semotchie with Shasha River	54	21 38	28 39	2,359
From the Junction of Semotchie and Shasha to Tati settlement, Southern, or Victoria and Albert Gold Fields is 54 miles W.N.W.				
Lee's House, Mangwe (lat. and lon.. E. Mohr and T. Baines, crucial station)	85	20 44	28 14	3,580
Hartley Hill, my house, Northern Gold Fields	269	18 11	30 49	3,798
Gauyana River	37	17 44	30 41	3,953
Total	1078			
Total viâ Hartley's Road...	1249			
The distance from Durban to my house at Hartley Hill, by Mr. Hartley's road, safe from fly, and healthy, is 1,211 miles, 7 furlongs—say ...	1212			
By direct route, with danger of fly and fever	1078			
Difference in favour of direct route	134			

ROUTE No. 11.

Distances and Positions from Pretoria, Trans-Vaal Republic, to the Marabastadt and Eersteling Gold Fields, by

T. BAINES, F.R.G.S.

PLACE.	Trochometer. Miles. Fur.	Latitude. Deg. Min.	Longitude. Deg. Min.	Height in feet.	REMARKS.
Mr. A. Brodrick's, Church Square, Pretoria	—	25 44	28 25	4,007	Mr. G. Moodie's longitude or Pretoria is 28 deg. 35 min.
Derde (third) Poort Magaliesberg ...	7 6	25 37	28 29	—	
To outspan north of Derde Poort ...	4 1	25 35	28 29	—	Mr. W. Leathern and T. Baines, with 4-horse cart, travelling rapidly with short outspans, and very little chance for observations.
Willem Prinslo (lang Willem)	11 3	25 26	28 25	—	
Apios River, opposite Mission at Saul's Kraal, Rev. Sachso, Berlin	11 4	25 16	28 26	—	
Fienaar's River, south side	6 2	25 11	28 26	—	
Klip Fontein, Enkeldo Boom, single tree, fir	5 4	25 6	28 26	—	
Ono hour south of Sand Fontein ...	13 3	24 56	28 31	—	On the Springbok Flats.
Mr. Hainard, on Zac De Beer's Farm ...	9 5	24 50	28 34	—	Zacharius De Beer (Oude Boethie).
Olsterhuysen's Poort, north end ...	3 6	24 48	28 38	—	
To Nylstroom, Mr. Van Nishen's House, a road turning north 3 6		24 42	28 36	—	Mr. Moodie's longitude of Nylstroom is 28 deg. 50 min.
Vor Doorn's 1 6		24 41	28 35	—	
Zac De Boor's 8 7		24 42	28 43	—	Zacharias (pronounced Sakrees.)
Loop Lino to north	14 4				

ITINERARY. 175

ROUTE No. 11.—Continued.

Zacharias De Beer, pure gift	6 0	as above.	—	De Beer, Pure Gift, or Rank Poison—so named from the Makaow, or Cattle Poison, which grows on his farm or Steel Spring.
Half-mile past Modemolulu, or Melie Fontein	10 5	21 49	28 52	
150 yards short of Bad's Loop or Bath Rivulet	6 7	24 35	28 56	
Outspan on Flat	14 7	24 21	29 4	
Gna Boom, Euphorbia Fontein... ...	3 6	24 21	29 6	
West side of Moordennai's Drift on the Nylstroom, marked tree	12 2	21 16	29 16	The Nile River or Magholiquain, i.e., fierce Crocodile—flows to Limpopo Village, abandoned during war with Makapan and other tribes, about 1869.
Carl Smit's House, Pieter Potgieter's Rust	7 2	24 11	29 18	Quartz Reefs and Clay Slate.
Rivulet in Kloof	6 1	44 9	29 23	
Past Yzerberg to Turf Fontein	12 0	24 2	29 30	4,882	Yzerberg, or Iron Mountain, affects the compass several miles.
Mr. Goodwin's House, Marabastadt ...	6 0	23 58	29 31	—	Perhaps six houses in Main Street.
Pretoria to Marabastadt	159 5				
Back to Mr. Button's at Eersteling 11		24 6	—	3,800 or 4,000	Makaria Reef, very rich quartz, and alluvial workings.
To Turf Fontein 4	0 7				
Pretoria to Eersteling, viâ Turf Fontein	152 4				

ROUTE No. 12.

Distances from Pretoria to Eersteling, via Kameel Poort or Eastern road, with light or waggon travelling at least 3 miles per hour, or more, say 3¼, CAPT. F. ELTON *and 25 others.*

	Hours.	Min.
From Pretoria ...		
Piennar's River drift ...	3	0
Grey's Farm and Store, Fransche Poort ...	1	0
Carl Minnoar's, cross two spruits and spruit near farm ...	1	20
De Waal's Farm, Elands River taking left-hand road ...	2	15
Hodgson's Farm, cross Hartebeeste River ...	2	0
Next spruit ...	2	50
Cross do. ...	2	35
Cross Kameel River, good drift ...	2	0
Through Kameel Poort ...	2	15
Spruits of Elands River, Makapan's range above Sebedelis can be seen ...	3	20
To Elands River, good drift, runs to Olifants River ...	2	20
Dronk Fontein (Kraal oxen on account of lions), bush country ...	2	50
Pan, on right, dry at end of winter ...	3	40
Klip Fontein, on left, dries in very dry seasons ...	2	5
To Sebedelis Kraal, through bush to intermediate water ...	6	50
Cross Inkumpi River, or Sebedelis River, drift good, descent stony	0	55
Through Melie Gardens to spruit of Inkumpi, Stryd Poort ...	1	40
Cross spruit three times to Bath spruit, clear stream, blue granite	1	50
Venter's Farm, cross spruit steep, in and out, but not bad ...	1	30
Button's Farm, Eersteling or Girslling Gold Field, Natalia Reef	1	40
	47	55
Taken at 3 miles per hour ...	3	0
Gives miles ...	142	0

In comparing this with my route along the Nylstroom, Capt. Elton has inadvertently added the 11 miles from Marabastadt to Eersteling, making my distance 170½ miles, instead of deducting 7 miles, which should make it only 152½ from Pretoria, viâ Turf Fontein to Eersteling.

ROUTE No. 13.

Distances from Durban, Natal, to Lydenburg and the Geelhoutboom, or McMc and Pilgrim's Rest Gold Fields; Mr. WILLIAM LEATHERN'S *route.*

	Miles.	Feet above the sea
From Durban to Pietermaritzburg is accounted	54	Durban 22 Pietermaritzburg 2,080
Plough Hotel, Pietermaritzburg, to corner of Mr. Handley's Store, Greytown, by trocheameter (T. Baines)	45½	Town Hill 3,700 Kelly Hill 5,000
Utrecht, at the drift opposite the town (T. Baines)	115½	3,526
Marthinus Wesselstroom, east of the church (T. Baines)	35¾	5,300
Lat. 27 deg. 22 min. Total	250¾	
Height above the sea 5,300 feet	—	6 miles north
There are inns along the road as far as Marthinus Wesselstroom	—	5,727
Marthinus Wesselstroom in Wakkerstroom District to Mr. Buhrman's—Vaal River	42	
John Joubert's	14	
Spruit north of Gideon Joubert's	10¼	
Mr. Clarke's, at Lake Chrissie, New Scotland	15	Klipstafel is 6,328
Here the track crosses the road from Pretoria to Dideen and Delagoa Bay, and attains an elevation of more than 6,000 feet; the sources of Vaal River, Olifants River, and Umkomati, or Manice, or King George River, rising from Klipstafel, a few miles west		The high lands are called 7,000
Flat up in the hill near Vander Merwe's	15	
Gabriel Stoltz, Komatie River	17	
Potgieter's on Elands spruit	13¼	
Blaawebosch Kraal spruit	4¼	
Christian Vourie	7½	
Top of Krokodil Rivier Hill	3	
To this side of Krokodil Rivier	11⅓	
Sarel Vilgoens	13½	
Lydenburg	2	5,825
Total miles	419¾	
Road to McMc—		
Lydenburg, east to Spitzkop		7,100
Thence north to Geelhoutboom or McMc		4,750
Total	42	(A. Bellvill*)
Road to Pilgrim's Rest—		
Lydenburg, north, cross Spekboom River to Kruyger's Post	2	Perhaps a little lower
Thence south-east to John Muller's		
Cross Blyde (Blythe or Joyful) River to Pilgrim's Rest	1	
Total	38	

ROUTE No. 14.

Route from Durban, Natal, to the Lydenburg Gold Fields; Mr. J. McLean's *route.*

	Miles.	Feet above the sea.
Durban to Maritzburg, by omnibus, numerous Hotels along the road	54	Durban 22 2,080
Maritzburg to Umgeni Waterfall, Howick Hotel	14	3,230
		Houtbosch Raand
Currie's Hotel (below Houtbosch Raand)	12	4,400
Mooi River, Helen Bridge Hotel	12	4,230
Bushman's River do. Estcourt, Alice Bridge Hotel	22	3,562
Colenso, Tugela River, drift and pont (3,436 ?) Hotel	22	3,000
Ladysmith Hotel	18	3,353
Knight's, no accommodation	15	
Thomas's Hotel	14	
Inyangane, George's Hotel	16	
Newcastle Hotel (height a few miles north of the town)	14	3,936
	—— 213	
Cruikshank's Mill, no accommodation	9	
Lang's ditto	9	varying
Harrison's ditto	12	5,000
Castrop's Sand Spruit Store	9	or 6,000
Robertson's Store	18	
	—— 57	

New Scotland route—

Swart's, no accommodation	10	
Vaal River, Buhrmann, no accommodation	10	
J. Joubert ditto	14	
G. Joubert ditto	9	
Clarke's, Lake Chrissie ditto (Klipstapel)	18	6,323
Stein ditto	10	
Vander Merwie ditto	15	
Cross Umkomatie River to Stoltz ditto	7	
Potgieter's ditto	12	
Vouries ditto	9	
Crocodile River	18	
Lydenburg	18	5,825
	—— 150	

Total distance—Durban to Lydenburg	420	
Lydenburg to De Klerks	16	
Thence to McMc	14	
	—— 30	4,750

Summed up thus... 450

Durban to Newcastle	213
Robertson's	57
Lydenburg	150
McMc	30
	450

Lydenburg to Pilgrim's Rest, Villiers & Truchard's Farms	20
Pilgrim's Rest to McMc	10
McMc to Delagoa Bay	150

ITINERARY. 179

ROUTE No. 15.

Distances from Pretoria to Lydenburg, given me by Mr. W. Leathern,
(six miles per hour on horseback).

PLACE.	Miles.	Latitude. Deg. Min.	Longitude. Deg. Min.	Height.
		APPROXIMATE.		
Pretoria, Church Square, latitude, Stellar; Boiling point, 204·4; Barometer, 26·22	—	25 44	28 25	4,007
To Diedrick Muellers, where New Scotland Road goes south-east (see preceding Table)	57¾	25 46	29 16	—
Olifants Rivier	17	25 37	29 35	—
Nazareth Berlin Mission Station (Cobalt Mine, reported Gold)	11	25 32	29 43	—
Van Wyk's Spruit (the house 1 mile south)	18	25 29	29 53	—
Botha (cross Bothasberg)	12½	25 27	30 9	—
Nicholaas Grobler, near Steal Poort River	9	25 26	30 23	—
Groote Zuckerbosch Kop, near Steinkampsberg	15	25 23	30 31	—
Enter long valley source of Spekboom River	15	25 18	30 40	—
Down the Valley, cross the River five times	12	25 11	30 44	—
Lydenburg (Lat., by St. Vincent W. Erskine)...	12	25 4	30 52	5,825
Total ...	179¼			

	Miles.	Lat. Deg. Min.	Long. Deg. Min.	Height.
Lydenburg to McMc, J. McLean	30	—	—	—
Do. to Pilgrim's Rest, do.	20	24 49	31 2	—
From Pretoria to Nazareth is reckoned	90	—	—	—
Nazareth to Lydenburg	90	—	—	—
	180			

Distances from the Diamond Fields to Lydenburg Gold Fields, given me by Alfred Belville, F.R.G.S.

	Miles.	Latitude. Deg. Min.	Longitude. Deg. Min.	Height.
Diamond Fields to Potschefstroom	204	26 43	27 44	3,900
Pretoria	94	25 44	28 25	4,007
Lydenburg, viâ Bolsabelo, M.S. ...	158	—	—	5,825
Total	456	25 4	30 52	—
Lydenburg to eastern edge of Drakensberg	14	—	—	—
Devil's Knuckles	6	—	—	—
McMc	21	—	—	—
Total Diamond Fields to McMc	497			

Returning, Mr. Belville crossed Olifants River in latitude 25·4·30.

N 2

ROUTE No. 16.

Distances from Pretoria, Trans-Vaal Republic, to Delagoa Bay, given me by Mr. William Leathern.

	Miles.	Latitude. Deg. Min.	Longitude. Deg. Min.	Height above the Sea.
		APPROXIMATE.		
Pretoria, seat of Government, Trans-Vaal Republic, on sources of Apies Rivier, south of Maghaliesberg, observed at Mr. Brodrick's, Church Square. Boiling point 204·4. Barometer 26·62		Stellar. 25 44	28 25	4,007
Van Meulins (on horseback, 6 miles per hour)	6	25 44	28 31	—
Ballantine, cross Pienaars River	4¾	25 46	28 37	—
Botha, in Poort, south of Grays at Fransche Poort	5	25 47	28 43	4,500(?)
Marthinus Prinslo, cross Honden (or Dog) Spruit	15	25 50	28 55	—
Solomon Prinslo	3	25 49	28 57	—
Salamo Vermaak	9	25 47	29 4	—
Cross Wilge or Willow River, source of Rhenoster River	6	25 46	29 9	—
Piet Forster	6	25 49	29 16	—
Diedrick Muller, a branch road, goes N.E. to Lydenburg	3	25 46	29 19	—
Isaac Holsthuysen's	12	25 50	29 32	—
Piet Holsthuysen's, cross Olifants Rivier	3	25 51	29 35	—
Lydenburg Road crosses this track	21¼	25 59	29 52	—
Cross Little Olifants River	4	26 1	29 55	—
Lodewyk de Jager	9	26 3	30 3	—
De Toto	9	26 6	30 11	—
Marthinus Steyn, Thee Spruit	4	26 7	30 14	—
Clarke's, at Lake Chrissie, New Scotland	16	26 10	30 26	6,328
Here cross the road from Natal to Lydenburg — Hamilton (New Scotland) — Umpolosi River	10	26 15	30 36	—
Stony Spruit (with waggon, about 2½ miles per hour)	6	26 15	30 43	—
Jas. Mac Arthur's, Stony Spruit	6	26 14	30 47	—
Next outspan (not far from Holnek?)	5	26 15	30 52	—
Spruit of Umbolosi — beginning to descend	10	26 17	30 57	—
Elandsridge, Dumbarton — gentle descent	6	26 19	31 2	—
Batabelas Baaken — the hill N.E.	9	26 22	31 9	—
Hell Gate, near the borders of New Scotland	5½	26 24	31 11	—
Sapan's Kraal	6	26 26	31 14	—
Buffel's Nek	5	26 29	31 15	—
Buffel's Kraal	6	26 32	31 16	—
Norbombas Flat	4	26 35	31 16	—
Dideen, where Songhaan lives	7	26 39	31 15	—
Umbolosi, Mnyama Poort, in Lebombo	60	26 15	31 56	1,300
Bemban River (Mattol or Dundas River)	35	25 58	32 31	—
Lorenzo Marques, English River, Delagoa Bay	9	25 58	32 37	—
Total	325¾			

Mr. Moodie states the distance as—
Pretoria to New Scotland ... 130 — — —
Thence to Delagoa Bay ... ... 110 Miles — —

Total 240

The Railroad from Delagoa Bay to Pretoria, on the line explored by G. P. Moodie, will probably pass through Umbolosi, M'nyama Poort, up Elandsrid ge, near Hol Nek, and along this line to Pretoria. Probably Mr. Moodie avoided the turn south to the Dideen. This line now surveyed by Mr. R. Hall.

ROUTE No. 17.

Distances from Marthinus Wesselstroom in Wakkerstroom District, Trans-Vaal Republic, to Delagoa Bay, given me by Mr. W. Leathern.

PLACE.	Miles.	Latitude. Deg. Min.	Longitude. Deg. Min.	Height.
Durban, Port Natal to	—	29 52	31 1	22
Marthinus Wesselstroom (T. Baines)	250¾	27 22	{ 30 22 } { 30 13 }	5,300
Pass Pietstoup, Hendrick, Vesagie, Carlstoup, and Veldtman, under Slang Apiesberg, to cross the Umkonto or Assegai River, good drift	30	27 7	30 38	5,000
Pass Shobbakin, Audries Botha, Derby (late Mr. McCorkindale's residence), to Umkompies River	27	26 56	30 57	—
Dwandwar (an Amaswasi Chief) ...	12	26 49	31 5	—
Cross Great Usutu River	3	26 47	31 7	—
Cross Little Usutu River	12	26 41	31 14	—
Dideen, Kraal of the King Songhaan Erskine makes Dideen lat. 26·34, lon. 31.20.	3	26 39	31 15	—
Cross Umtelaan and Umyelegasi River, near Maloys Kraal ...	15	26 29	31 23	—
Cross Umbolosi Umthlope (white Umbolosi) to Martin's Well ...	3	26 27	31 25	—
Large Mountain near Umlebar ...	6	26 23	31 28	—
Cross Umbolosi Mnyama (black Umbolosi)	6	26 20	31 34	—
On the Great Umbolosi, I think Osborne's "Gold Valley" is on a tributary some miles N.W. Cross Umbolosi six times in three hours	18	26 13	31 47	—
Umbolosi Mnyama Poort, in Lebomba Range	12	26 15	31 56	1,300
Umbolosi Mnyama Drift	21	26 7	32 12	—
Cross Umbolosi Mnyama ninth and last time	9	26 3	32 20	—
Bamban River, Mattol River, Dundas River	12	25 58	32 31	—
Lorenzo Marques, on English River, Delagoa Bay	9	25 58	32 37	—
Total Marthinus Wesselstroom to Lorenzo Marques	198			
Durban to Marthinus Wesselstroom	250¾			
Total Durban, viâ Marthinus Wesselstroom to Lorenzo Marques, Delagoa Bay	448¾—say 450 Miles.			

ROUTE No. 18.

Trocheametric Distances from Pilgrim's Rest to Delagoa Bay, by D. R. Wilson (from America), and Dr. Graham. Sketch of road by Mr. Compton.

Location	Miles from Pilgrim's Rest.	Lat. Deg. Min.	Long. Deg. Min.	Height in feet.
		Approximate.		
Pilgrim's Rest is a valley on the sources of the Blyde (Blythe or Joyful) River, about 10 miles from Treur, or Weeping River, so called because a party of the early Dutch emigrants lost each other at the one and re-joined at the other, say between 1836 and 1840 (lat. and lon. approx., Bellville)	—	24 49	31 2	—
McMc, on source of Badenhoff's Spruit, Sabia River	10	24 54	31 1	4,750
Sabia Falls, 150 feet, on Sabia River	27	24 59	31 4	3,600
First Camp on Spruit, north of Spitzkop	33	25 4	31 8	—
Second, west of a ridge (whose highest point is 4,900 feet)	39	25 5	31 12	—
Sand River	48	25 7	31 25	2,520
Water, red-topped grass	55½	25 10	31 29	—
South of Pretoriaskop (fly and fever prevalent south-east of this)	59	25 12	31 31	—
North of Saddleback or Long Mountain, water, 300 yards south-west	68	25 16	31 35	—
Compton's Old Camp, south of Buffelskop, water in rocks	76¼	25 21	31 37	—
Big tree and water hole	83	25 23	31 41	—
Camp Thankful, water holes, spiked grass	90¼	25 26	31 46	1,370
Krokodil Rivier, at Sebohomo, 90 yards wide and 4 feet deep, coarse sand and nodules of bed rock making eddies. Found gold in sand of creek and on bed rock—Dr. Wilson. Probable gold field—Dr. Graham. (More than probable fever—T. Baines)	95	25 28	31 47	1,350
Komati Rivier, Umkomogazi UmkomanziMauice, or King George River, 24 yards wide and 3 feet deep, quick sand, near Fabini	111	25 33	31 57	1,225
Compton and Hampton	119¼	25 35	32 3	—
The Divide, Portuguese and Trans-Vaal Boundary, on Libombo range, treaty of July, 1869	122¼	25 36	32 4	1,545
Black rock hole, granite, little stream	125¼	25 38	32 6	1,300
Over last wide topped range, low, flat	135¼	25 41	32 13	—
Kafirtown	157¾	25 49	32 26	—
Talala's Town, on Matloe or Madolo Marshy River, 8 or 10 miles further cross a stream with bridge of iron and wood running in near Lorenço Marques	162¾	25 52	32 29	—
Lorenço Marques, Portuguese town on English River, Delagoa Bay, surrounded by sand and mud banks, and encircled by water at high tides; cocoa nut and other trees about the town	173¾	25 58	32 37	—

Great caution should be exercised in using this road. I believe the only safe months are June, July, and August, and perhaps the first half of September; in the latter part of September, and to May inclusive, travellers are liable to fever, from which eight or ten persons had died up to March, 1874, and many were ill. The Tsetse fly abounds in this low country nearly to Pretoriaskop. Mr. Macdonald's expedition lost, I think, 114 oxen, and Mr. Arrowsmith reports a loss of 14. Donkeys are generally safe, but not quite so here. Goods are taken 10 or 12 miles up Matloe River in boats, and small slavers used to go 40 miles up the Manice, but the best remedy would be a railway up the ridge by Hal Nek, in New Scotland.

ROUTE 19.

Distances, Positions, &c., from Walvisch (or Whale-fish) Bay, on the West Coast of South Africa, to Lake Ngami, the Victoria Falls, and my house at Logier Hill, Zambesi. CHAPMAN'S *Trocheameter distances.*

PLACE.	Trocheameter. Miles Fur. Yards	Latitude. Deg. Min.
Walvisch Bay	—	22 53
Ookiep	36 0 166	22 43
Tincas	31 3 115	
Poortjie, or Pass Ouanies	10 1 157	
Platte Klip	13 0 120	
Witte Water	12 1 55	
Tsoubis	11 6 58	
Otjimbengue	21 7 41	22 20
	136 5 52	
Otjimonjebba	33 7 211	
Otjikango Katitie, Little Barmen	9 0 90	
Great Barmen	5 2 149	22 5
Otjithebba	15 0 0	
Gous da Gous	16 7 107	
Eikhams (warm springs) ...	12 0 120	22 23
Carry forward from Walvisch Bay to Eikham's	229 1 0	

Distances from Walvisch Bay to Victoria Falls and Logier Hill. From Great Barmen. Distances by CHAPMAN. *Latitudes by* BAINES.

PLACE.	Trocheameter. Miles Fur. Yards.	Latitude. Deg. Min.	Height.
Two miles beyond (near Wendhoek, formerly Wesleyan Mission, now abandoned)...	2 0 0	22 33	
One and a-half miles further ...	1 6 0	22 33	
Great Cheek Kraal, south of Elephant River	18 0 0	22 27	
Mount Secace, Kleine Bakjies, or Little Cheek	17 0 0	22 30	
Wegdraai, or Turnaway Bend...	11 0 0	22 29	
Pass through Witvlei, or Adullam	2 4 0	—	
Outspan, 2 or 3 miles beyond ...	2 4 0	22 25	
Trek all day and night, and reach Gobabies, or Elephant Fountain	26 direct	22 26	
Twass, from Elephants Fountain	48 2 132	22 35	
Otjikeko Appollos's werft ...	—	22 31	
Onweada Onganga		22 25	
Pit nearly dry		22 24	
Poortjie, or Small Pass ...	33 0 0		
Sand Fontein, Otjimathie ...	16 6 32		3,475
Elephant's Kloof, Otjimapa ...	9 4 144	22 11	3,525
Pit, no water	—	22 4	

PLACE.	Trocheameter. Miles Fur. Yards			Latitude. Deg. Min.		Height.
Reit Fontein, Kounobis, or Otjembende	57	1	117	21	54	3,633
Dog Hole Pit, water enough for dogs only (T. Baines) ...	8	5	2	21	56	
Along the dry river bed to Wahlberg Well, in Maramba Otjimbende, Gnathais...	24	0	201	21	56	3,600
200 yards south of Gnuegga, or Fort Funk, a pit of good water in depression of limestone	10	5	88	21	49	
Trocheameter choked with sand, say	17	0	0			
Ghanze Well in limestone, thorn grove, the water 350 yards north, the best altitudes gave 21 deg., 33 min., 14 secs.	15	4	43	21	34	
Patches of forest, dry pit! ...	12	5	52			
Thounce, Letsin, Pierie, or Wolf Fontein, the Stink Fontein of Anderson, ice at sunrise	15	0	107	21	17	
Total Eikham's to Thounce, or Stink Fontein	390	0	133			

Distances, &c., from Walvisch Bay to Victoria Falls and Logier Hill, Zambesi River, by T. BAINES.

PLACE.	Trocheameter. Miles Fur. Yards			Latitude. Deg. Min.		Height.
Thounce, or Letsia Pierie, to ...	—			21	19	
Morning Outspan	5	6	215	21	19	
Waterless Pit	5	7	165	21	14	
Koobie, the water due north 150 yards	10	5	175			
Koobie, the water 500 yards south. Observation Tree. Latitude by 12 or 14 stars. Variation 24 deg., 41 min., 27 secs. Lunar distances here.	0	4	38	21	7	3,475
Motjeerie-trees, Mahalapsie ...	5	0	0	21	4	
Outspan on flat grey sand and limestone, heavy rain ...	6	3	44			
Under a Motlopie-tree, Quarantine Vlei	6	7	26	20	59	
Total Distance from Eikham's to Quarantine Vlei ...	431	4	0			
From Maquata Hill, about a mile north of Quarantine Vlei to Seesie Vlei Scherm.	3	5	7			
A fine Vlei Massie Touka ...	6	1	109			
Bushy Vlei	7	5	176			
Pass Sebubumpi, and halt at Motenyani. Vlei, south of Lubelo Mountains	6	3	95			

ITINERARY.

PLACE.	Trocheameter. Miles Fur. Yards			Latitude. Deg. Min.		Height.
Grassy flat, with bush all round	9	7	204			
No water, 16 or 20 giraffes in sight, thick bush, found water at some distance ...	12	0	60			
Makhabana, south of Quaobic Hills	4	5	67	20	39	
Thick bush, without water ...	4	3	102			
Dry Vlei, Motjihaara-trees ...	7	2	121			
Outspan, without water ...	8	5	79			
Edge of the forest, south of Bo-tlét-le River	9	2	180			
Near Letsatsilebi's old place, south of the river, about 16 miles east of Lake Ngami	—	—	—	20	19	
Westward to Leshulatebes town at Lake	—	—	—	20	21	Baines
Ngami, 13 miles 4 furlongs 188 feet	—	—	—	20	21	Chapman.
Eastward back to our old camp	—	—	—	20	20	Livingstone.
Extra distance, by sweeping round to return, 13 miles 5 fur. 211 yards. Zougas Kraal and ferry are supposed to have been about here. Livingstone calls the river "Zouga," instead of Bo-tlét-le. From Leshulatebes town, west to Christmas-tree is 33 miles 5 fur. Chapman made the whole length of the lake 39 miles.						
From Letsatsilebi's old place to Island in river, east end ...	4	1	13			
South of river	3	4	207			
Short tract included in next distance						
South of river	5	5	36			
Pass Baobab, south of river ...	3	7	57			
Separation camp. Henry Chapman and J. A. Bell leave us here for Graham's town on the 23rd. Latitude observed on the 25th ...	—			20	9	
Pass Ma Tabbin, the Tamalukan river comes in from the north	5	7	6	20	7	
Called also Noka-e-a Lingalo (river of Lingalo)						
Thorn trees south of river ...	5	3	106			
Three-quarters of an hour stopped by heavy rain ...						
First valley like side channel of river, opposite Makata's new village	11	6	43	20	10	
Pass Samaganga's drift but keep south of river	7	5	110			
South of river	7	0	167	20	15	
Pass Samaganga's, halt at Kala Mabele (or two friends) south of river	6	4	148	20	18	

PLACE.	Trocheameter. Miles Fur. Yards			Latitude. Deg. Min.		Height.
Dora Karra, south of river	4	2	102			
Fine thorn trees, H. Chapman's old Kraal	8	3	219	20	18	
Cross the river at Khamma's ford, out-span a mile on road	4	0	72			
Near Bushman village	1	0	143	20	15	
Near Motjeerie tree	4	1	154	20	12	
Flat, with thorn trees	5	6	155	20	12	
Kill buffalo, and go on till noon north of river	5	1	28			
Moro-o-a Mahootoo, or the tree with legs, river in a sweeping curve, convex side to the north				No latitude, fever, and cloudy sky.		Waggon 2,515, River 2,455
Leave the Bo-tlet-le, which flows south-east	2	7	4			
Dense bush	6	2	20	20	12	
Ghonna, water in limestone, scanty drink for the men	0	3	175			
Dwarf palm bush, Vlei and Bushman's village	5	0	103	20	6	
Limestone country, passed the water	0	0	32			
Cross salt pans. northern Spruits of the Ntetwe	8	6	66			
North to Baobab on border of the pan	3	3	16	The Bushmen point E.N.E. to Khama Khamma.		
Clump of thorns north of the pan	2	1	41	20	6	2,675
Dwarf palm, good water, east of the salt pan	2	6	168			
Dwarf palm bush	10	1	136			
Kangyon, water half under Motjeerie tree	8	7	29	20	14	
Grove of Motjeerie and Melon patch	1	0	191			
Pass seven palms and thirty minutes beyond	6	2	20			
Under Baobab, near Kounyara	11	5	121	20	33	
Baobab, 200 yards north of Gnakou water	6	5	115	20	5	
Pass Raghopalie water	7	1	202	20	4	
Tsagobia, the water dish, 100 yards east	5	2	192	20	3	
Mahootoo Mahbe (ugly foot) north of the water	5	4	33	20	1	
Open flat with bush, a large pan north	0	4	95			
Metsebokluko (or bitter water) ¼ mile south	15	2	195	19	46	2,591
Mopani grove, sand ridge	10	0	124	19	43	
Thammaseitjie, water, W.S.W.	5	2	153	19	29	
Garuga, small pit on right, the trocheameter shews 3.0.12. too little, sand choking it, say perhaps	5	0	0			
Thorn country, vines bearing grapes in March, 1863	8	6	31	19	33	
Valley with wooded hill on left, beyond Gumkaabie	6	0	30			
Jerufa	10	1	0			
Thammafupu, water, ½ mile north-west and Leteba ¼ mile south	5	5	122	19	20	

ITINERARY.

PLACE.	Trochcameter. Miles Fur. Yards	Latitude. Deg. Min.	Height.
Thammaseitjie, the water ½ mile south	6 3 155	19 15	
Flat, with small thorns ...	11 4 37	19 6	
Large Mopani tree in forest ...	9 0 70	18 58	
Six-tree ring in valley, with Vleis in the wet season ...	8 3 30	18 55	
Vlei in open space of Mopani forest	4 2 74		
On plain with Mopani Forest 3,000 feet above the sea. Edge of the plain 3,500. Descend into valley of the Zambesi system	8 4 167	18 45	
Daka, rivulet of the Daka or Luisi River...	7 6 123	18 40	
Cross Bonka branch of Daka; cross Daka little rise near Bonka or N'Kumba ...	4 7 100	—	
Zimboya or Zibi Valley, hill on our left, one palm tree ...	10 5 192	18 33	
Pass waggon to Small River ...	5 4 63	—	
Pass through patch of fly, cross Matietsie River ...	8 0 89	18 20	
Quagga shot by Chapman ...	2 2 139		
Big tree, Bolungo River ...	8 0 134	18 23	
Break Disselboom in Spruit of N'yati River	4 4 125	—	
N'yati or Buffalo River ...	2 2 196	18 14	
Quagga shot by Chapman ...	1 1 7	—	
By waggon of Sechelis Ambassador, N'yati River, where we leave the waggon	3 3 128	18 12	
On foot, cross broad red sand hill, with Mopanies, infested by fly. Sleep under Motseebe tree, about	18 — —	18 30 / 16 0	The last probably the best.
Camp under anna-wood tree, abreast of the western end of the chasm of the Victoria Falls	7	17 55	
Camp at the Ferry above the Falls, say about two miles	2	17 54	2,460
Quarantine Vlei to Victoria Falls	497 2 190		
Walvisch Bay to Quarantine Vlei	660 3 —		
Total, Walvisch Bay to Victoria Falls...	1,157 6 185		

Summary of Distances from Walvisch Bay to Victoria Falls.

	Miles. Fur. Yds.	Latitude. Deg. Min.	
Walvisch Bay	— — —	22 53	Chapman.
	— — —	22 57	Capt. Galton.
To Eikham's	229 0 69	22 33	Baines.
Quarantine Vlei	431 3 144	20 59	Do.
Victoria Falls	497 2 190	17 55	Do.

Walvisch Bay to Victoria Falls, Total 1,157 6 183

My House on Logier Hill, about 60 miles east of the River Victoria Falls, on south side of Zambesi		18 4	Baines.
Height above the Sea, 1,550 feet		18 2	Mohr.

LONDON:
WHITE & FAWCETT, Printers, 17, Bloomfield Street, London Wall, E.C.

LEATH & ROSS, HOMŒOPATHIC CHEMISTS, LONDON.

6A.

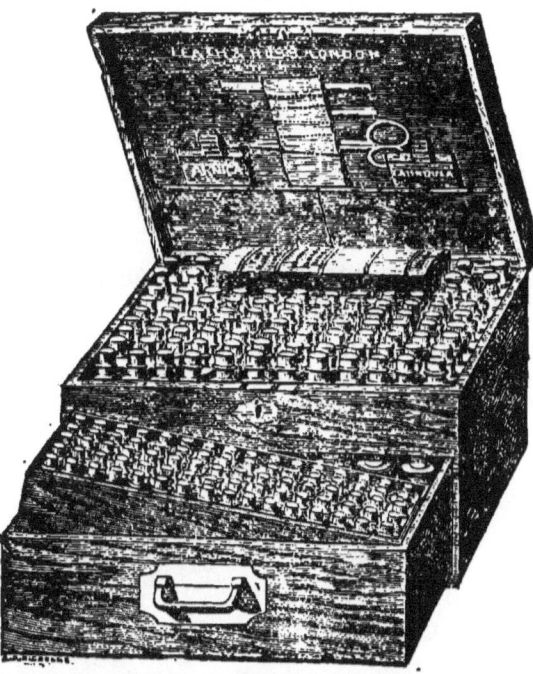

No. 6a, is a very handsome mahogany case, adapted to, and containing the new Edition of Laurie's Domestic Medicine, edited by Dr. Gutridge, and contains all the medicines that work prescribes the lid-dropping tube and top conductors scissors and tweezers, Arnica and Calendula Plaster, at the top of the case, the work handsomely bound in half, ninety-four chief remedies in 2-dram bottles; in the drawer, a tray containing the eighty remedies in the Appendix which includes the new American remedies, and all the latest additions to the Pharmacopœia. Underneath the tray are placed medicine spoons, oil silk, lint, &c., and at the back of the drawer, large bottles of the external tinctures, making altogether a most handsome case, and well suited for Missionaries owners of large estates or plantations, where numbers of hands are employed. Price, complete, £9, and sent carriage paid within the United Kingdom on receipt of a remittance for that amount.

No. 13 is a Morocco Globule case. It contains all the external and internal remedies prescribed in Laurie's Domestic Medicine, new edition. In a drawer lined silk velvet are all the external tinctures, in a sliding tray above the drawer the ninety-six remedies in the Appendix, which embrace all the latest additions to the Pharmacopœia, including the new American remedies; above are ninety-six remedies prescribed in the first part of Laurie's Domestic Medicine, in good-sized bottles; and in the lid are placed plaster and globule spoons, being a most portable and convenient case for travelling. All the Globules in this case are so prepared that four are equal to one drop of tincture. Price complete, and sent carriage paid on receipt of a remittance, for £6 6s.

LONDON:

LEATH & ROSS,

Homœopathic

Chemists,

No. 5, St. PAUL'S

CHURCHYARD,

AND 9,

VERE STREET,

OXFORD STREET.

Shippers and the Trade supplied.

Intending Purchasers will please quote the Number in ordering either of these Cases.

Full Descriptive Catalogue sent free to any part of the World.

THE GUARDIAN

FIRE AND MARINE

Insurance & Trust Company,

30, MAIN STREET,

PORT ELIZABETH.

CAPITAL ... £100,000 | RESERVED FUND £34,000

BOARD OF DIRECTORS:

J. W. SALOMON, Chairman.

F. S. Fairbridge,
A. J. Macdonald,
E. W. Engelken,

J. Walker,
W. Savage,
D. F. Stewart.

THE COMPANY UNDERTAKES

The Administration of Estates; the Agency and Management of the Affairs of Persons leaving the Colony; the Purchase and Sale of Landed Property; the Raising of Loans or the Investment of Capital.

Proposals in any of the Branches attended to daily.

MARINE POLICIES GRANTED, PAYABLE IN LONDON.

FRANCIS H. CARPENTER, Sec.

ÆGIS

ASSURANCE AND TRUST

COMPANY

OF PORT ELIZABETH

(LIMITED).

CAPITAL ... ... £125,000.

BOARD OF DIRECTORS:

A. BARSDORF, Chairman,
JOHN PATERSON, Deputy-Chairman.

| M. MACDONALD, | W. M. FARMER, |
| E. MORRIS, | A. O. HARWOOD, |

R. PETTIT.

SOLICITORS:

MESSRS. CHABAUD AND DYASON.

AUDITORS:

J. A. HOLLAND and A. WILMOT.

THE Business of this Company embraces:—Fire and Marine Insurance; the Insurance of Diamonds, Specie, and other Valuables by Inland Transport; the Guarantee of the Honesty and Integrity of Clerks and other Servants and Officials; the Administration of Estates; the Agency and Management of the Affairs of Persons leaving the Colony; the Investment of Capital; the Raising of Loans; the Sale and Puchase of Landed and other Securities.

R. S. SMITH, Secretary.

UITENHAGE
BOARD OF EXECUTORS

AND

TRUST COMPANY,

(LIMITED).

CAPITAL - - - - - - - - - £20,000

BOARD OF DIRECTORS:

F. LANGE, Esq., Chairman.

F. LEISCHING, Esq. | R. H. BLACK Esq.
S. J. VAN NIEKERK, Esq. | F. GERDS, Esq.

Auditors—H. W. BIDWELL, Esq., and JOS. REID, Esq

Trustees—F. GERDS, and F. LANGE.

Bank—Uitenhage Branch of Standard Bank.

The Company undertakes the Administration of Estates, the Agency and Management of the Affairs of Persons leaving the Colony, the Purchase and Sale of Landed Property, the Raising of Loans, or the Investment of Capital ; Fire and Life Insurances effected, &c., &c., the Collection of Accounts and Magistrate's Court Business.

HENRY N. CHASE, Secretary.

Cape of Good Hope Bank.

ESTABLISHED 1836.

DIRECTORS:
C. J. MANUEL, Esq., M.L.A., Chairman.

F. F. Rutherfoord, Esq. | Hon. J. Murison, Esq., M.L.C.
Thomas Watson, Esq. | James Ansdell, Esq.
W. J. Anderson, Esq. | Henry Reid, Esq.
C. R. Eaton, Esq. | E. M. Twentyman, Esq.

HEAD OFFICE:
74, Adderley Street, Capetown.

BRANCHES:
Port Elizabeth; Kimberley and Dutoitspan (Diamond-fields).

LONDON AGENCY:
London and Westminster Bank, Lothbury, E.C.

Drafts and Letters of Credit granted, payable in all the above-named places and in all the principal Towns in South Africa.

Advances made on approved Security, and Bills Negotiated or Forwarded for Collection.

Current Accounts opened on the same principles as those observed by other Bankers. Every person connected with the establishment signs a Declaration of Secrecy as to the accounts of its Customers.

Fixed Deposits, for long or short periods, received at rates of Interest which can be ascertained at the Head Office in Capetown, or at any of the Branches. Parties may lodge money upon an Interest Account who have no Current Account, and those who have Current Accounts may transfer any portion of their balance, for which they have no immediate use, to an Interest Account.

Colonial and other Securities of Constituents of the Bank received for safe custody, and Interest and Dividends collected as they fall due.

The Agencies of other Banks, and Parties residing at a distance, undertaken, and every description of Banking and Exchange business transacted at current rates.

W. FORSAITH,
Manager.

81, Main Street, Port Elizabeth.

THE STANDARD BANK

OF

BRITISH SOUTH AFRICA

(LIMITED).

SUBSCRIBED CAPITAL ... £2,400,000.
PAID-UP CAPITAL ... ... £600,000.
RESERVE FUND ... ... £150,000.

Head Office: 10, Clement's Lane, Lombard Street, London.

DIRECTORS.

Frederick Greene, Esq.   Daniel Mackenzie, Esq.
Geo. M. Kiell, Esq.   John T. Rennie, Esq.
Samuel Hyde, Esq.   Robert White, Esq.

Edward Wyld, Esq.

Manager . . ROBERT STEWART, Esq.
Secretary . . GEO. N. PLAYER, Esq.

BANKERS.

BANK OF ENGLAND.   THE ALLIANCE BANK, LIMITED.

Joint General Managers in } GILBERT FARIE, Esq,
the South African Colonies } H. C. ROSS, Esq.

Branches.	Managers.	Branches.	Managers.
Adelaide	M. D. Savory, Esq.	Grahamstown	Peter Gordon, Esq.
Aliwal North	R. W. Johnston, Esq	Hopetown	W. J. Nichols, Esq.
Beaufort West	C. K. Dorrington, Esq.	Kimberley (New Rush)	J. W. Harsant, Esq.
Burghersdorp	Selkirk Stuart, Esq.	King Williamstown	George H. Nitch, Esq.
Capetown	W. H. Doldge (acting)	Mossel Bay	Arthur Gates, Esq.
Cerys	J. Mitchell, Esq.	On It-stroom	J. Langermann, Esq.
Colesberg	Richard Seymour Esq.	Pietermaritzburg	F. A. Hathorn, Esq.
Cradock	W. S. Leigh, Esq.	Port Elizabeth	Lewis L. Michell Esq.
Dordrecht	J. F. Brown, Esq.	Queenstown	John E. Dell, Esq.
Durban	William Godaman Esq.	Richmond	John Maxwell, Esq.
East London	Lewis Evans, Esq.	Somerset East	F. R. Southey, Esq.
Fort Beaufort	James Tudhope, Esq.	Uitenhage	H. O. Edwards, Esq.
Graaff-Reinet	William Rhind, Esq.	Victoria West	H. G. McDiarmid Esq.

Standard Bank—continued.

AGENTS (Home and Foreign.)

Australia	Union Bank of Australia.
China	Chartered Mercantile Bank of India, London, and China. Oriental Bank Corporation.
England	Alliance Bank. Birmingham and Midland Bank. National Provincial Bank of England. Messrs. Gurney and Co., Norwich and Norfolk Bank.
Holland	Messrs. Meyer and Co., Amsterdam.
India	Chartered Mercantile Bank of India, London, and China. Oriental Bank Corporation.
Ireland	Hibernian Bank. The Munster Bank. The Ulster Bank.
Mauritius	Messrs. Blyth Bros. & Co.
New Zealand	Union Bank of Australia. Bank of New Zealand.
Scotland	North of Scotland Banking Company, Bank of Scotland. Commercial Bank of Scotland, National Bank of Scotland, Caledonian Bank.
United States	Messrs. Kidder, Peabody and Co., Boston. Messrs. Howard and Aispinwal, New York.
France	P. Gil, Paris.

THE STANDARD BANK OF BRITISH SOUTH AFRICA (LIMITED), LONDON,

Issues Drafts and Letters of Credit payable in England, the Cape Colony, Natal, the Diamond Fields, and elsewhere.

Receives Deposits at favourable Rates of Interest, which are regulated by the amount and length of time for which the deposits are made.

Open Current Accounts for the convenience of its South African constituents in London and at the various Branches.

Negociates and Collects Bills payable in any part of the South African Colonies or elsewhere where Banking Institutions exist.

Makes Advances on Shipments of Produce, &c.

Undertakes the Agency of Persons connected with the Colonies; and receives for safe custody Colonial Securities, Shares, &c.; drawing interest and dividends on the same as they fall due.

Undertakes all other descriptions of South African Banking and Monetary Business, and affords every facility to persons in their transactions with South Africa and elsewhere.

R. STEWART.
Manager.

10, *Clements Lane,*
Lombard Street, London.

ORIENTAL BANK CORPORATION.
(Incorporated by Royal Charter, 30th August, 1851.)

Paid-up Capital - - - - - - - £1,500,000.
Reserved Funds - - - - - - - 500,000.

Head Office, Threadneedle Street, London, E.C.

Court of Directors:
Chairman—George Arbuthnot, Esq.
Deputy-Chairman—Sir Wm. J. W. Baynes, Bart.

| M.-Gen. H. Pelham Burn | Duncan James Kay, Esq. | Lestock Robert Reid, Esq. |
| John Samuel Collman, Esq. | James Campbell, Esq. | W. Walkinshaw, Esq. |

Chief Manager—Charles J. F. Stuart, Esq.
Sub-Manager—Patrick Campbell, Esq.

Bankers:

| Bank of England | Union Bank of London | Bank of Scotland, London. |

Agents in Scotland:
R. Dundas Cay, Esq., 23, St. Andrews' Square, Edinburgh.

| Bank of Scotland | British Linen Company Bank |
| Commercial Bank of Scotland | National Bank of Scotland |

Agents in Ireland:

| Provincial Bank of Ireland | The National Bank |

Agent in Paris:
Mons. P. Gil, 6, Boulevard des Capucines.

Banks, Branch Banks, and Agencies:
In *India.*—Bombay, Calcutta, Madras, Pondicheery, Tellicheery
In *Ceylon*—Colombo, Kandy, Point de Galle, &c.
In *Straits' Settlements*—Singapore
In *China*—Hong-Kong, Shanghai, Foochow
In *Japan*—Yokohama, Hiogo
In *Australia*—Melbourne, Sydney and Inland Agencies
In *Mauritius*—Port Louis
In *South Africa*—Port Elizabeth and Inland Agencies

ESTABLISHMENT IN COLONY OF CAPE OF GOOD HOPE.
Port Elizabeth Branch.

Manager	..	..	..	..	..	..	..	Fred. W. Crozier
Visiting Officer of Agencies	..	..	..	..	..	David Don
Accountant	..	..	..	..	..	..	..	Alexander Watson

Inland Agencies.

Cradock	..	..	..	..	..	..	..	J. E. Green,	Agent
Graaff-Reinet	..	..	..	..	..	..	W. Meadway,	,,
Grahamstown	..	..	..	..	..	..	J. W. Ashburnham	,,
Kimberley and Dutoitspan (Diamond Fields)	..	..	W. Ross,	,,
King Williamstown	..	..	..	..	..	Chas. J. Dowell,	,,
Middelburg	..	..	..	..	..	..	..	Rob. J. Taylor,	,,
Queenstown	..	..	..	..	..	..	..	F. C. Bate,	,,
Uitenhage	..	..	..	..	..	..	..	George Kay,	,,

Correspondents in South Africa.

Capetown	..	..	..	..	..	..	..	Cape Commercial Bank
Pretoria (Transvaal)	..	..	..	..	..	Cape Commercial Bank
Pilgrims Rest (Leydenburg Gold Fields)	..	..	Cape Commercial Bank
Potchefstroom (Transvaal)	..	..	..	..	Cape Commercial Bank
Sommerset East	..	..	..	..	..	..	Somerset East Bank
Pietermaritzbury (Natal)	..	..	..	..	Natal Bank
Durban (Natal)	..	..	..	..	..	..	Natal Bank
Fauresmith (Orange Free State)	..	..	..	Fauresmith Bank
Bloemfontein (Orange Free State)	..	..	..	Fauresmith Bank

Oriental Bank—continued.

Foreign Correspondence.

Tasmania	Bank of Australasia
South Australia	Bank of South Australia
"	Bank of Adelaide
Western Australia	Western Australian Bank
New Zealand	National Bank of New Zealand
"	Bank of New Zealand
Valparaiso	Bank of Valparaiso
"	National Bank of Chili
Canada	Bank of Montreal
New York	Bank of Montreal
California	Bank of California

PORT ELIZABETH AGENCY—RULES OF BUSINESS.

CURRENT DEPOSIT ACCOUNTS.

1. Deposit Accounts are opened with sums not under £50.
2. Depositors in drawing on their Accounts must do so by the Cheque forms supplied by the Corporation.
3. Cheques drawn for sums under £1 will not be paid.
4. Cheques in which erasures or alterations have been made, or bearing a date subsequent to that of presentation, will not be paid.
5. The Corporation do not hold themselves responsible in respect of the *genuineness* of endorsements on Cheques altered payable to *order* (their own forms being in favour of *bearer*), nor of Cheques advised as lost or mislaid. They will do all in their power to protect Constituents in both these cases, but do not guarantee them against possible loss in consequence of forged endorsements or lost Cheques being paid.
6. Accounts are balanced half-yearly—on 30th June and 31st December—but Pass Books should be *frequently* sent to the Bank to be written up and compared with the Ledgers. Depositors must not make entries in their Pass Books.
7. No interest is allowed on Deposits re-payable on demand.
8. Over-drafts are not permitted, unless specially arranged for.

FIXED DEPOSITS.

1. Sums of £50 and upwards received for fixed periods. Interest allowed thereon according to arrangement.
2. No interest accrues after the term has expired.
3. Receipts are not transferable by endorsement or otherwise, except with approval. When to be renewed they should be sent in with the endorsement of the Depositor, at due date.

DISCOUNT AND ADVANCES.

The Corporation discount Private Bills or Notes payable in the Colony representing *bonâ fide* transactions, with two or more approved names; or bearing one name only, if accompanied by deposit of adequate collateral security.

Advances are made on Merchandize (not of a perishable nature), on deposit of Warehouse Receipts and Fire Insurance Policy; also on Government Securities.

EXCHANGE AND REMITTANCE.

Drafts are issued on London, *on demand*, or at 30, 60, or 90 days' sight, and on towns in Scotland and Ireland *on demand* only.

N.B.—Drafts for sums under £20 issued *on demand* only.

Drafts are also granted on any of the Branches or Agencies of the Corporation in India, Ceylon, China, Japan, Australia, or Mauritius; also on the Corporation's Correspondents in New Zealand, South Australia, Tasmania, Western Australia, and elsewhere.

Letters of Credit issued; also Circular Notes for the use of Travellers, negotiable in all towns of importance throughout the World.

Bills payable in Europe, or in any of the above places, are purchased, or remitted for collection.

Family remittances to England and elsewhere effected at stated times, full Christian names and addresses being furnished by Constituents. In case of remittances to married ladies, *their* Christian names, *not their Husbands'*, should be given on application for drafts.

SAFE CUSTODY.

The Corporation take charge of Government and other Securities, and realise Interest and Dividends for Constituents. Forms of Powers of Attorney supplied on application.

All letters should be addressed and remittances made payable to the "Oriental Bank Corporation," and not to individual officers by name.

Office hours, 9 to 3; Saturdays, 9 to 1.

FRED. W. CROZIER,

PORT ELIZABETH, April, 1875. *Manager.*

ALGOA BAY
Landing & Shipping Company,

(LIMITED.)

DIRECTORS.

WILLIAM HUME, Esquire (A. C. Stewart & Co.) Chairman.

AUGUST BARSDORF, Esquire (Lippert & Co.)

J. W. SALOMON, Esquire (A. Mosenthal & Co.)

EDWARD SLATER, Esquire (E. Slater & Co.)

GEORGE C. SMITH, Esquire (J. O. Smith & Co.)

G. H. WEDEKIND, Esquire, (Ebell, Wedekind, & Co.)

BANKERS.

ORIENTAL BANK CORPORATION.

MANAGER.

JAMES FORBES, Esquire.

ACCOUNTANT.

JOHN GLEN, Esquire.

EAST LONDON, CAPE OF GOOD HOPE.

FERGUSON & ATTWELL,

Shipping, Forwarding and Commission Agents,

EAST LONDON.

Offices:—Opposite Queen's Warehouse.

References: D. Lippert, Esq., London and Hamburg; Messrs. Arthur & Co., London and Glasgow; Messrs. White & Holmes, Mildmay Chambers, 82, Bishopsgate-street, London.

SOUTH AFRICAN DIAMOND FIELDS.

JAMES FERGUSON,

WHOLESALE MERCHANT,

KIMBERLEY,

Begs to announce to Storekeepers and others that he is Importing all kinds of

MERCHANDISE FROM THE HOME MARKETS,

And in order to effect a speedy clearance,

PRICES have now been further REDUCED. Builders will find

TIMBER, GALVANIZED IRON & HARDWARE, PLOUGHS, NO. 75 EAGLE,

For all the country are kept at the lowest standard of importation.
Implements for Households as well as for every Workshop.

Provisions, Groceries and Oilman's from first to last at unprecedented LOW PRICES, to fair margin for Retailers.

WINES & SPIRITS, best imported brands and qualities.
Clothing, Warm and Good for Winter, in the Newest Styles.
An Assortment of Boots, and Men's and Boys' Bluchers.

Soft Goods in general, replete with unusually low lines for Kafir Trade: Blankets, &c.

DIGGER'S UTENSILS, WITH GOOD STOCK OF MANILLA LINE.

COME ONE! COME ALL!!

INSPECT & SECURE BARGAINS. THE IMMENSE STOCK IS LANDED AT LOWEST RATES OF CARRIAGE.

MEALIE MEAL, FRESH AND FINE GROUND, SOUND AND SWEET.

JAMES FERGUSON,
KIMBERLEY.

SOUTH AFRICAN
Landing, Shipping, Forwarding,

AND

PRODUCE AGENCY,

JOHN HERLEY,

MARKET-SQUARE,

PORT ELIZABETH.

GEORGE ARMSTRONG,

WHOLESALE AND RETAIL

Ironmonger & Metal Merchant,

72, MAIN STREET, & PEEL STREET,

PORT ELIZABETH.

IMPORTS EVERY DESCRIPTION OF MEN'S AND BOYS'

CLOTHING,

Hats, Caps, Shirts, Ties, Scarfs, Hosiery, Boots, Carpet Bags, Portmanteaus, Umbrellas, Blankets, Perfumery.

WATERPROOF CLOTHING, DOESKINS, TWEEDS,

CORDS, MOLES, SHIRTINGS, FLANNELS, &c., &c., &c.

WHOLESALE & RETAIL

WEST OF ENGLAND

CLOTHING ESTABLISHMENT,

3 & 5, MAIN STREET,

PORT ELIZABETH,

CAPE OF GOOD HOPE.

Marchant & Compy.,

Wholesale and Retail Drapers,

MILLINERS, &c.

WEDDING & OTHER OUTFITS.

NEW GOODS

Per each Mail Steamer.

COUNTRY ORDERS HAVE IMMEDIATE ATTENTION.

---

75 & 77, MAIN STREET,

PORT ELIZABETH,

Cape of Good Hope.

DENTISTRY.

Messrs. Clinton & Stroud,

SURGEON DENTISTS,

29, *DONKIN STREET, PORT ELIZABETH.*

ESTABLISHED 1869.

JOHN GEARD & SON,

WHOLESALE & RETAIL

IRONMONGERS,

No. 9, MAIN STREET, PORT ELIZABETH.

DEALERS IN AMMUNITION.

KISCH BROS.,
PHOTOGRAPHERS,
DURBAN, NATAL,
HAVE ALWAYS ON HAND A LARGE SUPPLY OF
VIEWS OF ZANZIBAR,
MOZAMBIQUE, NATAL, AND EAST COAST,
AND OF
MR. T. BAINES'S PICTURES
OF THE MANY INTERESTING SUBJECTS OF
UP-COUNTRY EXPLORATIONS.

Charges Moderate.

ALL ORDERS PROMPTLY ATTENDED TO.

KISCH BROS.,
SMITH STREET, DURBAN, NATAL,

G. D. PEEK,

ARCHITECT,

HILL STREET,

PORT ELIZABETH,

CAPE OF GOOD HOPE.

JOHN CROOKS'
LEATHER STORE.

Always on hand a large supply of Leather of every description; also, Colonial made Boots, Shoes, and Veldtschoens. Wholesale and Retail.

SADDLER & HARNESS MAKER,

Coach, Cart, and Carriage Trimmer.

Saddlery and Harness of every description always on hand.

70 & 72, QUEEN STREET,
PORT ELIZABETH.

UITENHAGE TANNERY,
LATE J. BILLINGHAM.

Always on hand,

A LARGE SUPPLY OF
Various descriptions of
LEATHERS,
WHOLESALE & RETAIL.

JOHN CROOKS,
70 & 72, QUEEN STREET.

I. O.
RICHARD S. COOPER,
SCENIC AND DECORATIVE ARTIST,
PLAIN & ORNAMENTAL SIGN WRITER,
SOUTH STREET, NORTH END,
PORT ELIZABETH.

Scenery for Dramatic and other Entertainments, Banners, Bannerets and Devices for I.O.G.T. and other Societies, Transparencies, Illuminations, Gauze Wire, Perforated Zinc, Window and Office Blinds, Fanlights, Gilding on Glass, Wood, &c., Wagon and Stencil Plates, Photographic Backgrounds, &c., *supplied on the shortest possible notice*, Consulate Shields repainted and *restored to their pristine beauty*.

R. S. C. while thanking his Patrons for their kind and liberal support, has much pleasure in intimating that he has succeeded in securing the services of some most talented assistants, and is now prepared, in addition to the above Branches, to execute any orders entrusted to him in House Painting, Graining, Marbling, Glazing, and Paper-Hanging.

First-class Workmanship and Moderate Charges guaranteed.

The best Room Decoration for this climate is TEMPERA. Try it.

SPECIALITIE, SHORTLY EXPECTED,
SILK TO SUPPLY BANNERS,
(*All Sizes, without Seams*).
G.   Cords, Tassels, and Trimmings to match.   T.

NORTON'S PATENT
ABYSSINIAN TUBE WELLS.

This valuable invention supplies the most simple, rapid, and perfect means of obtaining

PURE WATER

for every purpose, from the smallest quantity for domestic use to the largest supplies for farming operations, water-works, &c.

They are simple in their construction, and easily driven; their cost is small, and they rarely or ever require repair. Full particulars may be obtained from

DEARE & DEITZ,
Sole Agents for the Colony of the Cape of Good Hope.

J. W. C. MACKAY,
BOOKSELLER AND STATIONER.
40, MAIN STREET, PORT ELIZABETH,
HAS ALWAYS ON HAND AN ASSORTMENT OF
STATIONERY AND FANCY GOODS,
AMONG WHICH WILL BE FOUND

Account Books—in various sizes, shapes, and rulings
Writing Papers—in Foolscap, Post, and Note (white and coloured)
Blotting do.—in Buff, Red, and White
Tissue do.—assorted colours
Inks—Writing, Fluid, Black, Blue, Red, and Copying
Pens—Steel and Quill (Gillott's and Mitchell's)
Inkstands—in Wood, Glass, and Papier Mache
Stationery Racks and Letter Cages
Spring Bill Files and Letter Clips
Rulers—Round and Flat, Solicitors' Green Silk
Music Books and Paper
Sealing Wax, India Rubber, Desk and Pen Knives
Drawing Pencils, Paper, and Copies
Photographic and Writing Albums
Chess and Draught Men, &c., &c.

☞ Parcels of MAGAZINES, PERIODICALS, and BOOKS received by each Steamer.

COUNTRY ORDERS PROMPTLY DESPATCHED.

J. W. C. MACKAY,
BOOK AND MUSIC SELLER,
40, MAIN STREET, PORT ELIZABETH,
HAS ALWAYS ON HAND A SELECTION OF
GENERAL LITERATURE, SCHOOL BOOKS AND MATERIALS,
AMONG WHICH WILL BE FOUND

BIBLES, CHURCH SERVICES, PRAYER & HYMN BOOKS,
HOUSEHOLD FAMILY PRAYER BOOKS,

POETICAL WORKS, | **BIOGRAPHICAL WORKS,**
HISTORICAL WORKS, | **MEDICAL WORKS,**
LAW WORKS, | **NOVELS,**
JUVENILE STORY BOOKS IN GREAT VARIETY,
SONG BOOKS AND LETTER WRITERS,
S C H O O L   B O O K S
IN
ENGLISH, FRENCH, LATIN, GERMAN, GREEK, AND DUTCH,
ALSO
MUSIC, SONGS, PIANOFORTE PIECES, AND INSTRUCTION BOOKS.

Homœopathic Medicines in all forms kept in stock.

☞ BOOKS and MAGAZINES, to Special Order imported by each Steamer.

IRON HOUSES.

GALVANIZED CORRUGATED IRON,

And all Galvanized and Zinc Goods.

FRED. BRABY & COMPY.,

LIMITED,

WORKS—LONDON, LIVERPOOL AND GLASGOW.

EXPORT OFFICE, 120, CANNON ST., LONDON

Catalogues and full particulars furnished on application, but all Orders must be sent through responsible merchants.

F. BRABY & CO., pay special attention to Quality Iron, and Colonists desirous of obtaining excellence in this respect will find it to their advantage to use the

"CASTLE" BRAND OF GALVANISED CORRUGATED IRON.

E. SLATER, JUN.,
ENGINEER, BLACKSMITH
AND
FOUNDRY WORKS.

N.B.—Castings of all descriptions to order. Machinery made on shortest notice, much lower than imported. Produce of all kinds received and placed to a favourable Market on Commission.

Pressing of Wool done by Steam.

Nos. 107, 109, 111, 113, 115, & 117,

QUEEN STREET, PORT ELIZABETH.

STEINMANN'S CONVEYANCES
TO GRAHAM'S TOWN,
LEAVE THE MASONIC HOTEL DAILY

(SUNDAYS AND THURSDAYS EXCEPTED),

At 5 o'clock a.m., and arrive in Graham's Town the same day.

PASSENGER CARTS TO

Somerset East, Graaff-Reinet, and Uitenhage.

For information, apply to

E. STEINMANN,
Masonic Hotel.

JOHN F. SMITH,

(Next Door to Kirkwood, Marks, & Co.).

RODNEY STREET, PORT ELIZABETH,

GENERAL DEALER AND IMPORTER.

GOODS & CONSIGNMENTS PURCHASED FOR CASH.

Temporary Office of the Grand Lodge of the
I. O. of G. T.

PETER FINLAY,

WHOLESALE AND RETAIL

Wine and Spirit Merchant,

61, MAIN STREET, PORT ELIZABETH.

EDGAR & HODSON,

Builders and Undertakers.

PICTURES FRAMED AND MOUNTED

In Maple or Gilt Mouldings.

ON HAND.

A Splendid Assortment of Maple and Gilt Mouldings, suitable for Picture Frames.

Architrave, Cornice, Door Panel, and Bead Mouldings.

Chance's Sheet, Picture, and Window Glass, all sizes, from 7×9 to 30×48 inches.

DOORS & WINDOWS, ALL SIZES.

All Work in the above Branches executed with promptitude and dispatch.

N.B.—CHARGES MODERATE.

Griffin's Green, Foot of Russell Road,

PORT ELIZABETH.

A. MASKELL.
(LATE CAPTAIN MASON.)

FIRST-CLASS
ACCOMMODATION FOR TRAVELLERS.

CAPACIOUS PREMISES AND GOOD STABLING.

Wines and Spirits of the Best Quality.

HIGHEST PRICE GIVEN FOR PRODUCE.

ADDERLEY-STREET,
PORT ELIZABETH.

Maynard, Walker & Co.,

73, 75, and 77, MAIN-STREET,

PORT ELIZABETH,

AGENTS FOR THE

ASSOCIATION OF HAMBURG UNDERWRITERS

AND FOR

Les Comites des Assureurs Maritimes du Havre, des Assureurs Maritimes de Paris.

FAIRBRIDGE & PETTIT,

FOREIGN

AND COLONIAL PRODUCE,

SHARE AND DIAMOND BROKERS,

&c., &c.,

49, MAIN-STREET,

PORT ELIZABETH.

E. HAYES,
BOOT & SHOE MAKER

Has taken over the Premises in Main-street lately occupied by Mr. B. HANSEN, and popularly known as the

"LITTLE WONDER,"

Together with all Goods and Stock-in-Trade appertaining thereto, comprising a miscellaneous assortment of Clothing, Shirts, Concertinas, Fancy Goods, &c., which will be offered at an alarming sacrifice, inasmuch as the advertiser intends concentrating all his energies of body and mind on the

BOOT AND SHOE TRADE.

And in soliciting the Patronage of the Public, he begs to assure them that cheapness, combined with durability and completeness of Workmanship will characterise his work. E. HAYES was seven years in the employ of the late WILLIAM PALMER, and two years with his successor.

Wholesale Orders for all descriptions of Bootware promptly executed. Also Repairs of all kinds neatly effected.

ADDRESS:—108, MAIN-STREET, PORT ELIZABETH.
OPPOSITE MESSRS. SAVAGE & HILL.

Sun Fire Assurance Company

OF LONDON.

The Undersigned are authorised to accept Risks against Fire on Property in Port Elizabeth :—

Wm. ANDERSON & Co.,

AGENTS,

MARKET SQUARE, PORT ELIZABETH.

FIRE ASSURANCE.

The Undersigned are vested with full powers to accept Risks in the above Branch of the

LONDON & LANCASHIRE

ASSURANCE COMPANY.

Head Offices:—11, Dale Street, Liverpool.

CAPITAL IN THE FIRE DEPARTMENT...............ONE MILLION.

Proposals entertained from any of the Principal Towns in the Colony.

Proposal Forms and Tables of Rates supplied on application.

Wm. ANDERSON & Co., Agents.

B. G. LENNON & Co.,
WHOLESALE AND RETAIL
CHEMISTS AND DRUGGISTS,
PORT ELIZABETH.

DEALERS IN

Patent and Dutch Medicines, Druggists' Sundries, Surgical Instruments, Glassware, Photographic Goods, Perfumery, Homœopathic Medicines, Soda Water Material, &c., &c.

BRANCH ESTABLISHMENT—GRAHAM'S TOWN.

Price List on Application.

KIRKWOOD, MARKS & Co.,
AUCTIONEERS, APPRAISERS,
AND
COMMISSION MERCHANTS.

SALES ON COMMISSION HELD BI-WEEKLY.

LAND AND STOCK SALES HELD IN ANY PART OF THE COLONY.

(ESTABLISHED 1859.)

F. B. BROWN,

AUCTIONEER, BROKER, LAND AND LAW AGENT.

Live Stock and Merchandise Sales every Thursday and Saturday Morning.

Cash Advances on Live Stock or Goods to be Sold. Large Consignment of Rough Goods always on hand—for Sale at Low Rates.

LOANS ON FARMS AND TOWN PROPERTIES.

Extensive Storage for the receiving and forwarding of Goods and Produce.

PUNCTUALITY AND DESPATCH.

WILLIAM POWELL,
BAKER, GROCER, DAIRYMAN,
AND
GENERAL DEALER,
QUEEN-STREET,

PORT ELIZABETH.

FAMILIES SUPPLIED WITH GOOD WHOLESOME BREAD.

A Good Supply of Vegetables and Fresh Milk every Morning.

FRESH GARDEN SEEDS
OF EVERY DESCRIPTION ALWAYS ON HAND.

NOTE THE ADDRESS:
OPPOSITE RUSSELL ROAD.

Union Boating Company of Port Elizabeth

(LIMITED).

DIRECTORS:

JOSEPH SIMPSON, Esq., Chairman

F. S. FAIRBRIDGE, Esq.

E. W. ENGELKEN, Esq.

E. MORRIS, Esq.

A. L. BLACKBURN, Esq.

A. TAYLOR, Esq.

JAS. SEARLE, Manager.

A. F. TANCRED, Secretary.

BANKERS:

ORIENTAL BANK CORPORATION.

SOLICITORS:

Messrs. CHABAUD & DYASON.

CITY OF GLASGOW
LIFE ASSURANCE COMPANY.

Incorporated by Special Act of Parliament.

Subscribed Capital - - - - £600,000
Annual Revenue upwards of - - 156,000
Existing Assurances - - - - 4,332,295

THE CITY OF GLASGOW LIFE ASSURANCE COMPANY

Has now been conducted for thirty-six years with much success, which is attributable not only to the perfect security which it affords for the due fulfilment of every contract, but likewise to its extensive and influential connections, and to the liberality of its dealings.

Full particulars of Rates and Premiums, &c., which are very favourable to insurers, can be obtained from

GEORGE DUNCAN, *Agent.*

Main Street, Port Elizabeth.

"PHŒNIX HOTEL,"
PORT ELIZABETH.
GUTHRIE & Co., PROPRIETORS.
AGENTS FOR
COBB AND COMPANY'S COACHES,

Which leave Port Elizabeth every Morning for all parts of the Colony.

THE PHŒNIX HOTEL is admitted to be the largest and best conducted Hotel in the Colony. It adjoins the Post-office and H.M. Customs; is opposite the Town Hall, Museum, and Library, as well as the principal Newspaper Office, and only a few steps from the Public Market, Breakwater, and Bathing Place.

JESSE SHAW'S
Celebrated African Herbal Preparations.

DIAMOND AND GOLD DIGGERS, AND THE PUBLIC GENERALLY.

DYSENTERY,

Cured by the new Medicine SPECIFIC prepared almost entirely from Colonial Herbs, and which, since its preparation has never been known to fail. No Digger should leave for the Fields without a good supply, and no house ever be without a bottle of it.—Sold Wholesale and Retail by JESSE SHAW & Co., at Fort Beaufort, and their Agents, Messrs. Savage & Hill, Port Elizabeth; Howse, Reynolds & Co., Grahamstown; T. H. Grocott, Grahamstown; Richards, Glanville & Co., Grahamstown; S. White & Co., Cradock; Jas. Hodges, Queenstown; Whicher & Dyer, King Williamstown and Keiskama Hoek; J. B. Temlett, Alice; Jas. Verity, Adelaide; Cooper & Drummond, Bedford; J. Shaw & Co., Eland's Post; J. Mosel, Uitenhage; Austin Bros. & Co., Dutoitspan; Hill & Paddon, Klipdrift; R. Armstrong & Co., Brandford, O.F.S.; J. R. Windell & Co., Fauresmith; Spiller & Bekker, Wipener;—Leach, Poplar Grove, O.F.S.; Peacock & Weir, King Williamstown.

SHAW'S SPECIFIC FOR DYSENTERY.
NEW TESTIMONIALS OF CURE.

To Mr. J. SHAW.   Fort Beaufort, April 11.

DEAR SIR,—I have not words sufficiently strong enough to express to you my thanks for the relief I have obtained from your medicines, after being under the care of several medical men in Grahamstown from whom I found no relief. I was recommended to buy your "Specific," and I am now, thank God, perfectly cured, and would strongly recommend it to all sufferers of the same complaint (Dysentery).

I remain, dear sir, yours very truly,
CHARLES ROTING, Wagonmaker at Mr. Bulgin's.

I purchased at Messrs. SHAW & Co.'s some bottles of "The Specific." Having given them a fair trial, I feel compelled that I ought to acquaint others with its merits. During my visit to the Diamond Fields, I witnessed a case where a person was suffering extremely om Dysentery. A friend advised a dose of "The Specific;" after a couple of doses the sufferer was quite cured.

Chancery Hall, Adelaide, April 10, 1874.   T. NILAND, Jun.

Testimonials in favour of Jesse Shaw's "Sure Cure," a Certain Remedy for Snake Bites, &c.

MR. MULLER, near Fort Beaufort, writes us:—"Your 'SURE CURE' has cured a dog of ours, which was bitten of a Puff Adder, and its head was swollen in a frightful manner. It was quite well in a day and a half."

At Fort Beaufort a Native was bitten in the foot, which swelled in a fearful manner; but with one single dose, and application of the 'SURE CURE,' was quite cured on the same day.

Near CAPTAIN BLYTH'S, in the Transkei, on the Chief ZAZELA'S Location, a little girl was bitten in four places, in different portions of the body, by a Night Adder during sleep, and whose body became callous and cold. She took and used the Tincture twice only and was quite cured.

MR. S. J. RADEMEYER, writes us from the Orange Free State, dated, "Clith Roe," near Rouxville:— "Dear Sirs,—I have much pleasure in bearing testimony of the usefulness and complete success of your Tincture for Snake Bites, called 'SURE CURE.' I have used it many times, and so have my neighbours, until the bottle is nearly empty, and in each case it has succeeded in quite curing. It is what is called a 'SURE CURE,' and quite equal to Croft's."

THE "SURE CURE."
A new Tincture of African Plants, and a certain Remedy for the Bite of Snakes, Insects, and all Species of Reptiles.

Manufactured only by JESSE SHAW, at Fort Beaufort,
AND SOLD ONLY BY HIS ADVERTISED AGENTS.

N.B.—Beware of Imitations! This Tincture has been sold for years, but never before Advertised. Do not entrust life to cheap Preparations.

PRICE, 7s. 6d. AND 10s. 6d. PER BOTTLE.

Fort Beaufort, August 28, 1876.   JESSE SHAW.

MERCHANTS,

COMMISSION AND FORWARDING AGENTS,

QUEEN STREET,

PORT ELIZABETH.

EASY CHAIRS, COUCHES, SOFAS,
DINING AND DRAWING-ROOM FURNITURE,
MADE OF THE BEST, WELL SEASONED WOOD,
Under Careful Supervision, and Properly Selected Materials suitable for all Climates.

JAMES LYLE & CO.,
57, BISHOPSGATE STREET WITHIN, LONDON, E.C.,

GENERAL FURNISHERS AND DECORATORS,
Wholesale and Export Upholsterers and Cabinet Manufacturers, and Furnishing Contractors for Mansions and Houses of all Classes.

During the last twenty-five years this Firm has Fitted and Furnished many first-class Criterions and Residences at Home and Abroad, the former including some of the handsomest Rooms in this Country, and the latter more especially at the Cape, China, and Japan. This wide experience has led to the command of every resource for ensuring Elegance, Utility, Economy, and unrivalled good taste, and for the expedition in the completion of all orders at moderate charges.

Theatres, Music Halls, Clubs, Hotels, Restaurants, and other Public Resorts Decorated and Furnished on the most Favourable Terms.

ESTIMATES PROMPTLY SUPPLIED.

See important notice in the *Times* of April 7th, and *Furniture Gazette*, April 17th, 1875.

FACTORY and WAREHOUSES: 24, CASTLE STREET, FINSBURY SQUARE.

OFFICES: 57, BISHOPSGATE STREET WITHIN, LONDON.

HOUSEHOLD FURNITURE.

G. BARTHOLOMEW & Co.,
CABINET-MAKERS AND UPHOLSTERERS,
WHOLESALE AND EXPORT.
ILLUSTRATED CATALOGUES FREE ON APPLICATION.
FOREIGN ORDERS MAY BE SENT DIRECT OR THROUGH ANY LONDON MERCHANT.

WAREHOUSES:—13 AND 14, PAVEMENT, AND ROPEMAKER STREET,
FINSBURY, LONDON.

REMOVED FROM 15, OLD BAILEY.

Honourable Mention for Printing Materials, International Exhibition, 1862.

"Standard" Printing Material and Composition Roller Works

ESTABLISHED 1825.

FREDK. ULLMER,

MANUFACTURER OF

THE "STANDARD" CYLINDER JOBBING MACHINES,

ALBION AND COLUMBIAN PRESSES,

GUILLOTINE PAPER-CUTTING,

PERFORATING, AND PAGING MACHINES,

TYPE, WOOD LETTER, BRASS RULE, and PRINTERS' JOINERY,

AND

MACHINERY & MATERIALS OF EVERY DESCRIPTION

FOR

PRINTERS, BOOKBINDERS, AND STATIONERS.

"STANDARD" STEAM WORKS,

CROSS STREET, HATTON GARDEN,

Leading into the Farringdon Road, London, E.C.;

Near the Farringdon Station of the Metropolitan Railway.

A LARGE STOCK OF SECOND-HAND MACHINES, PRESSES, &c., &c., ON SALE

SEE LIST FORWARDED FREE.

FREDERICK ULLMER'S New Illustrated List of Prices of Machinery and Materials is now ready, and will be forwarded free.

Type Specimen Book of New Founts, with weights and prices affixed, sent free Bookbinders' Specimen Book of New Rolls, Corners, &c., sent free.

H. W. CASLON & CO.,
Letter Founders,
AND
MANUFACTURERS OF PRINTING MATERIALS,
No. 22, CHISWELL STREET, LONDON, E.C.,

Supply every requisite for the Printing Office, of the best manufacture. After an experience of more than a century and a half, during which time the reputation of the Caslon Letter Foundry has been steadily maintained, H. W. C. & Co. confidently ask the continued support of their Customers.

TYPE.

BOOK AND NEWSPAPER FOUNTS
AND A VERY EXTENSIVE ASSORTMENT OF

Titling Letter, Scripts, Texts, Blacks, Ornamental and Bill Type, Borders, Corners, Casts, Brass Rules, Metal Rules, Clumps, Leads, Furniture, and Wood Letter.

ALL FOUNTS CAN BE SUPPLIED WITH ACCENTS, IF REQUIRED, FOR THE FRENCH SPANISH, AND PORTUGUESE LANGUAGES.

MACHINES AND PRESSES

of every description. Printing, Mitering, Cutting, Ruling, Paging, Numbering, and Perforating Machines, by experienced engineers.

PRINTERS' INK, JOINERY, &c.

Cases, Frames, Racks, Imposing Surfaces, Galleys, Composing-Sticks, Chases, Side-sticks, Reglet, Quoins, &c., &c., &c., all of the best manufacture.

SPECIMENS AND ESTIMATES ON APPLICATION.

The Type used in this Work was manufactured at the Caslon Letter Foundry.

Just Published. Price 13s. 6d.

THE GOLD REGIONS
OF
SOUTH EASTERN AFRICA,

By the Late Thomas Baines, F.R.G.S.,

WITH MAGNIFICENT MAP OF THE COUNTRY BETWEEN THE VAAL AND ZAMBESI RIVERS.

Comprising the Seat of War in the Transvaal, and the Gold Regions of Africa, to which is annexed a Map of the Cape Colonies. Numerous Illustrations accompanying the book, which supplies a truthful and excellent description of one of the most interesting and least known portions of South Eastern Africa.

The Book is published at a very low price, in order to secure a large circulation.

MR. BAINES was so well known and appreciated in Africa that in the Cape Colonies there are no fewer than 3,000 Subscribers to this work.

The Map—COLOURED—may be had separately, on thick paper, 10s. Mounted on cloth in case, 15s. Do. on roller, 20s.

LONDON :—EDWARD STANFORD, Charing Cross.
CAPE COLONY :- J. W. C. MACKAY, Port Elizabeth.

WHITE & FAWCETT,
STEAM PRINTERS,
Lithographers, Wholesale Stationers, Account Book Manufacturers,
AND GENERAL CONTRACTORS.

Shipping Orders carefully and promptly executed.

17, Blomfield Street, London Wall, LONDON, E.C.

N.B.—Printers of this volume.

PENS.   PENS.
THE BEST PEN AT A MODERATE PRICE
IS THE
EXPRESS.
FIRM, FREE, EXTRAORDINARILY DURABLE.
Wholesale of John Henry Best,
10, WARWICK LANE, LONDON, E.C.

BRUSHWARE!

EXPORT MANUFACTURERS
OF EVERY DESCRIPTION.

Rob. A. Rooney & Sons
27 & 28,
Bishopsgate Street, E.C.,
LONDON.

ILLUSTRATED PRICE LISTS ON APPLICATION.

INKS FOR HOT CLIMATES.

STEPHENS'
Writing Fluids & Copying Ink

Have obtained the Highest Awards every time they have been Exhibited.

PARIS,	HAVRE,	AMSTERDAM,	LYONS,
1867.	1868.	1869.	1872.
	VIENNA,	PHILADELPHIA,	
	1873.	1876.	

They embrace the higher qualities of

WRITING & COPYING INKS

And each possesses some special character adapted to the many different requirements of Correspondence and the Counting House. These distinctive features, and their general excellence, make them preferable to, and more widely useful than the ordinary class of manufactures.

Stephens' Blue Black Writing Fluid.
Stephen's Blue Black Copying Fluid.
Stephen's Scarlet Ink for Steel Pens.

The above are particularly adapted or hot climates, extremely fluid, but becoming intense and durable colours.

And Every description of Writing and Copying Ink, Quills, Gum Mucilage (to resist fermentation in hot climates), and Sealing Wax, Manufactured by

Henry C. STEPHENS, Chemist,
WHOLESALE AND FOR EXPORT, AT
171, ALDERSGATE STREET, LONDON, E.C.

SOLD BY ALL BOOKSELLERS AND STATIONERS

ADVERTISEMENTS.

JUSTIN BROWNE

CATALOGUE OF DESIGNS AND PRICES SENT FREE.

THE WHOLESALE DISCOUNT OF 25 PER CENT. ALLOWED TO MERCHANTS AND SHIPPERS.

Having had a long practical experience in the **MANUFACTURE OF PIANOS** expressly for exportation to extreme climates, has succeeded in producing an Instrument which combines English durability and soundness, with first-class quality of tone. Justin Browne can refer to customers whom he has supplied in New Zealand, Costa Rica, Peru, Calcutta, &c., all of whom have expressed the greatest satisfaction, and renewed their orders. His prices will be found to be extremely low in proportion to the quality of Pianos, and in comparison with those of other Houses where the same degree of soundness and durability is studied, the reason of the difference being, that in their case, selling as they do retail, there are heavy expenses for Show Rooms, Advertising, &c., which as a Wholesale Manufacturer he does not incur; having only factory expenses, he can offer an Equally Good Instrument at a much Lower Figure. Address—

Justin Browne, Pianoforte Manufacturer, 237 & 239, Euston Road, London.

EXPORT SPECIAL.

GEO. CARLEY & Co.,
30, ELY PLACE, HOLBORN,
LONDON, E.C.,

WHOLESALE WATCH AND CHRONOMETER MANUFACTURERS

IMPROVED KEYLESS WATCHES
SUITABLE FOR THE COLONIES.

HUNT & TAWELL

ATLAS WORKS, EARLS COLNE, ESSEX, ENGLAND,

MANUFACTURERS OF

HORSE GEARS

From One to Four Horse Power; specially adapted for Colonial use, and suitable for Driving.

| Mining Machinery, | Pumps, | Thrashing Machines, |
| Saw Benches, | Churns, | Chaff Cutters, |

AND ALL KINDS OF PLANTATION AND AGRICULTURAL MACHINERY.

CHAFF CUTTERS — All sizes, suitable for Hand, Horse or Steam Power. | **CORN DRESSING MACHINES.** | **BEAN, OAT and** Corn Bruising & Kibbling Machines.

ORDERS FROM ABROAD, EITHER DIRECT OR THROUGH A MERCHANT SHIPPER, WILL RECEIVE EVERY ATTENTION

Full Illustrated Catalogues Gratis and Post Free on Application.

THOMAS WEST,

Manufacturing Silversmith and Electro Plater,

JEWELLER,

Goldsmith and Watchmaker,

No. 3, LUDGATE HILL, ST. PAUL'S,

LONDON.

Sterling Silver Spoons and Forks.
Fiddle Pattern—Best Make.

	oz.	s.	d.	£	s.	d.
12 Table Spoons	30 at 7	8..11	10	0
12 Table Forks	30 „ 7	8..11	10	0
12 Dessert Spoons	20 „ 7	8..	7	13	4
12 Dessert Forks	20 „ 7	8..	7	13	4
2 Gravy Spoons	10 „ 7	8..	3	16	8
Soup Ladle	9 „ 7	8..	3	9	0
4 Sauce Ladles	10 „ 8	2..	4	1	8
Fish Knife and Fork			5	10	0
4 Salt Spoons, gilt bowls		1	2	0
Mustard Spoon, gilt bowl			8	6
12 Tea Spoons	10 at 8	2..	4	1	8
Sugar Tongs			15	0
Moist Sugar Spoon			12	0
Sugar Sifter		1	1	0
Butter Knife		1	8	0
6 Egg Spoons, gilt bowls		2	5	0
Asparagus Tongs		4	0	0
Salad Spoon and Fork		4	15	0
Cheese Scoop		1	16	0
Grape Scissors		2	15	0
Tea Caddy Spoon			10	0

West's Amalgamated Silver.
Thoroughly Plated on Hardest White Metal—Fiddle Pattern.

	£	s.	d.
12 Table Forks	1	16	0
12 Table Spoons	1	16	0
12 Dessert Forks	1	7	0
12 Dessert Spoons	1	7	0
12 Tea Spoons		16	0
2 Sauce Ladles		7	0
1 Gravy Spoon		7	0
4 Salt Spoons, gilt bowls		6	8
1 Mustard Spoon		1	8
1 Pair Sugar Tongs		3	6
1 Pair Fish Carvers	1	5	0
1 Butter Knife		3	0
1 Soup Ladle		12	0
6 Egg Spoons, gilt		10	0
1 Sugar Sifter		5	0
1 Cheese Scoop		6	0
1 Marrow Spoon		5	0
2 Pickle Spoons		5	0
1 Moist Sugar Spoon		2	6
1 Tea Caddy Spoon		2	6
1 Asparagus Tongs		15	0

Biscuit Boxes, Bread and Cake Baskets, Butter Dishes, Sauce Boats, Bedroom Candlesticks, Table Candlesticks, Breakfast Cruets to contain Salt, Pepper, Mustard; Card Cases, Cups for Children, Table Dishes, Dish Covers, Entrée Dishes, Dessert Fruit Knives and Forks, Cutlery of all kinds, Fish Knives and Forks, Fish Carvers and Slices, Cruet Frames, Liquor Frames, Egg Frames, Mustard Pots, Salt Cellars, Muffiners, Knife Rests, Nutcracks, Nutpicks, Pencil Cases, Penholders, Gold Pens, Tea and Coffee Services, Toast Racks, Waiters' Tea and Coffee Trays.

London made Gold and Silver Watches. Jewellery in every variety. Every article warranted of the very best quality and most moderate price.

THE "DENMARK PHÆTON," AS BUILT FOR H.R.H. The Princess of Wales. Price 34 Guineas.		THE "VICTORIAS," WITH LATEST IMPROVEMENTS, *ELEGANT, LIGHT & EASY* Price 70 Guineas.

HARNESS, SADDLERY,

AND

EVERY STABLE REQUISITE.

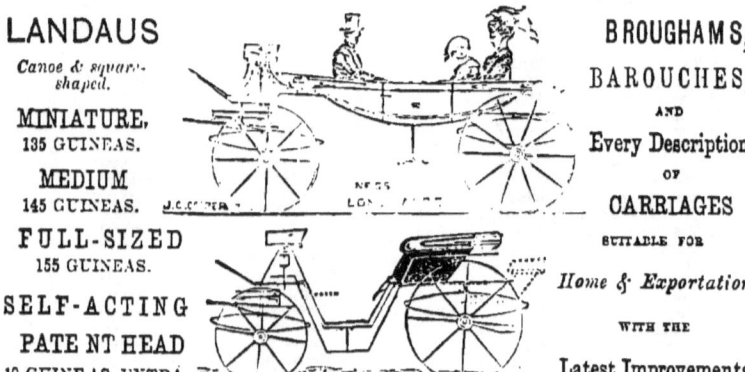

LANDAUS *Canoe & square-shaped.* **MINIATURE,** 135 GUINEAS. **MEDIUM** 145 GUINEAS. **FULL-SIZED** 155 GUINEAS. **SELF-ACTING** **PATENT HEAD** 10 GUINEAS EXTRA.	**BROUGHAMS,** **BAROUCHES,** AND Every Description OF **CARRIAGES** SUITABLE FOR *Home & Exportation* WITH THE Latest Improvements

DAVID NESS,

3, LONG ACRE,

LONDON, W.C.

In consequence of D. Ness's personal experience abroad, coupled with his large foreign connection, he is conversant with all classes of Carriages and Harness, and their suitability to each respective climate.

Price 3s. 6d., cloth gilt.
LIFE AND FINDING OF
DR. LIVINGSTONE,
CONTAINING THE ORIGINAL LETTERS
WRITTEN BY H. M. STANLEY,
To the "New York Herald."

New and enlarged edition, with an account of Dr. Livingstone's Death and Latest Discoveries.

PORTRAITS AND NUMEROUS ILLUSTRATIONS.

THE ROYAL PANOPTISCOPE.
Price 3s. 6d., in Box.

Portable and Handy for out-doors or in-doors.
Perfect for harmony of colours.
Infinite for outline of form.

This Scope is different to any hitherto invented; and whenever lifted to the eye a distinct artistic effect is produced. Recommended for every home of taste by the Society of Arts.
Merely crumple up a piece of paper, and the Panoptiscope throws it into a beautiful picture of geometrical proportions, with lights and shadows.

Just Published, with 420 various very Useful Receipts,—6s.

GUNTER'S MODERN CONFECTIONER.
THIRD EDITION.

A Practical Illustrated Guide to the Latest and most Improved Methods of Making the various kinds of Confectionery.

INCLUDING ICES.

The Receipts in this Book for Pastry, Cakes, and Sweetmeats are original, and have been used with uniform success by Mr. William Jeanes, Chief Confectioner at Messrs. Gunter's, Confectioners to Her Majesty, Berkeley Square. They are drawn up in style so plain as to be intelligible to servants and persons of moderate capacity.

THE EMPORIUM OF GAMES.

In commodious strong boxes, of assorted Games, for Juveniles. Three different sizes, all the articles of sound, strong make and good workmanship.

Emporium of Games.—No. 586. Contains 14 games; has Whipping Top, Shuttlecock, Boxwood Cups for playing at Ball, French Shuttlecock and Bandolcur, sets of Dibs, of Knuckle Bones, and Les Graces Cones, Pop-gun, Skittles for Carpet, Teetotum, Humming Top, Skipping Rope, Game of Jack Straw, Ball, and Boxwood Cup and Ball. Price 10 6. Smaller sizes, to same style, to sell 1,6, 2,6, 3 6 and 5 - each.

Designers' and Draughtsmen's Handbook of Ornament.
Illustrating and explaining the various styles of decoration. By W. Gibbs. With 150 different designs. Price 1s.- Most useful to students and schools of design.

The Land Surveyors' Ready Reckoner; or, Gentleman and Farmer's Guide to Land Measure. Showing how any person may become his own Surveyor, and accurately gauge the area of any piece of Land. By S. Thurlow. Price 2,- post free.

LONDON: DEAN & SON, 160a, FLEET STREET,
AND, BY ORDER, OF ALL STATIONERS AND BOOKSELLERS.

ILLUSTRATED BOOKS OF TRAVEL.
By the Rev. Samuel Manning, LL.D.

Just Published. **American Pictures, drawn with Pen and Pencil.**
Profusely Illustrated with superior Engravings from designs by eminent English and Foreign Artists. Handsomely bound in the best style of cloth, gilt. Imperial 8vo. 8s.

Swiss Pictures, drawn with Pen and Pencil. With numerous Illustrations by Whymper and others. Imperial 8vo. 8s., cloth elegant.
"In this edition there are so many improvements that this very beautiful volume is still more attractive and beautiful than ever."—*Standard.*
"The illustrations are particularly good."—*Daily Telegraph.*

"Those Holy Fields." Palestine Illustrated by Pen and Pencil. Profusely Illustrated. Imperial 8vo. 8s., cloth elegant.
"The author is aided by upwards of a hundred wood engravings, all admirably executed from sketches and photographs."—*Art Journal.*

Italian Pictures, drawn with Pen and Pencil. Profusely Illustrated. Imperial 8vo. 8s., cloth elegant.
"The more we turn over the pages of this book the more we like it. The plain descriptions and accurate drawings really tell us more about Italy than a library of inspired poems and a gallery of ideal paintings." *Times.*

Spanish Pictures, drawn with Pen and Pencil. With Illustrations by Doré and other eminent Artists. Imperial 8vo. 8s., cloth elegant.
"The letterpress is pleasant reading, and many of the sketches are of the highest excellence."—*Times.*

The Land of the Pharaohs. Egypt and Sinai: Illustrated by Pen and Pencil. With numerous fine Engravings. Imperial 8vo. 8s., handsomely bound, gilt edges.
"Extremely well written, with admirable illustrations."—*Guardian.*
"A highly interesting description of Egypt and Sinai."—*Public Opinion.*
"Full of spirited and highly finished engravings."—*Standard.*
No more charming book of its kind is known to us."—*Record.*

Life in the Southern Isles: Scenes and Incidents in the South Pacific and New Guinea. By the Rev. W. Wyatt Gill, B.A. With Maps and numerous Illustrations. Imperial 16mo. 5s. 6d., cloth boards, gilt edges.

Homes and Haunts of Luther. By the Rev. Dr. Stoughton, Author of "Stars of the East," &c. With numerous Engravings by Whymper and others. Small 4to. 8s., cloth boards, gilt edges.

The Realm of the Ice King. A Book of Arctic Discovery and Adventure. Numerous Illustrations. Imperial 16mo. 4s. 6d., cloth boards, gilt edges.

Madagascar and its People. Notes of a Four Years' Residence. With a Sketch of Mission Work among the Malagasy. By J. Sibree, jun. Map and Engravings. Crown 8vo. 6s. 6d., bevelled boards.

The Seven Golden Candlesticks; or, Sketches of the Seven Churches of Asia. By Canon Tristram. Engravings. 6s., bevelled boards, gilt edges.

Rivers of Water in a Dry Place. An Account of the Introduction of Christianity into South Africa, and of Dr. Moffat's Missionary Labours. For Young People. By the author of "The White Foreigners," &c. New Edition in Crown 8vo. With Illustrations. 3s., cloth boards.

London: The Religious Tract Society, 56, Paternoster Row.
MAY BE HAD OF ANY BOOKSELLER.

SIXPENCE MONTHLY.
THE LEISURE HOUR.
A FAMILY JOURNAL OF INSTRUCTION AND RECREATION.

"The 'Leisure Hour' has always been remarkable for its excellent sketches of travel in foreign lands."—*Scotsman.*
"The 'Leisure Hour' is a pleasant family journal."—*Illustrated London News.*
"The 'Leisure Hour' is full of healthy, interesting reading."—*The Graphic.*
"The 'Leisure Hour' is certainly among the best illustrated of periodicals."—*St. James' Chronicle.*

A HANDSOME ILLUSTRATED GIFT BOOK.
THE LEISURE HOUR VOLUME FOR 1876 *CONTAINS—*

Seventeen-Seventy-Six. A tale of the American War of Independence. By Francis Browne.
The Borderlands of Islam: Slavs and Turks, Servia, Bulgaria, Roumania, &c.
American Caricatures.
Arctic Expeditions of the Nineteenth Century. By Edward Whymper.
Boy and Man; or, Life at School and in the World.
Early Civilisation. By the Rev. Canon Rawlinson.
Palmyra and the Desert. By the Rev. W. Wright, late of Damascus.
The Grants of Lochside. By the author of "Christie Redfern."
The Crinkles of Crinklewood Hall. By Mrs. Prosser.
The Shadow on the Hearth; or, the Influence of Priestcraft in the Home.
Musical Papers. By the late Dr. Rimbault.
Antiquarian Gossip on the Months.
Natural History Anecdotes.
European Celebrities. With Portraits.

And a great variety of Miscellaneous Articles on Subjects of Popular Interest.
The Volume is profusely Illustrated with Engravings by Eminent Artists, and contains also Twelve Illustrations on Toned Paper. It consists of 848 imperial 8vo. pages, and forms a handsome gift-book.
Price 7s. in cloth boards; 8s. 6d. in extra boards, gilt edges; 10s. 6d. in half calf extra.

LONDON: 56, PATERNOSTER ROW; AND OF ALL BOOKSELLERS.

NEGRETTI & ZAMBRA,
Surveyors', Travellers' and Tourists' Requisites.

Transit Instruments, Theodolites, Dumpy and Y. Levels, Miners' Dials and Compasses, Clinometers, Prismatic Compasses, Land Chains, Measuring Rods and Tapes, Quadrants, Sextants, Mariners' and Pocket Compasses, Telescopes for Land and Sea Service, Binocular Field, Race and Marine Glasses, Meteorological Instruments for Observatory or Travellers' use, &c., &c,

ANEROID BAROMETERS,
Watch Size for Altitude Measurements, £5 5s., £6 6s. and £8 8s.

STAFF OFFICERS' FIELD GLASS,
SIX AND SEVEN GUINEAS, INCLUDING CASE,
Unrivalled for power and brilliant definition.
Smaller Sizes of this Model at £5 5s., £4 4s., £3 3s., and £2 2s.

NEGRETTI & ZAMBRA'S
ENCYCLOPÆDIC CATALOGUE
Of Surveying, Mathematical, Optical, Photographic, & Standard
METEOROLOGICAL INSTRUMENTS,
Containing very numerous Comparative Tables of Reference, and Illustrated
by upwards of ELEVEN HUNDRED ENGRAVINGS,
Royal 8vo., Cloth, gilt lettered, Price 5s. 6d.

NEGRETTI & ZAMBRA'S
Opticians and Meteorological Instrument Makers
TO HER MAJESTY THE QUEEN, H.R.H. THE PRINCE OF WALES,
The Royal Observatory, Greenwich; the Admiralty; Honourable Board of Ordnance; Board of Trade, &c., &c.

HOLBORN VIADUCT,
45, CORNHILL, & 122, REGENT STREET, LONDON.
PRICE LISTS UPON APPLICATION—POST FREE.

MILNERS'

QUADRUPLE PATENT

HOLDFAST AND FIRE RESISTING
SAFES, CHESTS,
STRONG ROOMS & STRONG ROOM DOORS,

OF ALL THE SEVERAL QUALITIES,

AND SUITABLE FOR THE DIFFERENT DEGREES OF RISK.

List 1. Milners' Double Fire Resisting Chambered Boxes, recommended for Safety from Fire only (not Violence or Robbery) in Dwelling Houses and detached Offices.

List 2. Milners' Double Fire Resisting Chambered Safes, made of Strong Wrought Iron Plates, but not equal to List 3 as Security against Robbery, nor recommended as such.

List 2. Milners' Fire Resisting Safes, specially arranged for the use of Registrars.

List 3. Milners' Holdfast, Fire, Wedge, Crowbar, Violence, Robbery, and Fraud Resisting Safes.

List 4. Milners' Extra Strong Holdfast, Fire, Wedge, Crowbar, Violence, Robbery, and Fraud Resisting Safes.

List 5. Milners' First Class Extra Strong Holdfast, Fire, Wedge, Crowbar, Violence, Robbery, and Fraud Resisting Safes.

List 6. Milners' Double First Class Extra Strong Holdfast Double Bankers' Safes, for the Securing (in what are too often only "so-called" Strong Rooms) of Bankers' Stores of Cash, Bullion, and other Valuables.

Milners' Strong Room Doors and Frames, and Ventilating Gates for Strong Rooms.

Milners' Strong Rooms for Banks, Private Mansions, &c. &c.

Milners' Fire Resisting Gunpowder Magazines, *as tested at Woolwich October 9th and 10th*, 1872, *under authority of the Home Secretary.*

Milners' Japanned Iron Cash, Paper and Deed Boxes (not Fire Resisting) with Patent Lever Unpickable Locks.

LIVERPOOL—PHŒNIX SAFE WORKS, AND
8, LORD STREET.
MANCHESTER—28, MARKET STREET.
GLASGOW—41 & 43, WEST NILE STREET.
BRMINGHAM—93, NEW STREET.
LONDON—MILNERS' BUILDINGS, CITY
(OPPOSITE MOORGATE STREET STATION.)

THE COLONIAL MAIL LINE,
CARRYING HER MAJESTY'S MAILS,
BETWEEN ENGLAND AND SOUTH AFRICA.

THE

ROYAL  MAIL

STEAM SHIPS.

"DUNROBIN CASTLE"	2811	Tons Register.
"EDINBURGH CASTLE"	2678	,, ,,
"WALMER CASTLE"	2446	,, ,,
"BALMORAL CASTLE"	2850	,, ,,
"DUBLIN CASTLE" (building)	2900	,, ,,
"WARWICK CASTLE" (building)	2900	,, ,,
"TAYMOUTH CASTLE" (building)	2100	,, ,,
"NEW STEAMER"	2900	,, ,,
"LAPLAND"	1269	,, ,,
"COURLAND"	1246	,, ,,
"ELIZABETH MARTIN"	1242	,, ,,
"STETTIN"	830	,, ,,
"MARITZBURG" (building)	900	,, ,,
"FLORENCE"	665	,, ,,

Between LONDON AND CAPE TOWN, PORT NOLLOTH, MOSSEL BAY ALGOA BAY, THE KOWIE, EAST LONDON AND NATAL.

☞ The Ocean Mail Steamers are despatched from London every alternate Tuesday, and from Dartmouth for Cape Town, every alternate Friday. From Cape Town they sail for Plymouth, every alternate Tuesday. Outwards and Homewards the Mail Steamers call at Madeira; and at St. Helena and Ascension at stated intervals. The Coast Mails Steamers of the Company leave Cape Town for D'Urban, Natal, and D'Urban for Cape Town, in connection with the Ocean Service, (calling at the Coast Ports) once a fortnight under contract with the Government.

For Freight or Passage apply to—
Anderson & Murison, Cape Town; Prince, Vintcent, & Co., Mossel Bay; Blaine & Co., Algoa Bay; Robt. Bertram & Co., The Kowie; J. J. Irvine & Co., East London; Samuel S. Ridge (at the offices of the Company) D'Urban, Natal; or to the Owners,
DONALD CURRIE & CO.,
3 & 4, FENCHURCH STREET, LONDON, E.C.

Union Steamship Company, Limited.

MAIL SERVICE.

The Royal Mail Steamers of the Union Steamship Company, Limited, leave Southampton every alternate Thursday, and Plymouth every alternate Friday for the following Ports : Madeira, St. Helena, Cape Town, Mossel Bay, Port Elizabeth (Algoa Bay), Port Alfred (Kowie River), East London, Natal, Delagoa Bay, Mozambique and Ascension. *via* Cape or St. Helena.

The Company's Steamers for England leave Port Elizabeth (Algoa Bay) every alternate Friday, and Cape Town every alternate Tuesday.

DIRECT PORT ELIZABETH SERVICE.

EVERY FOURTH THURSDAY, commencing with Thursday, 14th December, 1876, one of the Union Steamship Co.'s Steamers will leave Southampton direct for Port Elizabeth (Algoa Bay), calling at Plymouth for Mails and Passengers and proceeding to Natal.

These Steamers sail for England from Natal EVERY FOURTH SATURDAY, beginning with Saturday, 20th January, and from Port Elizabeth EVERY FOURTH FRIDAY, beginning with Friday, 26th January, 1877.

The Company's fleet comprises the following vessels, all of them fitted with every modern convenience :—

ATLANTIC SERVICE.

Name.	Tnge.	Name.	Tnge.
AFRICAN	2019	NYANZA	2128
ASIATIC	2066	NUBIAN	3078
AMERICAN	2474	ROMAN	1850
ANGLIAN	2206	SYRIA	1958
DANUBE	2038	TEUTON	2313
EUROPEAN	2272		

COLONIAL SERVICE.

KAFIR	982	NATAL	734

FARES.

To	ADULT PASSENGERS.	
	1st Class.	2nd Class.
	£ s. d.	£ s. d.
MADEIRA	19 10 0	13 13 0
ST. HELENA	31 10 0	21 0 0
CAPE TOWN and *Vice Versa*	31 10 0	21 0 0
MOSSEL BAY "	34 13 0	23 2 0
PORT ELIZABETH (Algoa Bay) "		
PORT ALFRED (Kowie River) "	36 15 0	24 3
EAST LONDON "		
NATAL "	38 17 0	26 5 0
DELAGOA BAY "	44 2 0	29 8 0
MOZAMBIQUE "	63 0 0	42 0 0
ZANZIBAR "	70 7 0	47 5 0

Union Steamship Company—Continued.

CHILDREN under twelve months old to be charged ONE-SIXTEENTH of full fare, and a sixteenth for every additional year of their age. Servants, second-class fare.

The Rates from England INCLUDE DOCK AND AGENCY CHARGES, AND A FREE PASS BY RAIL FROM LONDON TO SOUTHAMPTON for Passengers and Baggage, which can be obtained of the Company or their Agents in England.

Double Journey Tickets are issued at a reduction of Ten per cent. off two Single Fares.

For further particulars apply at the Company's Offices, Southampton ; to H. J. WARING, The Wharf, Mill-Bay, Plymouth ; to F. J. MERCER & Co., 11, Leadenhall-street, London ; or to any of the following Agencies—

AGENCIES—HOME.

LONDON—F. J. Mercer & Co., 11, Leadenhall-street.
PLYMOUTH—H. J. Waring, The Wharf, Mill-Bay.
MANCHESTER—Keller, Wallis and Postlethwaite, 73, Piccadilly.
GLASGOW—F. W. Allan, 120, Buchanan-street.
DUBLIN—Carolin and Egan, 30, Eden Quay.

COLONIAL.

MADEIRA—Blandy Brothers.
ST. HELENA—Solomon, Moss, Gideon & Co.
CAPE TOWN (Cape of Good Hope)—Union Steamship Co., Limited.
ALGOA BAY   „   „
MOSSEL BAY   „   —Fleming & Mudie.
PORT ALFRED (Kowie River)—Walker & Co.
EAST LONDON   „   Union Steamship Co., Limited.
KING WILLIAM'S TOWN—Whitcher, Dyer & Dyer.
QUEEN'S TOWN   „   —J. Hodges & Co.
GRAAFF-REINET   „   —Peacock, Humphreys & Co.
RICHMOND   „   —R. Mortimer & Co.
COLESBURG   „   —W. Warren & Co.
FORT BEAUFORT   „   —J. Shaw & Co.
DURBAN, NATAL (South Africa)—Escombe & Co.
KIMBERLEY (Diamond-fields, South Africa)—Hill & Paddon.
BARKLY   „   —Hill & Paddon.
BLOEMFONTEIN (O.F.S., South Africa)—White, Barlow & Co.
FAURESMITH (Orange Free State)—D. P. Jones & Co.
POTCHEFSTROOM (Transvaal Republic, South Africa) Reid & Co.
PRETORIA   „   —J. W. Beckett & Co.
DELAGOA BAY (East Africa)—Thos. Thompson & Co.
INHAMBANE   „   —The Handlescompagnie.
QUILLIMANE   „   —Senor Nunes.
MOZAMBIQUE   „   —Fabre & Son.
ZANZIBAR   „   —John Scott.

CONTINENTAL.

AMSTERDAM—De Vries & Co.
ANTWERP—Kennedy & Hunter.
BREMEN—J. H. Bachman.
HAMBURG—R. Carl.
HAVRE—Langstaff, Ehrenberg and Pollak.
PARIS—G. Dunlop & Co., 44, Rue des Petites Ecurie
ROTTERDAM—Kuyper, Van Dam and Smeer.

ANDERSON, ABBOTT & ANDERSON,
INDIA RUBBER MANUFACTURERS,
QUEEN VICTORIA STREET, CITY, LONDON.

THE REGULATION WATERPROOF CLOAK
CONTRACTORS
TO THE

Right Honorable the Lords Commissioners of the Admiralty, the War Office, Secretary of State for India, and London Metropolitan Police.

EVERY DESCRIPTION OF WATERPROOF COAT
For travelling in all parts of the world
WARRANTED TO BE AFFECTED BY NEITHER HEAT NOR COLD.

THE PATENT HYGIENIC VENTILATING WATERPROOF COAT,
Having the appearance of an ordinary Woollen-lined Coat
Especially suitable for Winter use.

THE POCKET SIPHONIA, weighing twelve ounces.
India Rubber Leggings, Caps and Boots.
LADIES' TRAVELLING CLOAKS AND RIDING COSTUMES,
Weighing only a few ounces.
LADIES' CANADIAN SNOW BOOTS AND WELLINGTONS.
Ground Sheets, Pocket Baths, Buckets & Basins.
CAMP BEDSTEADS, CORK BEDS, & MATTRASSES.

THE REGULATION VALISE (BED AND KNAPSACK COMBINED),
Sir Garnet Wolseley's Pattern.

Knapsacks & Packs, Air Beds, Pillows & Cushions. Waterproof Travelling Rugs.
PORTABLE INFLATING BOAT, FOR EXPLORING EXPEDITIONS,
Weighing about 20-lbs.
And all kinds of India-Rubber Goods for Sporting, Nautical, Surgical, Domestic, Mining, Agricultural and Mechanical purposes.

ANDERSON, ABBOTT & ANDERSON,
QUEEN VICTORIA STREET CITY, LONDON.

www.ingramcontent.com/pod-product-compliance
Lightning Source LLC
Chambersburg PA
CBHW032131230426
43672CB00011B/2299